Discourse, power and justice

'A timely, valuable and thought-provoking contribution to the emerging body of literature on the management of long-term prisoners in the UK, and on prisons and other organisations in the contemporary era of agency status, managerialism and privatisation.'

Alison Liebling,
Institute of Criminology, University of Cambridge

Discourse, Power and Justice is a distinctive and theoretically informed empirical study of the administration of the Scottish prison system. It is based on extensive research and combines theoretical innovation with detailed empirical evidence. The book is located at the confluence of two academic traditions and their associated literatures, socio-legal studies and the sociology of knowledge, which are combined to produce a novel theoretical framework.

The authors focus on the activities of those who manage the prison system. They identify the most important social actors in the prison system, located both historically and comparatively, and examine their characteristic forms of discourse. A number of crucial areas of decision-making are analysed in depth, including decisions about the initial classification of prisoners, transfers between establishments and the allocation of prisoners to different forms of work. Another major focus is on the different forms and mechanisms of accountability, and the book concludes with an analysis of recent policy changes.

Discourse, Power and Justice will be essential reading for both students and practitioners in sociology, social policy, criminology and law.

Michael Adler is Reader in Social Policy at the University of Edinburgh.
Brian Longhurst is Lecturer in Sociology at the University of Salford.

INTERNATIONAL LIBRARY OF SOCIOLOGY
Founded by Karl Mannheim

Editor: John Urry
University of Lancaster

Discourse, power and justice

Towards a new sociology of imprisonment

Michael Adler and Brian Longhurst

Routledge
Taylor & Francis Group
LONDON AND NEW YORK

For Jonathan and Benjamin
Bernadette, James and Tim

In memory of Ruth

First published 1994
by Routledge
2 Park Square, Milton Park, Abingdon, Oxfordshire OX14 4RN

Simultaneously published in the USA and Canada
by Routledge
711 Third Avenue, New York, NY 10017

First issued in paperback 2014

Routledge is an imprint of the Taylor and Francis Group, an informa business

Typeset in Baskerville by
Ponting–Green Publishing Services, Chesham, Bucks

British Library Cataloguing in Publication Data
A catalogue record for this book is available from the British Library

Library of Congress Cataloguing in Publication Data
Adler, Michael
Discourse, power, and justice: towards a new sociology of improvement/Michael Adler and Brian Longhurst.
p. cm. – (International library of sociology)
Includes bibliographical references and index.
1. Prison administration–Scotland.
2. Imprisonment–Scotland.
3. Criminal justice, Administration of–Scotland.
I. Longhurst, Brian, 1956–. II. Title. III. Series.
HV9649.S35A35 1994
365'.9411–dc20 93–46106
CIP

ISBN 13: 978-1-138-87992-8 (pbk)
ISBN 13: 978-0-415-04237-6 (hbk)

Publisher's Note
The publisher has gone to great lengths to ensure the quality of this reprint but points out that some imperfections in the original may be apparent

Contents

Figures

Tables

Acknowledgements

It is now almost eight years since we began the research on which this book is based. We have been given a great deal of help and support at every stage for which we are extremely grateful. We would first of all like to thank the Economic and Social Research Council for funding our research under its Crime and Criminal Justice Initiative and the Nuffield Foundation for a small grant which enabled us to complete the research when our ESRC funding came to an end. We would also like to thank the Scottish Office for supporting our proposal and, after some initial hesitation, for facilitating our research. We were treated exceptionally well wherever we went and would like to thank the officials (at the Headquarters of the Scottish Prison Service in Edinburgh) and the prison governors, industrial managers, education officers, social workers and prison officers (in many establishments throughout Scotland) for giving us access to files, for allowing us to attend meetings and observe them at work and for responding so frankly and informatively to all our questioning. We could not have hoped for better co-operation from those who assisted us in this way and would like to thank them for letting us into their world and helping us understand it. We hope that they will recognise the Scottish Prison Service in our account and feel that the assistance they gave us was put to good use.

A number of people contributed to the research itself. Alison Petch helped to draw up the original proposal and to get the project off the ground, while Ed Wozniak (Principal Research Officer in the Scottish Prison Service) played a vital role throughout the research by warning us of pitfalls, tempering our impetuousness and steering us in the right direction. We are most grateful to both of them. We are pleased to record the help we received from

David Goldblatt and Sheila Henderson with data collection; from Linda Jackson, Fiona Rutherdale and Maureen Young with coding; from John Ronxin for transcribing and summarising our interviews and from Alan Alexander with data analysis. Alan's contribution, which involved setting up and analysing five large data sets, was particularly invaluable and we were very fortunate to secure his services.

Earlier versions of some of the material in this book have appeared in a series of articles which we have written together. These have been included in the list of References although they are not specifically referred to in the text. The book itself has been substantially improved by the comments of the publisher's reader and by the exceptionally helpful suggestions we received from four colleagues and friends, each of whom read a draft of the manuscript from beginning to end. We are extremely grateful to Nick Abercrombie (University of Lancaster), David Garland (University of Edinburgh), Sue Morris (Scottish Office) and Ian Taylor (University of Salford), and hope that they will be able to see from the final version how seriously we took their advice and criticisms.

We owe a special debt of gratitude to one person who has been with the project from the start. Valerie Chuter, our long-suffering secretary and friend, has typed everything we have ever written, produced endless drafts of every chapter with great speed, unfailing accuracy and infinite good humour. We have appreciated her loyalty as much as her technical expertise.

Finally, a word of thanks to our colleagues in Edinburgh and Salford, who must often have wondered whether this book would ever materialise, and to our partners Ruth and Bernadette for their endless encouragement, forbearance and support. If we had not managed to complete the book we would only have had ourselves to blame.

Michael Adler
Brian Longhurst

Abbreviations

AA	Administrative Assistant
ASPG	Association of Scottish Prison Governors
AO	Administrative Officer
BASW	British Association of Social Work
BSU	Barlinnie Special Unit
CI	Chief Inspector – see HMCIP(s) below
DCI	Deputy Chief Inspector
DI	Disability Insurance (USA)
ECHR	European Convention on Human Rights/European Commission on Human Rights
EIS	Educational Institute of Scotland
EO	Executive Officer
FCO	Foreign and Commonwealth Office
HEO	Higher Executive Officer
HMCIP(S)	Her Majesty's Chief Inspector of Prisons (Scotland)
IM	Industrial Manager
LIB	Local Induction Board
LRC	Local Review Committee
LTP	long-term prisoner
MP	Member of Parliament
NCB	National Classification Board
PCA	Parliamentary Commissioner for Administration
PRC	Preliminary Review Committee
PSMG	Prison Service Management Group
PU	Protection Unit
ROR	Restoration of Remission
SACRO	Scottish Association for the Care and Resettlement of Offenders
SCCL	Scottish Council for Civil Liberties

SCDP	Standing Committee on Difficult Prisoners
SEL	Special Escorted Leave
SEO	Senior Executive Officer
SHHD	Scottish Home and Health Department
SPS	Scottish Prison Service
STP	short-term prisoner
STUC	Scottish Trades Union Congress
TFF	Training for Freedom
VLTP	very long-term prisoner
VT	vocational training
YO	young offender
YOI	Young Offenders' Institution

Introduction

This book is both a study of the management of long-term prisoners in Scotland and a new perspective on the sociology of imprisonment which has rather wider application. In this introduction, we describe how we came to write it, explain its relationship to earlier studies of imprisonment, and outline its structure and content.

THE ORIGINS OF THE STUDY

Our book draws on material from an ESRC-funded research project on administrative decision-making in the Scottish prison system.[1] In this project, which ran from 1985–8, we focused on adult, male, long-term (over eighteen months in Scotland) prisoners,[2] who constitute the largest and most problematic of the various groups which together make up the prison population,[3] and analysed in detail several major areas of decision-making. In each case we sought to establish what decisions were accomplished; why the system operated in the way it did; what problems were created by existing practices, for whom they were problematic and to what extent they gave rise to pressure for change; what obstacles there were to change; the effectiveness of the different forms of accountability; what alternatives to the existing system were being canvassed and what their implications for day-to-day administrative decision-making would be.

During the course of our fieldwork, we used three main research techniques: documentary analysis, observation and interviews. Documentary analysis included the study of files and other official records; observation entailed attending meetings of, for example, the National Classification Board and Local Induction Boards, and sitting in with various staff groups at Headquarters; while interviews were conducted with a wide range of individuals from inside and outwith the Prison Service. We conducted a total of fifty-five semi-structured interviews, eight with civil servants (including the Director and three Deputy Directors of the Scottish Prison Service), twenty-six with governor-grade staff, seven with industrial managers, four with education officers, five with social workers, two with members of the Inspectorate, one with officials of the Scottish Prison Officers' Association (SPOA) and three with individuals who had retired from the Prison Service.[4]

We were initially drawn to the study of day-to-day administrative decision-making by two interrelated sets of concerns. Notwithstanding the lack of consensus about the aims of imprisonment or the lack of agreement about the future direction of penal policy in Scotland, we were struck, as many others before us have been, by the ability of those who ran the prisons to produce a semblance of social order, at least for much of the time. Although the spate of violent incidents which took place in Scottish (and likewise English) prisons drew attention to the fragility of this social order, and has quite rightly been the subject of a good deal of attention, we felt that it was important not to lose sight of the fact that these incidents constituted the exception rather than the rule. At the same time we were struck by the secrecy which characterised the activities of the Scottish Prison Service (SPS) and the fact that so little information relating to day-to-day administrative decision-making was available to the public. As Cohen and Taylor (1979) pointed out (in their powerful critique of the Home Office) secrecy 'insulates prisons and their administration from the type of reasonable criticism which is regularly incurred by other institutions in our society' (ibid.:94). This seemed to us to be particularly unhelpful at a time when the future direction of the Scottish Prison Service was quite rightly becoming a matter of public concern.

It is clear that between 1985 and 1990 the Scottish prison system was in a state of crisis. In part this was caused by an increase in the numbers of prisoners incarcerated (see Chapters 1 and 9), but its most significant manifestation was in a series of prison riots and rooftop incidents. In October and November 1986 there were hostage-takings in Edinburgh and Peterhead prisons and in January 1987 an incident in Barlinnie prison in Glasgow. These were followed by another set of incidents in the autumn of 1987, in September at Shotts and Peterhead and in October at Perth. Serious disturbances took place in several Scottish prisons.[5]

Cavadino and Dignan (1992) have pointed out that there is something paradoxical about describing prisons as being in crisis when such a description has been applied for so long. However, between 1985 and 1990 the Scottish prison system did appear to be in a state of crisis inasmuch as there was a fierce power struggle between those who represented the status quo and others who were prepared to implement new ideas. A closer look at Cavadino and Dignan's (1992) argument should make our own position clearer.

Cavadino and Dignan identify what they call an 'orthodox account of crisis' which, they suggest, points

> to the following factors as implicated in the crisis: (1) the high prison population (or 'numbers crisis'); (2) overcrowding; (3) bad conditions within prison (for both inmates and prison officers); (4) understaffing; (5) unrest among staff; (6) poor security; (7) the 'toxic mix' of life-sentence prisoners, politically-motivated prisoners and mentally-disturbed inmates; (8) riots and other breakdowns of control over prisoners. These factors are seen as linked, with number 8 – riots and disorder – being the end product which shows there is a crisis.
>
> (1992:10–11)

Cavadino and Dignan suggest that such an account links together a number of factors in an overly mechanistic fashion. By contrast, they maintain that it is possible to outline a 'radical pluralist account of the prison crisis', which attempts 'to analyse the crisis in the context of the relationships between politics and economics, ideology and material conditions' (ibid.:28). Central to this account is the idea of a 'crisis of legitimacy' (ibid.:30). Cavadino and Dignan suggest that a penal system has to 'legitimate itself with three groups of people: with the public. . .with penal staff. . .and with the penal subjects' (ibid.:30).

Cavadino and Dignan's attempt to theorise the penal crisis is certainly worthwhile but their account of legitimacy omits one element which we regard as central: the legitimacy of the system with those who are in control of it. Indeed, their analysis of legitimacy would seem to rely on a particular version of the theory of ideology which focuses on the role of ideology in incorporating dominated groups to the benefit of dominant ones. As such, it neglects the many criticisms of this approach by Abercrombie, Hill and Turner (1980) (see also Hill 1990) and, in particular, plays down the importance of ideology in securing the coherence of dominant groups rather than incorporating the dominated (Abercrombie et al. 1980). Our position, which we develop in the course of this book, is that the period from 1985 to 1990 was one in which there was a vigorous struggle between dominant elements in the Scottish prison system over ideas and for control and that the outcome of this struggle was a reformulation of discourse about imprisonment and the emergence of a new form of social order.

The empirical part of our study was concerned with the Scottish prison system and the evidence we advance will be drawn from it. However, we would like to think that the theoretical approach we developed in the course of our research and which is deployed in this book is of more general application. We are convinced that our approach can be applied to other penal systems. The results will, almost certainly, be rather different, but similar sorts of processes, institutions and options are just as much the subject of concern for policy-makers and power-holders elsewhere. Indeed, comparative work from a common theoretical standpoint would be particularly helpful for those studying imprisonment. Hence, the relevance of our study clearly extends beyond Scotland. It also extends far beyond the empirical study of decision-making in raising much wider issues of power and control within the prison system.

Our theoretical position can be located at a confluence of two academic subdisciplines and their associated literatures: socio-legal studies of justice and, in particular, the delivery of justice in administration, and the sociology of knowledge, especially that branch which was influenced by the work of Karl Mannheim. These two subdisciplines represented the traditions in which we had previously worked (MA in socio-legal studies, BL in the sociology of knowledge) and the attempt to produce a synthesis between them should therefore come as no surprise. Whether or not it has been successful is for others to judge, but we are convinced that by subjecting the discourse of justice to critical scrutiny and analysing discursive conflict in terms of the struggles for power and ascendency between those groups of actors in the Scottish Prison Service who act as the carriers of these discourses, we have developed a new and distinctive approach to the sociology of imprisonment. In the next section, we relate our approach to earlier work in this tradition.

THE SOCIOLOGY OF IMPRISONMENT

In a recent article (DiIulio 1991), which reflects the ideas developed in his book *Governing Prisons* (DiIulio 1987), John J. DiIulio Jr advocates a reconciliation between two approaches to penology, i.e. between an 'old penology' which was in the ascendency in the nineteenth century and the early part of the twentieth century, and a 'new penology' which emerged from and eventually displaced its predecessor and which has been in the ascendency for most of the post-war period, at least until recently. Whereas the old penology focused more on prison administrators than on prison inmates and made prison governance the central and abiding focus of prison studies,

> the new penology stood the two main precepts of the old penology on their heads. In essence, whereas the old penology focused sympathetically on prison administrators, the new penology focused sympathetically on prison inmates, and whereas the old penology maintained that prisons must be governed strictly by duly appointed officials, the new penology maintained that prisons must be governed by the prisoners themselves.
>
> (Ibid.:72)

Although DiIulio gave examples of both approaches, he concentrates his critique on the new penology, accusing it of encouraging and intensifying the disturbances and riots which became such a common feature of prisons in Britain as well as the USA during the 1980s. Some of the most famous and influential studies of imprisonment are part of this tradition. Many of them took the form of case-studies and focused on a single prison. The tradition began with the work of Clemmer (1958, first published in 1940), reached its high point in the late 1950s and early 1960s with the contributions of Sykes (1958), T. and P. Morris (1963) and Mathiesen (1965), and has continued in the work of King and Elliot (1977), Jacobs (1977), Fleisher (1989) and Little (1990). Most of these studies included descriptions of the nature of the prison and the characteristics of the inmate subculture. This is especially the case with Clemmer's *The Prison Community* and the Morrises' *Pentonville*. Other texts in the 'tradition' such as Sykes's *The Society of Captives* and Mathiesen's *The Defences of the Weak* were more theoretically informed. However, despite the many differences between them, a core of concerns can be identified. While many different aspects of the prison were analysed, including work, education, and the social composition and nature of the officer force, the focus of concern was on the adaptation of prisoners to their environment and the nature of the inmate subculture.

These concerns were carried forward into debates about the 'prisonisation' of inmates and the determinants of and changes to inmate subcultures (e.g. Irwin and Cressey 1962; Irwin 1970). The extent of prisonisation was disputed and the degree of autonomy (from the concerns of prison managers and the wider culture) of inmate subcultures debated. Such concerns influenced subsequent prison research, such as that carried out by Cohen and Taylor (1972), and reappears in some of the later prison case-studies (e.g. Fleisher 1989; Little 1990). Although such studies are often extremely rich in detail about prison life, and, especially when supplemented by insiders' accounts (e.g. Boyle 1977 and 1985; Bettsworth 1989; Smith 1989), provide a sound basis for discussing the extent of prisonisation and the degree of autonomy of inmate subcultures, they are problematic in several senses. They tend, first, to be rather ahistorical; second, not to address themselves to wider theoretical debates (though they are by no means atheoretical) in as direct a manner as we would advocate;[6] and third, to neglect the analysis of those in power for a focus on the responses of the powerless. However, this tradition has been called into question by two other developments.

Over the past twenty or so years, increasing attention has been paid to the history of imprisonment. A certain amount of this history has been of a 'revisionist' type and locates the history of the prison in wider social and political movements (e.g. Ignatieff 1978). The work of Michel Foucault (especially *Discipline and Punish*), although it is not history in the conventional sense, has had a considerable influence on historical work (e.g. Garland 1985, 1990). Although our focus is on the nature of and changes in current penal practice, we recognise the importance of contextualising the present by studying how it developed into what it is today. Thus, we draw on historical work at several points in our work, in particular in charting the development of the penal discourses we identify in Chapter 2. (Fuller accounts of aspects of penal history in Scotland can be found in Cameron (1983) and, more recently, in Coyle (1991).)

Increasing attention has also been paid to wider theoretical issues. We have already mentioned the work of Foucault (1979) and no work on imprisonment can ignore his theoretical insights. For us, his importance lies in his analysis of imprisonment in terms of the integral and symbiotic relationship between power and knowledge. Although Foucault can be criticised for treating power as though it were 'a thing in itself' and for failing to investigate the aims of power and the roles of individual power-holders (Garland 1990:169–70), his emphasis on the importance of power relations can be followed. However, this leaves a good deal of further work to be done. In particular, this must involve paying attention to the detailed mechanics of power relations which are neglected in his more general account.

Foucault lists principles which 'have constituted the seven universal maxims of the good "penitential condition"' (1979:269) and, in the course of our book, we address many of these aspects of prison life. First, he maintains that imprisonment has, as one of its stated aims, the transformation of the individual. It is premised on reform or rehabilitation. He calls this the 'principle of correction'. Second, he argues that prisoners are classified, saying that 'convicts must be isolated or at least distributed according to the penal gravity of their act, but above all according to age, mental attitude, the technique of correction to be used, the stages of their transformation'. Third, he maintains that penalties (or sentences) can be altered according to the response of the individual prisoner. Fourth, Foucault claims that 'work must be one of the essential elements in the transformation and progressive socialization of convicts'. Fifth, since it has a similar function, education is to be provided in the prison. Sixth, the prison is to be supervised by a specialist staff. Finally, surveillance will be continued after the period of imprisonment has ended. To ensure reform, there have to be 'auxiliary institutions'. Assessing the current status of many of these principles will form an important part of our work.

Although our book takes account of a number of important bodies of literature we have somewhat different aims from those of earlier studies. Rather than focusing on the response of prisoners to prison, how they deal with the pains of imprisonment, or the nature of inmate subcultures, we have sought to draw attention to the roles of the powerful, their aims and the strategies they deploy in practice. With reference to an old, but still pertinent, debate, we side with Gouldner (1968) rather than Becker (1967) in choosing to study the powerful in preference to the poor. Thus we have adopted a position similar to DiIulio's, albeit for somewhat different reasons. For DiIulio, the essence of the 'new old penology' (the name he gives to the reconciliation of the old and the new penologies) is 'a focus on how to make prisons more safe and humane by improving their organisation and management' (1991:67). We have somewhat different normative concerns (see Chapter 10 below). However, these are secondary to our primary aims, which are to account for the achievement of a semblance of social order in a crisis-torn prison system, to identify the pressures for change and to analyse the causes and consequences of recent developments in penal policy. But, although our aims differ, our methods, which involve focusing on those in positions of power and authority and studying the prison system as a whole, are clearly very similar.

Our book contains very little by way of accounts of the characteristics of inmate subcultures, the nature of prison argot, the activities of prisoner 'barons', or the nature of sexual practices which make up much of the new penology. These are, in our view, quite legitimate objects of study although they are not of primary concern to us. Furthermore, in contrast to much of the literature, we were not particularly exercised by the detailed operation of any one prison. Rather, we wished to examine the working of the prison system as a whole.[7] Thus, for example, the procedures for allocating work at any one prison were not of particular interest to us, but the similarities and differences between such procedures in the different prisons were of considerable interest. In this way, and by examining the role of Headquarters, we were able to build up a picture of the system as a whole and the way in which it operated. Thus, to reiterate, we have shifted from a focus on the prisoner and the prison, to a concern with those who run the prisons and with the prison system as a whole and from the experiences of the powerless to the activities of the powerful.

THE STRUCTURE OF THE BOOK

The book is divided into ten chapters. In the first two chapters, we develop and set out our theoretical approach. A central contention of the book is that it is impossible to study imprisonment in general and the administration of prisons in particular without paying attention to the relationships between important social actors and those ideas, beliefs and forms of knowledge (which we refer to as discourses) which shape and structure the prison system. Chapter 1 begins to elaborate this position and has three main aims. First, in order to contextualise our discussion of important social actors in the Scottish prison system today, we provide a historical account of its development; second, we characterise its current institutional topography and identify the most important groups of social actors; and third, to further contextualise our study, we examine some historical and comparative trends in the use of imprisonment. While Chapter 1 focuses on institutions and actors, Chapter 2 examines discourse in a similar manner. We begin by showing how our approach to the study of discourse is derived from the work of Karl Mannheim. We then examine the separate discourses associated with the ends and means of imprisonment which we see in play in the Scottish prison system today and show how these can be combined to form a 'discourse matrix'. Each composite discourse is carried by a different group of social actors while the power struggles between these actors give rise to and explain the struggles for ascendency between different discourses.

Having identified the key actors and discourses in their historical context, we focus in Chapter 3 on what we take to be a core activity in any social system: classification. We relate the changing nature of the initial classification of adult male, long-term prisoners to wider changes in the penal system and argue that classification outcomes reflected the dominance of bureaucratic civil servants over the professional prison governors who actually carried out the classification procedure. To investigate this proposition further, and to examine the long-term effect of initial classification decisions, we discuss in Chapter 4 the nature of the prison population, the transfer of prisoners between establishments and their consequent prison careers, and, in more detail, the prison careers of life-sentence prisoners. We conclude that the evidence presented in this chapter reinforces the arguments about bureaucratic dominance identified in Chapter 3.

In the next chapter (Chapter 5) we expand upon this discussion through a consideration of prison regimes. We consider the variation in prison regimes within the prison system and show that the structuring of these regimes is effectively determined by prison governors. Other prison professionals, such as industrial managers, education officers and social workers, are subordinated to prison governors through the latter's control over the operationalisation of the prison regime.

Having examined the changing structures of power and discourse associated with classification, transfers, careers and regimes in Chapters 3–5, we then move on to analyse different forms and mechanisms of accountability in Chapters 6–8. We focus on three particularly important institutional mechanisms: in Chapter 6, we examine the petition system which exemplifies a bureaucratic mode of accountability; in Chapter 7, we look at the Prisons Inspectorate which represents a type of professional accountability; and in Chapter 8, we scrutinise the European Convention on Human Rights which embodies a form of legal accountability. Our analysis of power and discourse leads us to conclude that each of these mechanisms of accountability is problematic, a theme we take up in the conclusion to our book.

Chapter 9 examines recent developments in penal policy in Scotland, and analyses the sequence of responses to the crisis of 1985–90. These responses and, in particular, the move towards an 'enterprising' prison system and the attempt to develop a new mode of managerialism in Scottish prisons, are again explained in terms of the changing structures of power and discourse. In our final chapter (Chapter 10) we pull the different strands of our argument together and assess the contribution of our book to the sociology of imprisonment.

Chapter 1

Institutions, actors and trends in imprisonment

A central contention of this book is that it is impossible to study imprisonment in general, and the administration of prisons in particular, without paying attention to the relationship between important social actors and those ideas, beliefs and forms of knowledge (which we shall term discourses) that shape and contextualise imprisonment. We have already noted in the Introduction how our work has taken place at a confluence of subdisciplines in the social sciences and provided an initial statement of our perspective. This chapter begins to elaborate aspects of this position and is divided into three sections. First, to contextualise our discussion of the Scottish prison system today, we provide a brief historical account of its development; second, we characterise its current institutional topography and identify the most important social actors; and third, we examine some historical and comparative trends in the use of imprisonment. Hence, this chapter looks at institutions and actors in a comparative and historical context. The next chapter examines discourses in a similar way.

INSTITUTIONAL DEVELOPMENTS

Local prisons prior to 1835

The idea of using deprivation of freedom as a punishment for crime is a fairly recent one in Scotland. In mediaeval times, standard punishments were compensation or fines, followed by corporal punishment (including branding), outlawry and capital punishment. Prisons were, by and large, places where criminals were held pending trial or sentencing or until such time as an outstanding debt was paid. After trial, they were used to hold prisoners until sentence, which could have been corporal punishment, banishment or execution, was carried out. However, they were rarely used as places of punishment in themselves.

Compared with England, Scotland appears to have enjoyed a relatively liberal penal tradition (Coyle 1991). Capital punishment was used much less frequently in Scotland than in England;[1] transportation did not become available as a penal sanction in Scotland until 1776 and was never used much more than one-quarter as often as in England; and imprisonment itself was used less frequently and for shorter periods than in England. However, the prisons themselves were in a poor state. With few exceptions, notably the Glasgow Bridewell (or 'House of Correction') and the other institutions run by William Brebner, general conditions in the early part of the nineteenth century were appalling. Corruption was rife among an ill-disciplined, ill-trained and poorly paid staff; prisons were insecure dens where males and females, old and young, serious and minor offenders mixed together; there was no set regime, no established objective and little attempt at anything but containment. Although prison gradually became the main sanction available to the courts, the theory and practice of prisons hardly changed at all from the time when they were designed simply to hold people for short periods pending trial or sentence.

Before 1835 it made little sense to refer to a *prison system* in Scotland. Responsibility for providing and maintaining prisons fell within the jurisdiction of local government, i.e. on burghs and counties, with most of the responsibility falling on the burghs. However, by the beginning of the eighteenth century burghs had lost much of their wealth. Legislation introduced in 1819 enabled but did not oblige counties to contribute to the costs involved. Although some counties did contribute to the costs, there were substantial variations in the conditions of imprisonment from one part of the country to another, and most prisons were small, run-down and badly managed.

The growth of central control

The general state of prisons in Scotland prior to 1835 was certainly no worse than that in England and Wales and, because imprisonment was used less often, overcrowding in Scottish prisons was probably not as bad. Concern with the state of prisons persuaded the Government that it could no longer leave responsibility for prisons in the hands of the local authorities. The Prisons Act 1835, which empowered the Home Secretary to appoint up to five Inspectors of Prisons for Great Britain, marked the first move towards centralisation. Frederic Hill was appointed Inspector with responsibility for Scotland and, although he had no previous experience of prisons, was soon arguing for a uniform system of prison management to be applied across the country and for a few main prisons which could be used as a national facility.

Under the (Scottish) Prison Act of 1839, local accountability for prisons came to an end: a General Board, which was given overall responsibility for the management of prisons in Scotland, and County Boards, which assumed responsibility for day-to-day administration, were set up. The General Board, on which the judiciary was well-represented, had the power to authorise the building, use and closure of prisons and to suspend or dismiss staff employed by the County Boards. In 1840, the first set of Prison Rules came into force and in 1842, a new General Prison in Perth, which was later to become a model for the Scottish prison system, was opened.

The process of centralisation was taken a stage further by the Prisons (Scotland) Administration Act 1860 which abolished the General Board and replaced it with four managers. They became advisors to the Secretary for Scotland, while the County Boards reported directly to him. In effect, the Secretary for Scotland took over many of the functions of the General Board although day-to-day control over local conditions was still exercised by the County Boards. Although responsibility for financing the prisons remained with the local authorities, this arrangement did not last for much longer.

The consolidation of central control

Central control over what could now be called the Scottish prison system was completed by the Prisons (Scotland) Act 1877, which transferred all responsibility for prisons to the Secretary for Scotland and made prisons a charge on central government funds. The 1877 Act also made provision for the appointment of Prison Commissioners, who were to report annually to Parliament; and for the continuation of local involvement through the appointment of Visiting Committees, consisting of commissioners of supply, justices of the peace and magistrates, and the granting of authority to local magistrates to visit prisons in their locality. However, their influence on the management of prisons has always been fairly minimal.

One of the major consequences of the new legislation was that it enabled prisoners to be transferred from one prison to another. At the same time, prison staff, who had previously been employed by the County Boards, were transferred to government employment and became civil servants. In addition to the General Prison at Perth, the Commissioners took over direct responsibility for fifty-six county prisons in April 1878. Within one year of taking up office the Commissioners had reduced this number to forty-three; three years later there were only thirty-five remaining and by 1888 this number had been reduced to fifteen (Coyle 1991).

Much of the detail of the 1877 Act was re-enacted in the Prisons (Scotland) Act 1952, which remained in force until it was itself replaced by the Prisons (Scotland) Act 1989. Both the 1952 Act and the 1989 Act were consolidating measures which did not change the law but brought together all the legislative provisions that had hitherto been enacted. These included a series of statutes which restricted the power of courts to impose sentences of imprisonment or detention on first offenders, or offenders under the age of 21, and the Criminal Justice Act 1967, which introduced parole and allowed for the early release of prisoners sentenced to more than eighteen months. The contemporary significance of the 1877 Act is that it set up the administrative framework which, to a substantial extent, still applies today, and that it therefore marked the start of the present era of prisons.

The Prison Commissioners were abolished in 1928 and replaced by the Prisons Department for Scotland, which was in turn abolished in 1939 when its functions were transferred to the Secretary of State for Scotland. (The Secretary for Scotland acquired the status of Secretary of State in 1926.) Since then prisons have been administered through the Scottish Home and Health Department (now the Scottish Office Home and Health Department) which forms a part of the Scottish Office, and the Secretary of State exercises overall responsibility for all aspects of penal policy and administration.

Under Section 39 of the Prisons (Scotland) Act 1989, the Secretary of State for Scotland is empowered to make rules for the regulation and management of penal institutions and for the classification, treatment, employment, discipline and control of persons detained therein. The rules are promulgated as statutory instruments. As such, they must be laid before Parliament although they are rarely debated or voted on. There are separate sets of statutory instruments regulating prisons, detention centres and young offenders institutions. Because the existing rules date from 1952, they are now in urgent need of updating and revision.

In spite of the fact that new consolidating legislation has recently been introduced, there is considerable support for the view that an entirely new statutory framework which takes account of recent changes in policy and practice, is now required. However, this is unlikely to happen until the struggle over the future of imprisonment in Scotland is finally resolved. This is an issue to which we shall return in Chapter 9.

The displacement of the legal profession by the civil service

What, then, can we learn from this brief account of institutional developments? We have already emphasised the increasing centralisation which accompanied the evolution of the Scottish prison system. Of equal note have been the changes in the balance of power among those who have exercised a dominant influence over its development. In the early stages, the dominant influences were legal ones and, as Coyle (1991) has argued, prisons were clearly regarded as an integral part of the criminal justice system. Thus, when the General Board of Directors was appointed in 1839, it was to consist of the Lord Justice General and the Lord Justice Clerk (the two most senior criminal judges in Scotland), the Lord Advocate and the Solicitor General (the Government's two Law Officers for Scotland), and the Dean of the Faculty of Advocates *ex officio* and fourteen other persons, five of whom were to be Sheriffs Depute, i.e. local 'circuit' judges. Even when they were replaced by four Managers in 1860, two of the three *ex officio* appointments, the Sheriff Principal of Perth and the Crown Agent (the equivalent in Scotland of the Director of Public Prosecutions in England), held important legal offices while the Stipendiary Manager and Secretary to the Board, Dr John Hill Burton, was an advocate. This situation continued when the Managers were replaced by the Prison Commission and throughout the fifty-two years of its existence (from 1877 to 1929) the Sheriff Principal of Perth and the Crown Agent were *ex officio* Commissioners. However, their influence was not great and when the Prison Commission was abolished in 1928 and replaced by the Prisons Department for Scotland, and when this was incorporated into the Scottish Office eleven years later, the residual influence of the legal profession over the Prison Service disappeared as the civil service sought to impose its control over it. Although prison officers and prison governors already had the status of civil servants, they were henceforth accountable to civil servants and increasingly subjected to bureaucratic regulations. Moreover, their own lack of professional standing, as evidenced by the poor educational backgrounds of the prison officers and the very rudimentary training which they received and by the direct recruitment of generalists and the promotion of prison officers to governor-grade staff, meant that they were effectively unable to challenge the increasing control of prisons by the civil service.

Having set out, albeit rather briefly, the institutional history of the Scottish prison system, we now turn to the discussion of the current institutional relationships that characterise it.

ACTORS IN THE SCOTTISH PRISON SYSTEM

In this section, we give a topographic account of the main actors in the Scottish prison system. We divide the system into an inner core, an outer penumbra, a ring of political accountability, a ring of external influence and an outer ring of legal accountability.

The inner core

There are five potentially significant groups of actors within the inner core of the Scottish prison system: civil servants who are located in the Headquarters of the Scottish Prison Service in Edinburgh; prison governors; prison officers; several groups of prison professionals, most of whom work in individual establishments; and the prisoners themselves. In the late 1980s the Director of the Prison Service was a senior career-grade civil servant with the rank of Under-Secretary (Grade 3), and the 150 or so staff who worked at Headquarters were organised into a number of Divisions each under the control of a Deputy Director.[2] Although a unified grading system known as Fresh Start was introduced in 1987, a distinction could still be made between the erstwhile governor grades (now often called managers) and the uniformed staff. Each of the twenty-two establishments was under the control of a governor and, depending on its size, contained up to ten governor-grade staff. There were about ninety governor-grade staff, a small number of whom had jobs at Headquarters (usually about six), with the Inspectorate (two) or at the Staff College (two). There were, of course, many more prison officers – about 2,500 to deal with an average daily population of 5,000 or so prisoners. Finally, there were some sixty chaplains, fifty social workers, thirty full-time education officers, twenty-five medical officers and smaller numbers of psychologists and psychiatrists. In Scotland, unlike England and Wales, few of these professionals were actually employed by the Prison Service – on the whole, they were engaged from external agencies to provide a service on a contractual basis.

Different groups of staff exercise power in different circumstances. In terms of day-to-day activity in the halls or in the workshops, the two most important groups are prison officers and prisoners, and what does and does not go on can, in the first instance, be understood in terms of a power struggle between these two groups. On the other hand, in terms of the specific services which they can provide and, in some cases, the particular decisions which they can influence, the power of some of the professional groups can be considerable. However, with respect to the large majority of administrative decisions which affect the prison careers and the quality of life of prisoners, prison governors and Headquarters personnel, in particular those in the casework branches, are the most important groups of staff. In fact, as we shall demonstrate, the nature of the decisions that are taken not infrequently reflect the outcome of a power struggle between these two groups of actors.

To argue that prison governors and Headquarters staff have the greatest influence on administrative decision-making is, however, not to deny that other groups also influence decisions. Prison officers are clearly involved in such decision-making, in that they write reports and make recommendations on a wide range of issues, for example, a prisoner's suitability for a change of work party, an upgrading of security category, or a move to semi-open or open conditions. However, their recommendations and opinions are nearly always 'translated' by the more powerful governor grades. As we show in Chapter 5 below, in spite of their status in the world outside, the position of many of the prison professionals is actually very similar to that of the prison officers. The position of the prisoner is not so different either. Although adult, male, long-term prisoners can now express a preference for one of the three 'prisons of classification' (Glenochil, Perth and Shotts), and may ask for a change of work party, they have few legally enforceable rights and must always persuade someone in authority to support their request. Thus, as we have already mentioned in the Introduction, prisoners do not feature prominently in our analysis which focuses on those who exercise the greatest influence over administrative decision-making.

In Figure 1.1, each of the five groups of actors within the inner core of the Scottish prison system is represented by a segment of a circle.

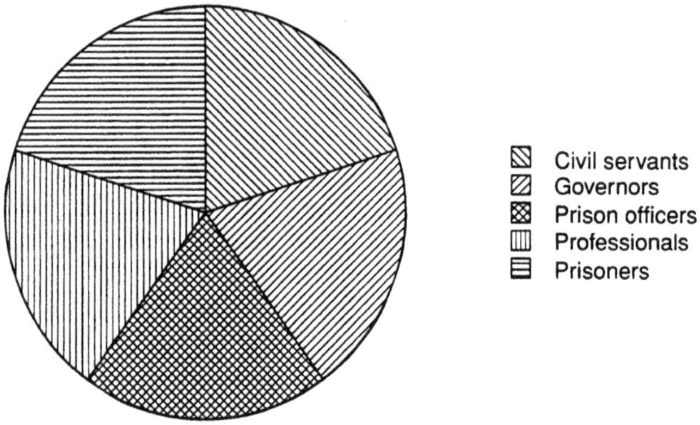

Figure 1.1 The inner core of the prison system

The outer penumbra

In addition to an inner core, the prison system also has an outer penumbra. This comprises three institutions which, although technically outside the Scottish Prison Service, are established by statute and are regarded as having a legitimate input into its workings. The first of these is the Parole Board, introduced by the Criminal Justice Act 1967, which has far-reaching effects on the operation of the penal system and, in particular, on the management of long-term prisoners. It is appointed by and accountable to the Secretary of State. Prisoners serving more than eighteen months are eligible for parole after twelve months, provided that they have served one-third of their sentence. The future of the Parole Board and of parole in Scotland has been reviewed by the Kincraig Committee (SHHD 1989a) which made forty recommendations, including: limiting parole to those prisoners serving more than five years; changing the eligibility date for the parole to halfway through a sentence; maintaining that those prisoners serving more than five years should be released on licence two-thirds of the way through the sentence; suggesting that those serving five years or less would have conditional automatic release halfway through sentence; abolishing Local Review Committees; and ending the remission and forfeiture of remission systems. Although it may well come to exercise a lesser role in future, at the time of our research the Parole Board was the main embodiment of the principle of rehabilitation. Of course, it is also concerned with the safety of the public, but this concern is directly related to its main focus on the rehabilitation of the individual offender.

The second institution is the Prisons Inspectorate, introduced by the Criminal Justice Act 1982. The Chief Inspector, who comes from outside the prison system, is also appointed by and reports directly to the Secretary of State. He is assisted by a Deputy Chief Inspector, who is a senior prison governor, and an Inspector, who is a governor with in-charge experience, and draws upon the services of a civil servant. The Inspectorate visits each penal establishment on a regular basis and produces three to four detailed reports on particular establishments per year. It also produces an Annual Report and has, in addition, undertaken a small number of thematic studies and a special inquiry into the spate of violent incidents in Peterhead Prison (see Chapter 7 below). However, it has no remit to inspect the civil servants working at Headquarters. Hence, the Inspectorate does not really inspect the whole of the prison system. The Inspectorate is primarily concerned with the physical conditions in which prisoners are held, the facilities available to them, the morale of staff and the efficiency of individual establishments. The influence of the Inspectorate is hard to assess: they themselves claim, citing examples of changes that were brought about as a result of their inspections of particular establishments, that their influence can be considerable, but others are less convinced.

The third institution consists of Visiting Committees (McManus 1986), most of whose members are appointed by the local authorities in the areas served by the prison. They can carry out inspections and members have the right to enter the prison whenever they like. They also have limited powers of adjudication which are now rarely used, but their overall impact on decision-making for individual prisoners and, more generally, on the prisons is slight.

In Figure 1.2, the outer penumbra of the Scottish prison system is represented by a ring surrounding the inner core and each of the three groups is represented by a segment of the ring.

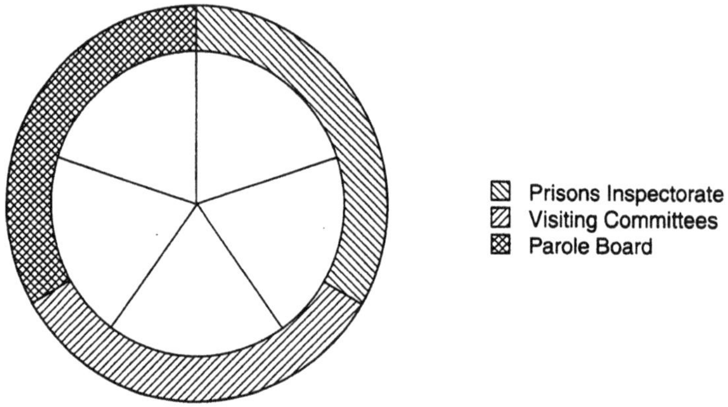

Figure 1.2 The inner core and outer penumbra of the prison system

Political accountability

The various groups and institutions comprising the inner core and outer penumbra of the prison service are all accountable to Scottish Office ministers who are responsible for formulating policy and, when they deem it to be necessary, for proposing legislation. However, as we have shown, legislation is resorted to relatively infrequently. As far as policy is concerned, there was something of a vacuum until 1988. The Director and the Deputy Directors constituted the Prison Service Management Group, but this tended to serve as a forum for collective management rather than a policy-making body. In the aftermath of the *May Report* (Home Office 1979) several Working Parties were set up by the Scottish Office but few of their deliberations led to new policy initiatives. During the late 1980s, a constellation of events, in particular an unprecedented series of rooftop incidents in 1986 and 1987 in which several prison officers were taken hostage and substantial damage was done to the fabric of a number of establishments, made the case for a radical re-think of policy that much more urgent. However, policy, in effect, remained the preserve of one of the Deputy Directors who, until recently, also had substantial casework responsibilities. Critics of what appeared to be a rudderless Department stressed the need to set up a policy unit within the Scottish Prison Service. Although this was never formally established, the number of Headquarters staff dealing with policy issues has certainly grown and, from 1988 onwards, there has been a far greater emphasis on policy-making (see Chapter 9 below).

Using the mode of representation already used to depict the inner core and outer penumbra of the prison system, Figure 1.3 shows them to be surrounded by an outer ring of political accountability.

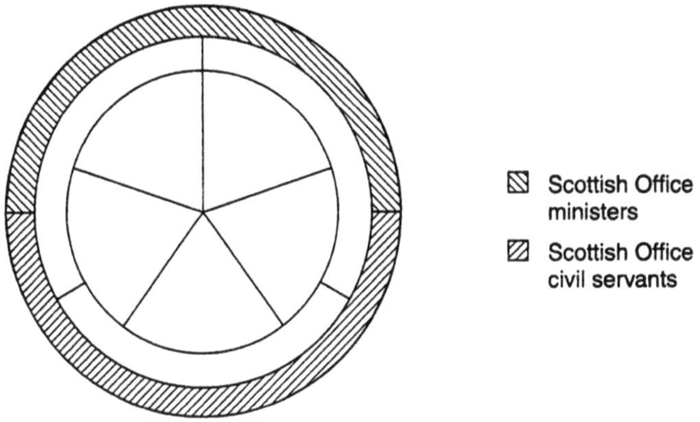

Figure 1.3 The politically accountable prison system

External influences

Governments and Government departments do not operate in a vacuum but are themselves subject to numerous external influences. In the case of prisons, these influences correspond, at least in part, to the five groups of actors which comprise the inner core of the prison system. Thus, governors are represented collectively by the Association of Scottish Prison Governors (ASPG) and by the Prison Governors' Branch of the Society of Civil and Public Servants, while officers are represented by the Scottish Prison Officers' Association (SPOA). There are a number of pressure groups and voluntary organisations which, in different ways, claim to speak for and represent the interests of prisoners and their families. Among the more prominent in recent years have been the Scottish Association for the Care and Resettlement of Offenders (SACRO), the Scottish Council for Civil Liberties (SCCL), the Howard League for Penal Reform (Scotland), the Gateway Exchange and Families Outside. The various professions are represented by their professional associations – in the case of medicine, the Royal Colleges and the British Medical Association; in the case of education, the Educational Institute of Scotland (EIS); and in the case of social work, the British Association of Social Work (BASW). However, these do not greatly influence penal policy in Scotland. In addition, as Richard Kinsey has pointed out, 'not one of the political parties has a clear and identifiable view of the purposes, effectiveness and future of imprisonment' (Kinsey 1988:104). Thus, political parties are not a major source of influence. Nor, moreover, is public opinion, despite the interventions of the popular press, most notably the *Daily Record*.

From the above, it would seem that ministers and their civil servants are relatively free to determine prison policy. They are not likely to be seriously troubled by Parliament or its Committees although they may come under pressure to keep broadly in line with developments in England (the recent review of parole in Scotland is a good example of this) and may have difficulty securing resources from the Treasury.

In Figure 1.4, the external influences on policy-making are represented by a further ring, outside the ring of political accountability.

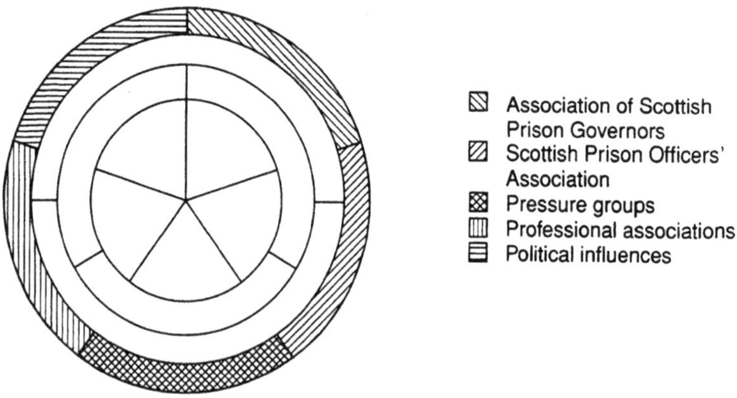

Figure 1.4 The politically accountable prison system in context

Legal accountability

Finally, beyond these external influences, comes an outer ring of legal accountability. This comprises the Scottish criminal courts, the superior civil courts (the Scottish Court of Session and the House of

Lords), the European Commission on Human Rights (ECHR) and the European Court, and the Parliamentary Commissioner for Administration (PCA). The criminal courts are in a rather different position from the other institutions in the outermost ring. Although the Government appears to regard their sentencing decisions as binding as far as the prison system is concerned and makes no serious attempt to influence them, it is not clear that it has to adopt this stance. Decriminalisation, diversion and the development of additional non-custodial disposals in place of imprisonment would undoubtedly affect sentencing and reduce the number of prison admissions. In fact, one could argue that the Government treats the criminal courts (even for policy purposes) as if they were entirely external, belonging to the outer ring of legal accountability when they could be treated, at least in part, as internal to the policy-making process and as part of the outer penumbra of the prison system.

The other three institutions rightly belong to the outer circle. For whatever reason there have, as yet, been only two cases of judicial review involving prisoners in the Scottish courts (the Thompson and Leech cases) and both of these were unsuccessful. However, there have been a number of such cases in the English courts and, where there has been an appeal to the House of Lords, the decision is regarded as binding in Scotland (English decisions in the Divisional Court and the Court of Appeal, although not constitutionally binding, are, in addition, rarely ignored). There have been a number of Scottish appeals to the ECHR and the European Court (for an analysis of these cases, see Chapter 8 below). European Court decisions, from wherever they originate, are binding on all the countries (including the UK) which have ratified the European Convention on Human Rights and have, *inter alia*, had some indirect impact on prisons in Scotland, leading, for example, to changes in the rules relating to prisoners' correspondence and access to legal advice (Fawcett 1985). However, it is worth noting that none of the Scottish cases has had a successful outcome. Finally, a number of cases of alleged maladministration have been taken to the Parliamentary Commissioner for Administration (PCA). Although PCA decisions are not legally binding, they are normally treated as though they are and, in a few cases, have led to minor changes in administrative procedures.

In Figure 1.5, which represents the criminal justice system as it applies to prisons, the system is enclosed by an outer ring of legal accountability.

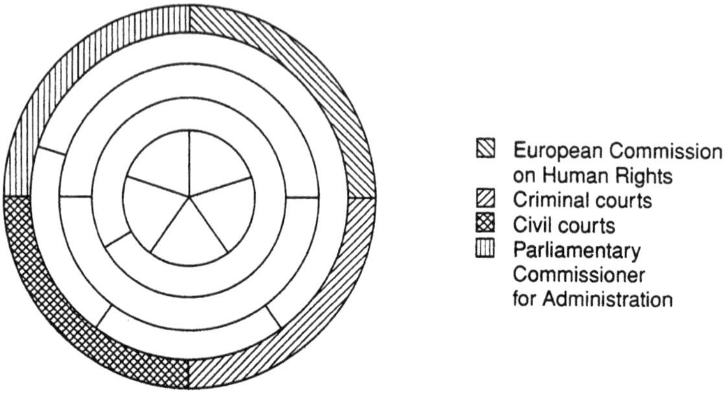

Figure 1.5 The criminal justice system as it applies to prisons

A simplified representation of the prison system

The main problem with this topographical representation of the prison system in its broad political and legal context is, of course, that it is far too complex for current analytical purposes. However, this defect can be remedied, as it is possible to produce a simplified version of the map by including only those actors and institutions which have a significant and direct bearing on administrative decision-making.

In such matters, the most important groups of actors in the inner core are officials, who are located in the Headquarters of the Scottish Prison Service in Edinburgh, and governors, who are mainly to be found in the various penal establishments. Within the outer penumbra of institutions whose activities impinge directly on the Prison Service, the most important are the criminal courts which decide who is sent to prison and for how long,[3] and the Parole Board which recommends who should be released before completing their sentence. Within the layer of political accountability which surrounds the Prison Service, the Scottish Office, i.e. ministers and their advisers, play key roles. Finally, within the layer of legal accountability, judicial review in the domestic courts and applications to the European Commission Human Rights are (actually or potentially) of particular importance. However, there is no need to distinguish these institutions here. Figure 1.6 represents a simplified representation of the prison system.

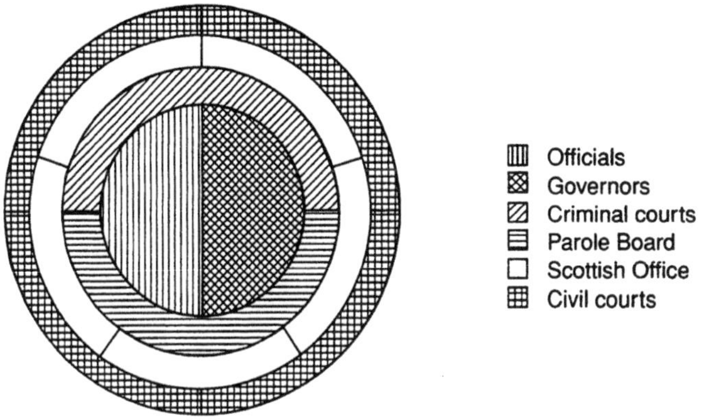

Figure 1.6 Simplified model of the criminal justice system as it relates to prisons

So far we have characterised the current institutional structure of the Scottish prison system and its historical development. Our final task in this chapter is to contextualise this discussion further by considering the changing trends in the use of imprisonment in Scotland.

TRENDS IN THE USE OF IMPRISONMENT

We look first at the changing use of imprisonment in Scotland since the turn of the century and then compare the use of imprisonment in Scotland with its use in other jurisdictions.

Changes in the use of imprisonment over time

Judicial statistics relating to penalties imposed by the courts were not available until 1897. Since then, it has been possible to study trends in the use of available sanctions. Table 1.1 sets out changes in the absolute and relative use of imprisonment and other forms of detention, the fine, admonishment and probation between 1897 and 1978. In 1897, the most common penalty was the fine (imposed in 71 per cent of guilty pleas or verdicts), followed by admonishment/caution (15 per cent), imprisonment and other forms of detention (9 per cent) and probation (1 per cent). By 1978, the *absolute numbers* of sentences of detention and of admonishment/

Table 1.1 Changes in the absolute and relative use of available penalties, 1897 and 1978

Absolute numbers	*1897*	*1978*	*% change*
Detention	10,329	11,132	+7.8
Fines	80,137	175,352	+118.9
Admonishment/caution	20,003	20,230	+1.1
Probation	1,230	2,654	+115.8
Other	1,015	1,745	+71.9
Relative numbers	*%*	*%*	
Detention	9.16	5.27	-42.5
Fines	71.10	83.10	+16.9
Admonishment/caution	17.74	9.58	-40.5
Probation	1.09	1.30	+19.3
Other	0.90	0.82	-8.9

Source: Young (forthcoming)

caution were much the same (they increased by 8 per cent and 1 per cent respectively). However, this contrasts with very large proportional increases in the number of fines (119 per cent) and probation orders (116 per cent). As a result, the *relative number* of guilty pleas/verdicts which received sentences of detention fell by 42.5 per cent, admonishment(s)/cautions fell by 40.5 per cent while those who were fined or given a probation order increased by 17 per cent and 19 per cent respectively. The availability of community service (introduced by the Community Service Offenders Act 1978) and compensation orders (introduced by the Criminal Justice (Scotland) Act 1980) have made little difference to the overall picture. Thus, in 1988, there were only 3,351 community service orders (1.9 per cent of all guilty pleas or verdicts) and 1,670 compensation orders (0.9 per cent). The relative use of other penalties was largely unchanged – 138,509 offenders (78.2 per cent of those who pled guilty or were found guilty) were given a fine, 15,561 (8.8 per cent) were admonished/cautioned, 14,008 (8.1 per cent) were given a custodial sentence while 3,115 (1.8 per cent) were put on probation (SHHD 1990a).

The comparative use of imprisonment in different jurisdictions

At any one time, Scotland has proportionately more people in prison than just about any other Western European country. Table 1.2, which is based on Council of Europe statistics and refers to

Table 1.2 Prison populations in Western Europe, as at 1 September 1988

Country	*Detention rate per 100,000 inhabitants*	*% unconvicted*	*Unconvicted detention rates*	*% convicted*	*Convicted detention rates*
N. Ireland	114.2	18.5	21.13	81.5	93.07
Scotland	99.3	16.6	16.48	83.4	82.81
England/Wales	96.7	20.4	19.73	79.6	76.97
Turkey	95.6	36.4	34.80	63.6	60.80
West Germany	84.9	19.0	16.13	81.0	68.77
Portugal	83.0	27.8	23.07	72.2	59.93
France	81.1	35.9	29.11	64.1	51.98
Austria	77.0	18.1	13.94	81.9	63.06
Spain	75.8	33.2	25.17	66.8	50.63
Switzerland	73.2	23.8	17.42	76.2	55.78
Denmark	68.0	17.1	11.63	82.9	56.37
Belgium	65.4	33.2	21.71	66.8	43.69
Italy	60.4	29.8	18.00	70.2	42.40
Sweden	56.0	11.2	6.27	88.8	49.73
Ireland	55.0	2.9	1.60	97.1	53.40
Norway	48.4	11.1	5.37	88.9	43.03
Netherlands	44.0	15.9	7.00	84.1	37.00

Source: Council of Europe (1990)

1988, places Scotland behind Northern Ireland but ahead of all the other members of the Council of Europe, including Turkey.

Although the total number of prisoners per 100,000 inhabitants in Scotland (shown in Column 1) was exceptionally high, the number of unconvicted (or remand) prisoners per 100,000 inhabitants (shown in Column 3) was actually lower than in most of the other countries.[4] This was probably due, at least in part, to the limits on the amount of time for which prisoners can be held on remand in Scotland.[5] The corollary of this is that the number of convicted prisoners per 100,000 inhabitants (shown in Column 5) was much higher in Scotland than anywhere else except Northern Ireland.

The prison population is a product of the number of receptions into prison and the mean period of detention in prison. Table 1.3, which is shorter than Table 1.2 because several countries did not submit the relevant data to the Council of Europe, summarises the available data. As may be seen from Column 1, Scotland imprisoned

Table 1.3 Prison receptions and mean periods of detention in 1988

Country	*Reception rate per 100,000 inhabitants*	*Mean detention period (months)*
Scotland	695.3	1.7
Northern Ireland	346.9	3.9
England and Wales	292.7	4.0
Turkey	262.7	4.4
Austria	204.6	4.5
Ireland	204.3	3.2
Finland	190.3	4.6
Belgium	175.5	4.5
Spain	175.2	5.2
West Germany	149.5	6.8
France	149.3	6.5
Netherlands	137.1	3.5
Italy	118.4	6.1
Portugal	100.9	9.9

Source: Council of Europe (1990)

substantially more people than any other European country.[6] At the same time, Scotland made proportionately much greater use of short sentences of imprisonment. The contrast with some other countries is indeed stark: while Scotland and, albeit to a lesser extent, England and Wales, and Northern Ireland, imprisoned large numbers of offenders for short periods; France, West Germany and Italy imprisoned considerably fewer people although they served much longer prison sentences.

Further examination of the Scottish statistics reveals a simple explanation. Among convicted prisoners, almost half (9,700 out of 20,540 or 47.2 per cent of receptions in 1988) were imprisoned for fine default. These prisoners usually spend very short periods (measured in days and weeks rather than months and years) in prison and therefore contribute much more to the prison reception rate than they do to the prison population rate. The very large number of fine defaulters creates considerable administrative and logistical problems for the prison service and calls into question whether sentencers pay sufficient attention to an offender's circumstances when they impose a fine, whether our systems of collection and enforcement are as efficient as they could be (Nicholson and Millar 1989) and whether imprisonment should be the only (or the main) remedy in the case of default (McNeill 1986).

Over the period 1970 to 1988, the average daily population and

Table 1.4 Trends in average daily population and in receptions, 1970–88

Year	Average daily population	Receptions (1) Remand	Receptions (2) Sentenced
1970	5,005	16,689	20,351
1971	5,338	18,102	22,035
1972	5,220	17,247	21,139
1973	4,810	16,132	18,419
1974	4,689	16,831	19,354
1975	4,951	17,324	19,674
1976	4,886	16,210	18,116
1977	4,871	16,296	17,540
1978	5,062	16,640	17,592
1979	4,585	14,400	14,447
1980	4,860	13,884	16,933
1981	4,518	13,550	15,939
1982	4,891	16,072	20,552
1983	5,052	15,286	20,183
1984	4,753	16,048	19,555
1985	5,273	18,985	24,252
1986	5,588	18,107	23,220
1987	5,446	17,111	22,186
1988	5,229	15,000	20,540

Source: Kelly (1987) and, for 1987 and 1988 figures, Scottish Home and Health Department (1990b)

the number of receptions of remand and sentenced prisoners have fluctuated in ways that do not suggest a simple explanation. This is illustrated in Table 1.4. More striking perhaps than these fluctuations have been several long-term changes in the composition of the prison population. These are illustrated in Table 1.5, which compares the average daily population, subdivided into five categories of prisoner, in the 'peak' years of 1971 and 1986. Although the average daily population in 1986 was almost the same as in 1971, the average number of remand prisoners increased by 45 per cent (from 702 or 13 per cent of the prison population in 1971 to 1,017 or 18 per cent in 1986) and the average number of fine defaulters increased by 9 per cent (from 302 or 5.7 per cent in 1971 to 329 or 5.9 per cent in 1986). By comparison, the number of young offenders (YOs) and the number of adult short-term prisoners (STPs) both fell markedly between 1971 and 1986 – the former from 1,587 (30 per cent of the total) to 1,010 (18 per cent), the

Table 1.5 Comparison of average daily population in 1971 and 1986

Average daily population	*1971*		*1986*		
	number	*%*	*number*	*%*	*% change*
Total	5,338		5,588		
subdivided into:					
Remand	702	13.2	1,017	18.2	+44.9
Fine defaulters	302	5.7	329	5.9	+8.9
Sentenced – YOs (under 21)	1,587	29.7	1,010	18.1	–36.4
Sentenced – adult STPs (18 months or less)	1,619	30.3	1,317	23.6	–18.6
Sentenced – adult LTPs (more than 18 months)	1,128	21.1	1,915	34.3	+69.8

Source: Kelly (1987)

latter from 1,619 (30 per cent) to 1,317 (24 per cent). At the same time, the number of adult long-term prisoners (LTPs) increased by 70 per cent (from 1,128 or 21 per cent of the population in 1971 to 1,915 or 34 per cent in 1986). This change, which may well reflect the imposition of longer sentences for drug-related offences and a reduction in the availability of parole for certain long-term prisoners[7] is especially significant and has been particularly marked in recent years. This build-up in the number of adult LTPs and, in particular, in those serving three years or more, is shown in Table 1.6.

Table 1.6 Changes in average daily population, 1984–8

	1984	*1985*	*1986*	*1987*	*1988*
Remands	942	1,092	1,017	938	844
Fine defaulters	258	308	329	287	275
YOs (under 21)	1,000	990	1,074	987	902
Adult STPs (less than 18 months)	1,386	1,523	1,532	1,456	1,411
Adult LTPs (18 months or more)	1,367	1,617	1,915	2,017	1,930
of which:					
adult VLTPs (3 years and over)	(1,079)	(1,311)	(1,498)	(1,603)	(1,545)

Source: Scottish Home and Health Department (1990b)

These increases in the number of LTPs serving eighteen months or more and in the number of very long-term prisoners (VLTPs) serving three years or more are very striking and contributed to the problems faced by the Scottish prison system. The reason for this is that, to prevent overcrowding, it is not enough for the available accommodation to match the number of prisoners. Apart from the fact that some accommodation is always out-of-service, different 'types' of prisoner have to be held separately and require different types of accommodation. Classification and categorisation are all-important within the Scottish prison system: not only are male prisoners held separately from female prisoners; YOs are separated from adult prisoners, remand prisoners from sentenced prisoners, long-term prisoners from short-term prisoners, prisoners deemed to require high security from prisoners deemed to require medium or low security, etc. Mismatches between particular types of prisoner and the available accommodation meant that prisoners (in particular LTPs and VLTPs) were often subjected to inappropriate regimes while certain establishments frequently held volatile mixes of inmates.

The Scottish penal estate

At the time of our research (1985–8), the Scottish prison system comprised twenty establishments whose roles are described in Table 1.7.

One prison (Cornton Vale) catered for all categories of female prisoner (see Carlen 1983 and Dobash et al. 1986 for two recent studies of this prison). Nearly all female prisoners were detained here, although three other prisons contained facilities for holding a small number of female prisoners on remand. The other nineteen prisons held male prisoners: eleven were 'local' prisons and held remand and/or short-term prisoners (serving sentences of eighteen months or less); ten, including the Barlinnie Special Unit, held long-term prisoners (serving more than eighteen months) and six held young offenders.

Several of the largest prisons were built in the nineteenth century. Many of them were in very poor condition and, for example, lacked sanitation in the cells. However, others were in modern accommodation and had much better facilities. Most of the prisons provided a high level of security and the two open prisons and one open Young Offenders' Institution (YOI) only held a very small proportion of the total population (together they

Table 1.7 Roles of prison establishments in 1987

Establishments	*Description*
1 *Prisons*	The main purpose of classification of prisoners is to associate those of a similar character. Where in any case it is considered that a prisoner would be unsuitable for the category in which he would normally be placed by reference to his age, aptitude, length of sentence, etc. he may be allocated to another category.
Aberdeen	For local prisoners serving sentences of eighteen months or less.
	For older prisoners serving sentences of over eighteen months allocated to an ordinary prison.
Barlinnie	For local prisoners serving sentences of eighteen months or less.
	Includes a Special Unit (up to 8 inmates) for the treatment of certain long-term prisoners with propensities of violence towards staff.
Cornton Vale	For all categories of female prisoners.
Dumfries[1]	For local untried prisoners. Until June 1987 a training prison for prisoners serving sentences of eighteen months up to three years.
Dungavel	For selected prisoners who by their behaviour and outlook are considered suitable for less restrictive conditions.
Edinburgh	For local prisoners serving sentences of eighteen months or less.
	For certain prisoners serving a sentence of over eighteen months.
Friarton	For category 'C' inmates serving sentences of up to nine months.
Glenochil[2]	For prisoners serving sentences of over eighteen months.
Greenock[1]	Until June 1987 a prison for prisoners serving sentences of three years or more considered suitable for trade training.
Inverness	For local prisoners serving sentences of eighteen months or less.
	For certain prisoners who require to be held for a time under a more stringent regime than that at other prisons.
Low Moss	For selected prisoners serving sentences of six months or less.
Noranside[3]	For selected prisoners who by their behaviour and outlook are considered suitable for open conditions.
Penninghame	For selected prisoners who by their behaviour are considered suitable for open conditions.
Perth	For local prisoners serving sentences of eighteen months or less.
	For prisoners serving sentences of over eighteen months.

Table 1.7 (continued)

Establishments	*Description*
Peterhead	For prisoners serving sentences of over eighteen months who are not allocated to a mainstream prison.
Shotts[4]	For prisoners serving sentences of over eighteen months.
2 *Young Offenders' Institutions*	For young persons not less than 16 years and not more than 21 sentenced to be detained in a young offenders' institution.
Castle Huntly	For youths of all sentence ranges likely to respond to more individual methods of training in open conditions.
Cornton Vale	For all female young offenders.
Dumfries[1]	For youths serving sentences of eighteen months and over including those detained without limit of time.
Glenochil[2]	Until June 1987 a young offenders' institution for youths serving sentences of over nine months and youths serving shorter sentences assessed as high security risks.
Greenock[1]	For youths serving sentences of eighteen months and over including those detained without limit of time.
Noranside[3]	Until May 1987 an open institution for youths of all sentence ranges.
Polmont	For youths serving sentences of less than eighteen months (other than those assessed as high security risks).
3 *Detention Centre*	
Glenochil	For male young offenders ordered under the provisions of Section 207 and 413 of the Criminal Procedure (Scotland) Act 1975, as substituted by Section 45 of the Criminal Justice (Scotland) Act 1980, to be detained in a detention centre for a period of at least twenty-eight days but not exceeding four months.
4 *Remand Institution*	
Longriggend	For youths under 21 years of age remanded to Barlinnie Prison for examination or trial.

Notes: 1 Changed use from prison to YOI in June 1987.
2 Changed use from YOI to prison in June 1987.
3 Changed use from YOI to prison in May 1987.
4 Phase II opened in June 1987.

Source: Scottish Home and Health Department (1989b:Appendix 1)

contained 344 places out of a total 'design capacity' of 5,505, i.e. 6.25 per cent of the total).

The geographical location of the twenty establishments is shown on Figure 1.7. It will be seen that most of the establishments are in the central belt. However, there was a substantial mismatch between the location of many of the establishments which held long-term prisoners and the areas from which they were drawn. This is illustrated most vividly by the fact that most of the LTPs in Peterhead came from Glasgow.

CONCLUSION

In an attempt to contextualise the Scottish prison system as it exists today, we have traced its historical development, charting the emergence and consolidation of central control and the displacement of the legal profession by the civil service as the major source of power and control. We then sought to identify the major actors within the prison system. In addition to the civil servants, who are located at Headquarters in Edinburgh, these include prison governors, who preside over establishments, the criminal courts, which decide who is sent to prison and for how long, the Parole Board, which decides who should be released and at what point in their sentence, the Scottish Office and other government departments, and the European Commission on Human Rights. Next, we looked at the changing use of imprisonment in Scotland and compared this with its use in other jurisdictions. Although the number of people sent to prison in Scotland is much the same today as it was at the turn of the century, this now represents a much smaller proportion of those who are sentenced by the courts. In spite of this, Scotland sent proportionally more people to prison and held proportionally more people in prison than almost all other European countries. We identified some of the reasons for this and described the recent increase in the number of long-term (eighteen months or more) and very long-term (three years or more) prisoners in Scotland. Finally, we showed how the attempt to accommodate these prisoners within the existing penal establishments caused serious problems which contributed to the crisis faced by the Scottish Prison Service in the late 1980s.

With these preliminaries accomplished, we now turn to a characterisation of the various discourses which are associated with different groups of actors in the Scottish prison system.

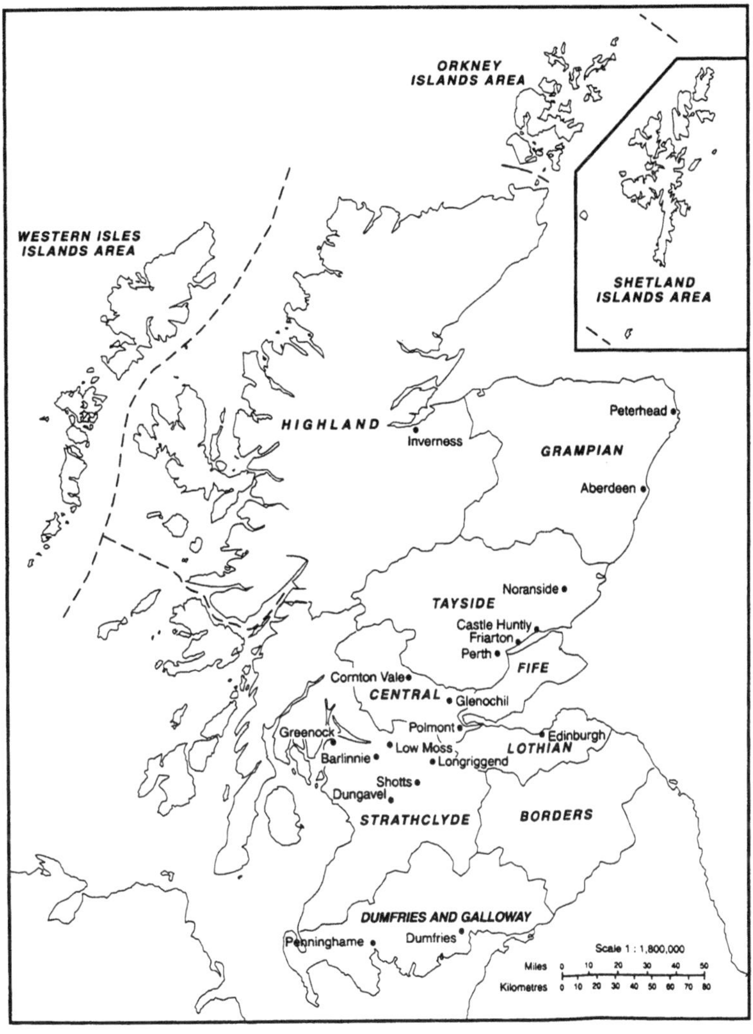

Figure 1.7 The location of penal establishments

Chapter 2

Discourses and discursive struggles

We argued at the beginning of Chapter 1 that an examination of the relationship between actors and discourses is crucial to our discussion of long-term imprisonment in Scotland. In that chapter we focused on the institutions and actors in historical and comparative perspective. In this chapter, we elaborate this position and, in so doing, seek to accomplish several aims. We begin by detailing how our approach to the study of knowledge in society is derived from the work of Karl Mannheim. Having outlined this approach, we then connect the discussion of institutional actors from the previous chapter with an examination of the ends and means discourses which we see in play in the Scottish prison system. We shall conclude this part of our discussion by showing how these means and ends discourses can be combined to form a discourse matrix of imprisonment in Scotland. We shall use this matrix all through our analysis, but at this point it will help to locate the principal actors identified in Chapter 1 in discursive space.

FROM KARL MANNHEIM TO THE SOCIOLOGY OF PENAL DISCOURSE

The form of the sociology of knowledge which we deploy in this book is derived from the suggestive work of Karl Mannheim. This has been the subject of a revival of interest recently (see, e.g. Kettler et al. 1984; Loader 1985; Woldring 1986) which has rescued his project from some of the more shortsighted criticisms which have been made of it.[1] In some earlier work, Longhurst has argued that Mannheim can provide a framework for contemporary analysis (Abercrombie and Longhurst 1981 and 1983; Longhurst 1984, 1988 and 1989; see also Dant 1991). Mannheim directs our attention to three aspects of the relationship between knowledge and society: the relationship between knowledge and power which is rooted in an inherently competitive conception of social life, the relationship between forms of knowledge and their specific manifestations; and the relationship between social groups and the forms of knowledge they adopt and develop. We shall briefly examine each of these aspects of the overall relationship in turn.

Knowledge, power and the nature of social life

For Mannheim, social life is inherently competitive (Mannheim 1952). He believes that competition is not simply an economic phenomenon, but affects all sectors of society. At times Mannheim comes close to suggesting that competition is a universal characteristic of human association. Mannheim stresses the political nature of human competition and argues that the competitive nature of human life is structured into established and relatively stable patterns of domination. However, for Mannheim, such domination is resisted by those who are subject to it. Thus, Mannheim is particularly exercised by the nature of social struggles for power. We follow him in stressing the importance of the struggles between different social actors and contend that the most useful way to view social life is in terms of the struggle for power and domination between different social groups. However, as Mannheim made clear, this does not mean that a Hobbesian war of all against all is always in evidence; rather, at particular moments, certain patterns of accommodation can occur. We would suggest that struggles between social groups can result in a continuing struggle of a manifest kind, in separation, in fusion or in alliances.[2] Separation implies that social groups recognise (not necessarily consistently or explicitly) that their interests can best be served by not engaging with others. For example, in the prison context, this would be the case where prisoners develop a form of culture which is separate and, to a large extent, autonomous from that of the prison staff. The two groups might be said to inhabit different worlds to avoid overt forms of conflict. Such a situation is often implied by some of the case-studies of imprisonment to which reference has already been made. Mathiesen's (1965) development of the concept of censoriousness points to the rather different case of two groups in some respects sharing the same world. Here, the dominated group censors the group in power for not delivering them their rights and dues. Groups can also fuse to form what is, in effect, a single group. In the prison context, it might be argued that some of the 'helping' or 'caring' professions have fused with each other to form what is, in effect, a single group. Finally, and perhaps most interestingly, groups can form alliances. In the prison context, governors may form alliances with officers or with the civil servants working in Headquarters. It may also be the case that officers form alliances with certain groups of prisoners. It has often been remarked, for example, that officers collude with certain inmates to ensure that sex offenders are brutalised in prison. Such alliances are likely to shift, making this a particularly interesting focus of attention. Indeed, it is a thought-provoking exercise to analyse the changing nature of the alliances made between the different groups in the penal context. However, our fundamental aim here is to point to the conflictual nature of social life, the importance of power and domination in such conflicts, and the fact that accommodation and alliances may result from them.

Mannheim also points to the discursive nature of social domination, showing how the use and development of certain forms of belief relate to positions in social hierarchies and patterns of domination. Thus, according to Mannheim, domination is of a discursive nature. As in the later work of Michel Foucault, power and knowledge are held to be intimately related. We are also much concerned with the discursive nature of social domination, which is particularly evident in the case of prisons. An institution, which in many respects seems to be built upon violence and brutal repression is, we would argue, also structured and maintained by discursive relations and interactions. This is because many of these relations of domination are structured and reproduced through the mobilisation of particular attitudes and forms of belief.

Forms of knowledge and their specific manifestations

In discussing forms of knowledge, Mannheim makes a broad distinction, using different terms at different points in his work, between the style, structure or form of a type of knowledge or belief and the nature of its specific manifestations (Longhurst 1989:35–47). He develops this view both theoretically and in his substantive study of conservative thought (Mannheim 1953 and 1986). Mannheim looks at the relationship between forms and specific manifestations of thought from two different points of view, which depend, in part, on the purpose of the analytical exercise. The first of these is concerned with the process of interpretation. Mannheim is concerned to address the methodological question of how the analyst can move from the specific manifestations of a form of thought to identifying and elucidating its general structure. He draws on debates in hermeneutics and produces a version of a hermeneutic circle or spiral. The parts are interpreted in the context of the whole, the whole is understood in terms of the parts and so on, until as complete a picture as is necessary for the research purpose is built up.

However, there is a second aspect to this difference between the general characteristics of thought and its specific manifestations, as the former acts as a resource for those engaged in struggles in particular social situations. So, for example, the conservative style of thought exists as a resource for those seeking to formulate particular conservative statements or engage in conservative political practice in a given context. Hence, statements and specific manifestations of discourse are built up by individuals and groups in the course of the struggles they are engaged in. One of the most important resources they can call on is the general style of the type of belief or practice that is being developed. The operation of these processes in Mannheim's work on 'Conservative Thought' is represented diagrammatically in Figure 2.1.

In earlier work, Longhurst (1989) has suggested that these two different levels of thought could be termed conceptual structure and discourse, with the conceptual structure level having much in common with Weber's characterisation of an 'ideal type' or with Althusser's notion of a 'problematic'. Although we adopt this general approach in this book, we do not say a great deal about the conceptual structure of the forms of discourse we identify. Rather we spend a good deal of our time in outlining the nature of the particular discourses we see in play in the Scottish prison system. These are generated in part from the beliefs, responses and actions of those involved in struggles within that system. However, specific discourses in the penal context can be related to more generic discourses of the same type, e.g. the discourses of specific actors can be related to generic discourses of normalisation or professionalism, but also to the conceptual structure, or deeper proto-discourse associated with these forms of thought. However, the interpretive task of moving from the whole to the parts remains a crucial part of the analysis.

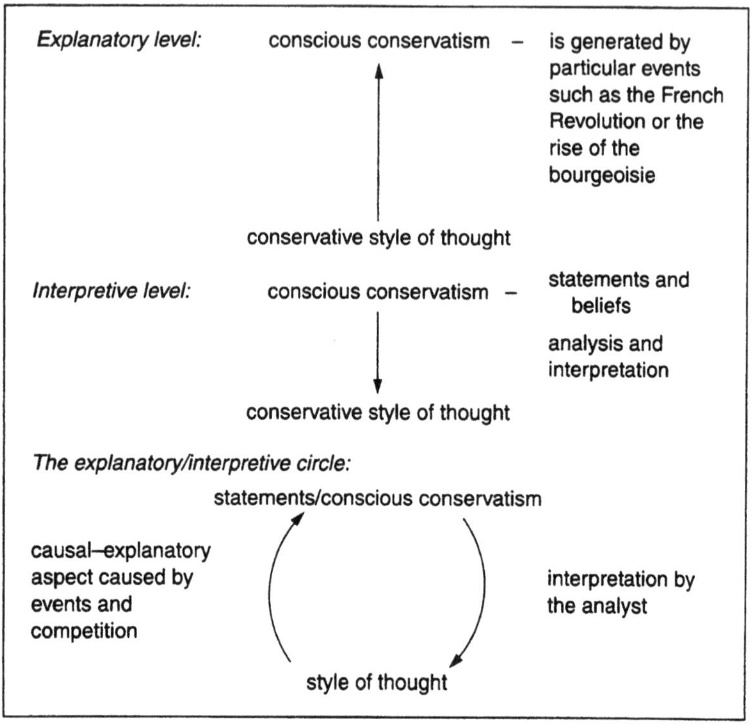

Figure 2.1 Explanatory and interpretive arguments in 'conservative thought'
Source: Longhurst (1989:63)

Social groups and forms of knowledge

Mannheim, like many other sociologists of knowledge, is concerned with the issue of why it is that particular groups adopt or develop particular forms of thought or types of knowledge. Mannheim rejects the concept of interest as an explanatory mechanism. However, his motives are themselves influenced by his lack of regard for certain forms of Marxism, which analyse the relationship between economic interests and ideology in a crude and reductive fashion. Although Mannheim is very critical of the Marxist approaches (Abercrombie and Longhurst 1983:9; Longhurst 1989), the concept of 'commitment' which he uses in his sociology of knowledge is actually rather close to some conceptualisations of 'interests' which are increasingly prominent in the contemporary sociology of scientific knowledge (e.g. Barnes 1977). Hence, once the economistic origins of the concept of interest have been removed, it is possible to see that there are many similarities between Mannheim's concept of commitment and the concept of interests advanced and utilised in much current research in the sociology of knowledge.

It is important to recognise, however, that the relationship between interests and the formulation and utilisation of types of knowledge has a certain circularity. That is, the different location of social groups opens up the possibility of different interests and the analysis of knowledge and belief can then take place relative to those socially generated interests. However, interests are themselves also constructed, or partly constructed, through appeals to such forms of thought. The relationship between social location, interests and forms of thought is interactive.

The sociology of power and discourse

Our general position is, thus, that groups of social actors in specific social settings produce discourses that reflect and construct their social interests in the course of competitive struggle. In any case-study, the analyst will be interested in the conflicts and accommodations between the most significant groups of social actors in a particular social domain; in our case it follows that we will be focusing on the conflicts and accommodations between social groups in the Scottish prison system.

Social groups are engaged in struggles over resources, which are distributed unevenly across society and in particular social settings. The social locations of groups in society offer a range of alternative strategies of action. Discourses, which we define as relatively coherent sets of ideas and symbols, are partly the product of such actions and strategies. It is possible for the analyst to identify the patterns and structures of such discourses, which in turn act as resources to be used by social groups engaged in struggle. Further, such discourses affect the nature of domination – the result of struggles – and give it a particular cast. Thus, for example, the dominance of rehabilitation discourse in penal systems throughout much of the twentieth century affected the nature of the ordering of the power struggles within such systems.

Power is crucial to our perspective as it is the cement which binds the different elements of this scheme in the sociology of knowledge together. Struggles take place over power, and discourses are constructed and reconstructed in the course of such struggles, which reflect and give effect to the interests of the groups engaging in them. Power is at the heart of social life. Three bodies of literature have influenced our thoughts in this realm.

First, there is the well-known discussion of power in the literature of political sociology. Lukes's (1974) account of three different views of power (a one-dimensional view which focuses on decisions over which there is some observable conflict of interest, a two-dimensional view which focuses on mechanisms which prevent decisions from being reached on issues where conflicts of interest are apparent, and a three-dimensional view which focuses on ways in which issues are kept out of politics altogether and where conflicts of interest are latent rather than actual) has lost little of its influence since it was first published. However, as Clegg (1989) has maintained, such an approach can be seen as representing the culmination of a particular tradition of writing on power whose origins can be traced back to the work of Thomas Hobbes. For Clegg, this tradition reached something of an end-point in the Marxist discussions of false consciousness and in the debates around the nature of 'real' interests. Further, as he recognises, the critique of the dominant ideology thesis (Abercrombie et al. 1980 and Abercrombie et al. 1990) introduced further difficulties. Of particular interest for us is the importance that should be attached to actual cases of decision-making. We contend that a concern with forms of power that are not reflected in decisions, to which Lukes rightly draws our attention, should be reintegrated with the analysis of decision-making. It is in this manner that any analysis will appreciate fully all the dimensions of power. This is, of course, an important part of Lukes's view.

The second obvious influence on us is the work of Michel Foucault. Again, many aspects of Foucault's work, in particular the alleged integral relationship between power and knowledge, as illustrated in his discussions of imprisonment and sexuality (Foucault 1979 and 1981) are now part of everyday sociological currency. Clegg (1989) maintains that this is one of the most recent manifestations of an alternative tradition of writing on power. This tradition, whose origins can be traced back to the work of Machiavelli, is concerned with the strategic deployment and implications of power. To see society as saturated by power, as Foucault sometimes does, is both to state an important truth and to say little at all.

It is the differential exercise of power and the pervasiveness of power relations which are of most importance, particularly within organisations. Our case-study can be read in this way since it is concerned with the uneven distribution of power in a particular institution and with the conscious and unconscious strategies adopted by the major social actors in that institution.

The concept of power has been very influential in one of the most sophisticated branches of sociological investigation: the sociology of scientific knowledge, which is the third important influence of our work. Here, Foucault's insights, and those of many others, have been extended and revised both theoretically and substantively in many directions. For example, Barnes (1988) has written generally on power, its role in structuring society, and the way in which the social should be seen as knowledge, and some detailed explorations of the relationship between power and knowledge can be found in Law (1986).

Schroeter (1990) has maintained that the sort of approach deployed in this book, derived from Mannheim, will be critical of such recent developments. If, the argument goes, Law (1986) is correct to say that the debate on the sociology of knowledge only reached stage one with Mannheim, then a focus on Mannheim must entail a backward step or a critique of recent efforts. This seems to us to misunderstand the nature of Mannheim's contribution. The approach we deploy in this book, which is derived from his work, seeks to pay attention to decisions, strategies, the relation between power and knowledge, the complex manner in which social groups and forms of thought are related, and the structure of power. Our work actually represents a confluence of concerns. Like Lukes, we suggest that decision-making is an important manifestation of the exercise of power, but that this should be seen in the context of struggles between groups of social actors and the strategies they deploy.

We can now begin to apply this discussion through an examination of the Scottish prison system by linking the historical and contemporary analysis of institutional actors outlined in the previous chapter to the analysis of discourse and power. We focus on the discourses of different actors and the struggles between competing discourses associated with different actors. We distinguish between discourses which are concerned with the ends of imprisonment, i.e. with what prisons are for, which we refer to as *ends discourses*, and discourses which deal with the means of imprisonment, i.e. with how prisons should be run, which we refer to as *means discourses.* Within the Scottish prison system, three distinctive ends discourses, those of rehabilitation, normalisation and control, and three means discourses, those of bureaucracy, professionalism and legality, can be identified. We now characterise each of these in turn, beginning with ends discourses.

DISCOURSES ON THE ENDS OF IMPRISONMENT

Many commentators have run reform and rehabilitation together, but it is important, both analytically and historically that they be separated (Hudson 1987). While reform was an important influence on the nineteenth-century prison, rehabilitation came into its own in the twentieth century.

Reform, hard work and moral training

As we have seen, the origins of the system of imprisonment which exists in Scotland today are to be found in the nineteenth century. When it was no longer possible or acceptable to exile offenders from the rapidly rising urban populations, alternatives had to be found. The same reasoning which led to the poorhouse (for the destitute) and the asylum (for the mentally ill) also produced institutions (prisons) for criminals. In effect, exile was continued, the main difference being that the new penal colonies were located within, rather than outside the society in which the crime had taken place.

The new institutional involvement of the state required a new penal philosophy. Several years before a similar system was introduced into the Philadelphia Penitentiary in North America and subsequently achieved prominence as the 'Philadelphia System of Imprisonment', William Brebner introduced a system of separation of prisoners in the Glasgow Bridewell (Coyle 1991). Subsequently the separate system, which was based on the principle of keeping prisoners separate from each other and locating them in separate cells where they were given a fixed amount of work to do each day was introduced into Perth Prison (and likewise into Pentonville Prison in London). Prisoners were subjected to regimented daily routines and were required to carry out hard work within their cells. At the same time, great importance was attached to practical and moral training. The entire system of labour and discipline was enforced by a staff of wardens, taskmasters, educators and ministers. Each prisoner was visited several times a day for the purpose of training, education and religious exhortation. Solitude, a sparse diet and repressive labour were intended to deter the prisoner, while education and the various forms of social and moral training aimed to reform him (or her).

One of the reasons the state developed the orderly prison was to provide the individual with the opportunity to reform on the basis of his or her free will. The prison as we know it was founded on these principles (see, e.g. Foucault 1979) and the famous penal reformers such as John Howard and Elizabeth Fry desired better penal conditions so that 'better' people would result after reforming themselves with the help of others. However, in the late nineteenth century the prison began to change (Garland 1985).

Under the influence of the first Prison Inspector for Scotland, Frederic Hill, useful labour came to replace repressive labour in Scottish prisons. Thus, by the late 1880s, Barlinnie (Glasgow) and Edinburgh Prisons (which were two of the largest in Scotland) only applied the separate system and hard labour to a small proportion of their inmates: the majority experienced the associated system and were employed on a variety of 'useful' tasks within the prison.

Under the Penal Servitude Acts of 1853 and 1857, inmate labour was employed on a large number of public-works projects in Britain and the colonies. From the mid-nineteenth century until at least the beginning of the twentieth century, the Scottish prison system represented an amalgamation of the separate system and penal servitude. However, the use of inmate labour for public works in Scotland was slow to develop. By the last quarter of the nineteenth century, concern began to be expressed about the effects on Scotland of the 'export' of inmate labour to England and in 1888 the first convict prison (Peterhead) was opened for prisoners serving sentences of penal servitude.[3]

From reformation to rehabilitation

The major report on English prisons, the *Report of the Gladstone Committee on the Prison System*, which was published in 1895, did not apply to Scotland. However, many of its recommendations reflected day-to-day practice in Scottish prisons and, in the end, it probably had just as much impact on Scotland as on England. Reformation was officially recognised as one of the primary aims of the penal system, alongside retribution and deterrence. However, this no longer meant what it had done during the previous fifty to sixty years and its new meaning was effectively captured by the concept of rehabilitation. With the development of disciplines such as criminology, psychology and psychiatry, reform was superseded by rehabilitation as the state actively sought to change the criminal using these new forms of knowledge (Garland 1985). The Gladstone Committee stressed the importance of recognising the individual needs of each inmate and of developing better systems of classification, and recognised the importance of productive work for 'reformation'. It also took a particular interest in the treatment of young offenders and proposed a system of penal reformatories with an indeterminate release date and with release on licence which anticipated the borstal system that was subsequently introduced.

Post-Gladstone developments were just as slow to develop in Scotland as in England and mainly affected young offenders. The Prevention of Crime Act 1908 made provision for the establishment of borstal institutions, modelled on the English public school system and committed to the provision of training for young persons aged 16 to 21. The first Scottish borstal opened in buildings previously occupied by a private boarding school at Polmont in 1911 and, in the inter-war years, a great deal of effort went into the development of effective approaches to the treatment of young offenders. As far as adults were concerned, attempts were made to humanise and liberalise the prisons – separate confinement was ended but, although open prisons were set up in England in the 1930s, there were no parallel developments in Scotland. Although the reality was frequently rather less impressive than the rhetoric, there were few challenges to the new discourse of rehabilitation.

The Second World War interrupted the reform–rehabilitation tradition. However, after the war, it was given further impetus by the provisions of the Criminal Justice (Scotland) Act 1949 which finally abolished the old concepts of hard labour and penal servitude; by the opening of Scotland's first open prison (Penninghame) in 1953; and by the introduction of home leaves (for selected long-term prisoners nearing the end of their sentence) and Training for Freedom (which enables some long-term prisoners to work outside the prison for up to six months prior to their release). While 'old style' reformation could be effected through punishment alone, 'new style' reformation or rehabilitation implied that reform had to accompany punishment (Hudson 1987). Thus, borstal training, open prisons, home leaves, Training for Freedom and, in particular, parole (which was introduced by the Criminal Justice Act 1967 and enables selected long-term prisoners who have already served part of their sentence in prison to serve the remainder of their sentence under supervision in the community) all reflect a commitment to rehabilitation.

The primacy of reform was enshrined in Rule 5 of the Prisons (Scotland) Rules 1952, and likewise in Rule 3 of the Young Offenders (Scotland) Rules 1965, which set out the objectives of the Scottish penal system. The same statement of objectives appears in Rule 1 of the (English) Prison Rules 1964:

> the purposes of training and treatment of convicted prisoners shall be to establish in them the will to lead a good and useful life on discharge and to fit them to do so.

Rule 5 (and likewise Rule 3) remains in force today and, to this extent, a commitment to rehabilitation is still part of the official discourse of the Scottish Prison Service.

The focus of rehabilitation discourse is on the 'deviant individual' who is deemed to be psychologically disturbed, socially maladjusted or otherwise out of step with the rest of society in some way. The nature and degree of the deviance were to be ascertained by the new disciplines. The aim of the prison as a state agency was to socialise the individual back into society. Ultimately, advocates of rehabilitation believed that this would lead to a reduction in crime and hence to the protection of society.

From rehabilitation to normalisation

Confidence in rehabilitation discourse (or in the 'treatment model' as it is often called) began to wane in the late 1960s and 1970s (Martinson 1974). Many critics attempted to show that prisoners were not reformed by their experiences in prison, although others retorted that, in spite of official discourse, prisons had never taken rehabilitation seriously. But the critics had seized the initiative and it became harder to justify the differential treatment of different prisoners.

Consequently, in the early 1970s rehabilitation discourse and practice came under attack both from those who thought it unjust and from those who thought it insufficiently punitive. As summarised by Hudson (1987), adherents of the 'justice model' held that the punishment should be proportionate to the crime, rather than the individual's response to prison. Hence, they argued, sentences should be determinate, there should be 'an end to judicial and administrative discretion' and 'disparities in sentencing' should be eliminated. In addition, prisoners should be protected by the 'due process' of law.

It can be seen, therefore, that the justice model was primarily concerned with sentencing and said relatively little about the nature of the prison itself. Discussions of the implications of the justice model for imprisonment are often very truncated compared with discussions of its implications for other aspects of criminal justice (Fogel 1975) and this is the case even with book-length studies (e.g. Morris 1974).

The justice model was originally developed by critics of the treatment model on both the political left and the political right. However, the most interesting criticisms of it have tended to come from the left. That being said, it is important that some of the 'progressive' possibilities of the justice model are not lost in the deluge of criticism from this direction. David Greenberg (1983) in particular has defended *Struggle for Justice* (American Friends Service Committee 1971) on which he collaborated, as a document that proposed a political strategy based on an assessment of the current political forces which, despite subsequent events, still has contemporary relevance (Greenberg 1983:314). In general, Greenberg stresses that 'only after the prisoners' movement and the wider radical social movements that supported it faltered in the early 1970s were the ideas of the justice model taken over by conservative and middle-of-the-road thinkers, who stripped the ideas of their radical implications' (Greenberg 1983:316). For Greenberg, many of those who have criticised the justice model from the left have wrenched it from its social and political context. Some (e.g. Clarke 1982) have criticised the philosophical bases of the model, laying bare its misunderstandings of its supposed antecedents and sources. Others have examined the relation of the model to wider developments in capitalism, such as the 'crisis of hegemony' (Paternoster and Bynum 1982) or seen the model as mirroring the nature of capitalism (Norrie 1982). While these critiques illustrate many of the problems of the model, we wish to draw attention to other issues. As we have already mentioned, the justice model focuses on sentencing and the operation of the criminal justice system and is rather less concerned with the specific functioning of the prison, i.e. with how prisons might be organised along justice model lines. In Britain, the most interesting application of justice model type thinking to the prison came in King and Morgan's unsuccessful attempt to persuade the May Committee (Home Office 1979), which had been set up in 1978 after a long period of deteriorating industrial relations in the English prison system, to adopt the philosophy of 'humane containment' (King and Morgan 1980). They argued, first, for the 'minimum use of custody', i.e. that prison sentences should be short and 'used only as a last resort'. Second, they maintained that prisons should operate with the minimum security level needed, calling this the principle of the 'minimum use of security'. Hence, far more prisoners would serve their sentences in less restrictive conditions. High security is not only expensive but also deprives prisoners of contact with their families. Third, they argued for the 'normalisation' of the prison, which they explained as follows:

> By this rather inelegant phrase we mean that as far as resources allow, and consistent with the constraints of secure custody, the same general standards which govern the life of offenders in the community should be held to apply to offenders in prisons.
>
> (Ibid.: 37)

Normalisation discourse seeks to obviate the negative effects of prison, merely aiming to ensure the individual will not become 'worse' during the period of incarceration. This contrasts in an extreme way with rehabilitation discourse which maintains that the individual can get 'better' in prison. The focus in normalisation discourse is on the normality of the incarcerated individual. He or she is seen as a normal individual who happens to have committed a crime, for which he or she has been punished (by being sent to prison) but for whom the experience of the prison itself should not be punitive. The contrast with the 'deviant' individual in rehabilitation discourse is striking. In its Report, published in 1979, the May Committee concluded that 'the rhetoric of treatment and training has had its day and should be replaced' (Home Office 1979:para. 427). However, it refused to espouse the normalising discourse of 'humane containment' on the grounds that this concept was far too negative to serve as the aim of imprisonment, and instead advocated its own concept of 'positive custody'. Unfortunately, it was not immediately obvious what this meant. The Scottish Prison Service set up a number of Working Parties to formulate detailed policies in the light of the Report's recommendations but these did not lead directly to any new policy initiatives or any revisions to the 1952 Prisons (Scotland) Act or the Prisons (Scotland) Rules. Since the early 1980s the pendulum has continued to swing away from rehabilitation and the 'treatment model' and towards 'normalisation' and the 'justice model'.

Control

Another form of discourse which we see as particularly important is that of control. The development, nature and ramifications of control discourses in society have been elegantly and illuminatingly discussed by Stanley Cohen (1985) who detects their increasing prevalence in the 1980s. Cohen's purpose is primarily critical, which means that he does not, as King and Morgan do, construct an alternative penality (Garland and Young 1983; Garland 1985).[4] With respect to imprisonment, the issue of control has often been entangled with that of security (and indeed also with order – see Young 1987). Security was a particularly salient issue in English prisons in the 1960s, which saw the publication of the *Mountbatten* (Home Office 1966) and *Radzinowicz* (Advisory Council on the Penal System 1968) *Reports*. However, the issue of control and, in particular, the control of 'difficult' or 'troublesome' prisoners has increasingly come to the fore. A more recent expression of this concern with control can be found both in England (see, e.g., Home Office 1984) and in Scotland (see, e.g. SPS 1988b). Of course, control is an inherent problem in prisons and all prisoners are inevitably subject to various forms of control. However, it is significant that, in the version of control discourse encountered in Scotland the 'difficult' prisoner has recently become increasingly prominent.[5]

Control discourse tends to stress conformity. It is not concerned with the rehabilitation or reform of the individual (with the demand that the prisoner should really change) or with the normalisation of the prison (with the demand that prisoners should be treated as much like individuals in the community as possible). Rather, it maintains that the individual should conform to whatever measures are deemed to be necessary for the maintenance of order and discipline in the prison. As such, it is particularly concerned with the protection of prison staff, in particular prison officers. The short-lived complete 'lockdown' of all prisoners in Scotland following the spate of rooftop incidents in 1986 and 1987 reflected the complete domination of control discourse over other forms of discourse. Although it would be very difficult to maintain such a situation for very long, control discourse can always be identified in debates concerning the 'ends' of imprisonment.

The characteristic features of the ends discourses

The characteristic features of the three competing forms of ends discourse most frequently encountered in Scotland are summarised in Figure 2.2 below.

Discourse	Rehabilitation	Normalisation	Control
source of legitimacy	improving the individual	prevention of negative effects of prison; treating prisoners like individuals in the community	control of disruption; 'smooth functioning'
focus	'deviant' individual	'normal' individual	'disruptive' individual
dominant concerns	socialising the individual back into society through the provision of training and treatment	minimum security; contact between the prisoner and his or her family; improved living conditions	good order and discipline; protection of prison staff

Figure 2.2 Characteristic features of three competing forms of 'ends' discourse

Here, the structures of rehabilitation, normalisation and control discourse are set out along three dimensions: their source of legitimacy, their focus and their dominant concerns. Rehabilitation is concerned with the reform of the individual and in this respect it tends to be an individuating discourse (see Abercrombie et al. 1986 for a discussion of this concept), with its aims being the rehabilitation of the individual back into society through the actions of the state as expressed by its representatives or agents. Any idea of a parallel need for wider social change tends to be omitted. Thus, the focus of rehabilitation discourse and strategies is, as already mentioned, on the 'deviant individual' who is in some way deemed to be out of step with the rest of society. Rehabilitation discourse in the penal context has as its prime aim the use of the prison to socialise the offender back into society. Ultimately, it is thought that this will lead to a reduction in crime and hence to the protection of society. Rehabilitation reached its highest level of influence in the Californian prison system in the 1960s, but has since diminished in importance. The well-known case of George Jackson who was given an indeterminate sentence for robbery, repeatedly denied parole and subsequently died in a violent incident at San Quentin Prison illustrates some of its problems (Jackson 1971).

Normalisation discourse is obviously very different. It seeks to prevent some of the negative effects of prison, hoping that the individual will not become 'worse' during the period of incarceration. As already noted, this contrasts in an extreme way with rehabilitation discourse which maintains that an inmate can get 'better' in prison. Normalisation argues for making the prison regime as much like 'normal' outside life as is possible, given the nature of the prison as a 'closed institution'. The familiar adage that prisoners are sent to prison as punishment rather than for punishment is central. The specific concerns of normalisation discourse follow from this; it does not attempt the rehabilitation of the offender, although it may seek to ensure that opportunities are available for 'facilitated change' (Morris 1974) if the prisoner desires to take advantage of them.

Control discourse is different again. Here the control of disruption and the smooth running of individual establishments and the prison system as a whole are of paramount importance. 'Good order' and 'discipline' are perceived to be threatened by the 'disruptive' individual who is the focus of the discourse. However, the implementation of a control strategy can have important effects on the nature of imprisonment for other types of prisoners. In particular, it can have important 'knock on' effects on the potential for normalisation. An important source of support for this discourse stems from its attention to the protection of prison staff, in particular prison officers.

DISCOURSES OF THE MEANS OF IMPRISONMENT

Jerry Mashaw and administrative justice

Having analysed ends discourses, i.e. discourses concerned with what prisons are for, we now move on to consider means discourses, i.e. discourses concerned with how prisons should be run. Our discussion here is influenced by the work of Jerry Mashaw (1983), who in analysing the specific nature of the United States Disability Insurance (DI) scheme, reorients the study of administrative decision-making by integrating the normative concerns of administrative law (which set out standards for 'good' administrative decision) with the positive concerns of organisation theory (which deal with how organisations actually work).

Mashaw examines many criticisms of the unpopular DI scheme. For example, it was criticised for not having adequate management controls, for not providing a good service, and for failing to ensure 'due process' or respect claimants' rights. Mashaw argues that these criticisms reflect different normative conceptions of the DI scheme, i.e. different views of how the scheme should be run. Thus, they correspond to three normative models or ideal types of organisation as follows: the first set of criticisms corresponds to the model of organisation as a bureaucracy; the second corresponds to the model of organisation as a profession; while the third corresponds to the model of organisation as a legal system. Bureaucracies, professions and legal systems are all ideal types. Thus, in terms of the terminology outlined earlier, they each have their own conceptual structure. Each is associated with a different set of organisational characteristics. Based on Mashaw's approach, we can identify different modes of decision-making, legitimating goals, systems of accountability and types of remedy associated with each model. These are set out in Figure 2.3.

According to Mashaw, each of these models is also associated with a different conception of administrative justice defined as 'those qualities of a decision-making process that provide arguments for the acceptability of its decisions' (Mashaw 1983:24). This is because, in each case, one appeals to different organisational characteristics to assess the acceptability of an administrative decision. Thus, there is one form of administrative justice associated with bureaucracies, another with professions and another with the legal system.

Model	Mode of decision-making	Legitimating goal	Nature of accountability	Characteristic remedy
bureaucracy	applying rules	accuracy	hierarchical	administrative review
profession	applying knowledge	service to client	interpersonal	complaint to professional body
legal	weighing-up arguments	fairness	independent	appeal to court or tribunal

Figure 2.3 Different models of organisation and their distinctive characteristics

Mashaw contends that the three models of administrative justice are competitive but not mutually exclusive. Thus, they can and do co-exist with each other, but the greater the influence of one, the less will be the influence of the others. This insight enables us to identify the trade-offs made between the three models in particular instances, and to see whether different sets of trade-offs might be more appropriate.

Although Mashaw's analysis derives from his case-study of the United States Disability Insurance (DI) scheme, it has wide general application. Thus it can be applied to the administration of the Scottish Prison Service.

Means discourses in the administration of Scottish prisons

Different forms of penal discourse, associated with each of Mashaw's three ideal types or conceptual structures, are all encountered in Scotland. The bureaucratic discourse associated with civil servants derives its legitimacy from its claims to fairness and impartiality. In contrast, governors' discourse is primarily 'professional' although, despite the recent interest in managerial techniques, it is clearly 'grounded' in experience rather than in some esoteric body of knowledge. As such it derives its legitimacy from the governors' claims to understand prisons and prisoners. They know the prisoners because they see them every day or on a routine basis. Likewise, on the basis of their experience, they know how the prison operates. One of the striking things about governors' discourse is their claim to knowlege about their establishments and the prisoners in them, despite their recognition of the distance between themselves and prisoners, and the autonomy of the prison subculture. Governors' discourse stresses their experience and the knowledge they have acquired from actually dealing with prisoners and from being responsible for the running of prisons.

Whereas bureaucratic discourse focuses on the prison system as a whole, professional discourse concentrates on the individual establishment. Further, while bureaucratic discourse has, as its primary concerns, the achievement of uniformity, consistency and fidelity to the rules, professional discourse emphasises leadership, experience and judgment as means of enhancing the institutional ethos. Bureaucratic discourse advocates the direct administrative accountability of establishments to Headquarters and thus of governors to civil servants, while professional discourse envisages a greater degree of decentralisation and negotiated forms of accountability.

While the bureaucratic and professional discourses associated with civil servants and governors are the dominant forms of means discourse, there is a third type. This is the legal or juridical discourse associated with the courts and the legal system which is evident in relatively muted form in Scotland today, though, as we have seen, it was more important in the past. This form of discourse derives its legitimacy from the rule of law. It focuses on the individual prisoner and its primary concerns are with protecting prisoners' interests and strengthening the means available to individual inmates to assert their 'general' and 'special' rights (Richardson 1984). This form of discourse stresses that prisons should be held accountable to the rule of law as interpreted by the courts. The characteristic features of the three competing forms of means discourse are summarised in Figure 2.4. Although the identification and characterisation of the different means discourses summarised in Figure 2.4 is clearly important, it only tells part of the story. Just as Mashaw can be criticised for assuming a greater degree of consensus about the ends of the DI scheme than was actually the case (Boyer 1984; Maranville 1984; Gilboy 1988), so an isolated analysis of means discourses could be criticised for exactly the same reasons. However, the response to such criticism is to combine our analysis of means discourses with our earlier analysis of ends discourses, since the latter attempts to identify and characterise the different extant discourses relating to the ends of imprisonment.

Discourse	Bureaucracy	Professionalism	Legality
source of legitimacy	fairness impartiality	intimate knowledge	rule of law
focus	on the system	on establishments	on individual prisoners
dominant concerns	uniformity, consistency, fidelity to the rules	leadership, experience, judgment, enhancing the institutional ethos	respect for prisoners' rights
accountability for decisions	internal	negotiated	external

Figure 2.4 Characteristic features of three competing forms of 'means' discourse

DISCOURSE MATRIX: ACTORS AND DISCOURSES

Discourse matrix

When we combine our analyses of ends and means discourses, we obtain an overall picture of the discursive structure of the Scottish prison system. We shall call this overall picture a *discourse matrix.* This 3 × 3 matrix is set out in Figure 2.5.

	Rehabilitation	Normalisation	Control
Bureaucracy	1	2	3
Professionalism	4	5	6
Legality	7	8	9

Figure 2.5 Discourse matrix for the Scottish prison system

It is possible to locate, *inter alia,* significant actor; institutional and administrative practices, and policy statements on this matrix. Further, it is possible to chart changes in policy and practice in terms of moves from one cell to another or from one area of the matrix to another.

Using this matrix, it is possible to identify individuals and groups whose discourses exemplify each of the cells. Thus, the discourses associated with Cells 1–9 are exemplified by the following:

Cell 1 Parole Board
2 Headquarters – Administration Division
3 Headquarters – Operations Division
4 Barlinnie Special Unit
5 Most prison governors
6 Scottish Prison Officers' Association (SPOA)
7 'Left realist' academics, Scottish Council for Civil Liberties (SCCL)
8 Rights-orientated governors, Scottish Association for the Care and Resettlement of Offenders (SACRO)
9 Judges and Courts.

These will now be discussed in more detail.

Actors and discourses

We have argued above that the penal system is the site of struggles between different social actors mobilising, constructing and re-interpreting particular discourses. Thus, for example, the Parole Board has recently been the site of conflict between professional-rehabilitative and bureaucratic–normalisation forms of discourse. Local Review Committees (LRCs) may always have emphasised professional rather than bureaucratic concerns, but the current proposals for the revision of the parole process reflect a movement away from local, professional inputs, towards a more centralised and more bureaucratic system; indeed they also reflect the continuing decline of rehabilitation generally (Home Office 1988; SHHD 1989a). However, the Parole Board is still associated with rehabilitation, albeit in a muted and bureaucratic form, and can thus be located in Cell 1 in the matrix.

The Headquarters of the Scottish Prison Service is dominated by a bureaucratic logic and a desire for increased central administrative (if not financial) control. Administration has increasingly come under the sway of a normalising discourse. However, operational considerations seem to be dominated by control discourse. While we do not accept the claim, which was not infrequently made in the past, that HQ is dominated by Operations Branch (Hutchinson 1988), the centrality of control discourse in this particular sector is clear. However, for HQ as a whole, the dominant forms of discourse are clearly those associated with Cells 2 and 3 in the matrix.

Moving on to professional discourses, the combination of professional with rehabilitation discourse can be seen in the philosophy and practice of the Barlinnie Special Unit (BSU) which can therefore be located in Cell 4 of the matrix. We do not wish to go into detail here as much has already been written on this topic (for example: Boyle 1977; Boyle 1985; Coyle 1987; Whatmore 1987; Stephen 1988; Cooke 1989a, 1989b). What is clear, however, is the commitment of those involved with the Special Unit to rehabilitation and the important role that professionals have played in its development. In fact, the struggle between these professionals and central control is a subtext of many of the accounts of the Special Unit. A strong commitment to rehabilitation and an enhanced role for the helping professions constitutes an approach that some of those connected with the Unit would like to see generalised across the prison system as a whole (Murray 1987).

Some of the most prominent governors in Scotland have argued for a normalisation strategy which has at its heart a stress on the quality of the relationship between the prison officer and the inmate (Coyle 1986 and 1991). Composite discourses of this kind can best be located in Cell 5 of the matrix. The combination of control with professionalism characteristic of Cell 6 is best exemplified in the Inverness Segregation Unit (Wozniak 1989) but can also be seen in some of the proclamations of the Scottish Prison Officers' Association (SPOA) (Renton 1987).

Moving on to examine legal forms of discourse, the combination of an appreciation of the value of prisoners' rights with a desire for some kind of rehabilitation of offenders as represented by Cell 7 has been espoused by 'left realists' (e.g. Matthews 1987 and 1989; Taylor 1991). Indeed, it has been argued by at least one proponent of this position that those committed to prison should in some way be forced into rehabilitation programmes, though these would not be of a 'traditional' nature (Kinsey 1988).

The combination of legal and normalisation discourses has been adopted by those governors who have a particular regard for human rights issues in the penal context and also by some academics. A good deal of current debate seems to be conducted in these sorts of terms. We have already mentioned King and Morgan's arguments for normalisation (King and Morgan 1980), others have focussed on rights (Richardson 1984 and 1985; McManus 1988) or on accountability (Maguire et al. 1985). The precise weighting to be given to the different versions of this composite form of discourses will vary from case to case but they can all be located in Cell 8.

The final cell in our matrix (Cell 9) is that which combines legal discourse with an emphasis on control. The established agents of the legal profession and the legal system would seem to occupy such a position. The courts appear to be particularly sympathetic to the concerns of those who are in charge of prisons and consider the rights of prisoners in this light. This characterisation of the concerns of the Scottish courts certainly helps to explain their rather dismal record in respect of prisoners' rights.

CONCLUSION

We have already seen in Chapter 1 that the institutional history of the Scottish Prison Service can be written in terms of two themes: centralisation and the displacement of the legal profession by the civil service as the dominant influence over the service. We are now in a position to argue that a key consequence of this power struggle was the emergence of a bureaucratic form of discourse which became, and remains, the dominant form of administrative or means discourse. Institutional changes were likewise associated with changing ends discourses. The separate system, which was pioneered by Brebner and adopted, first, into Perth Prison and, subsequently, throughout the Scottish Prison Service during the nineteenth century, reflected a confluence of two separate but related penal discourses: deterrence and reform. This should not be taken to imply that these were the only discourses of imprisonment. It is clear that they co-existed with a powerful control discourse which emphasised order and discipline for their own sake. However, while this control discourse remained constant, the discourses of deterrence and reform were gradually transformed during the course of the twentieth century into a discourse of rehabilitation. Although there was always an enormous gap between rhetoric and reality, rehabilitation became, along with control, one of the two dominant forms of penal discourse. However, more recently, and particularly since the announcement by the May Committee in 1979 that 'the rhetoric of treatment and training had had its day', rehabilitation discourse has been in decline while a new discourse of normalisation, which rejects some of the more grandiose aims of imprisonment, has emerged to take its place. This new discourse is now, arguably, in the ascendancy.

In the chapters that follow, we trace the implications of discursive struggle, i.e. the struggle for ascendancy between different forms of discourse, and use the discourse matrix outlined above to illuminate various facets of administrative decision-making in the Scottish prison system. We turn first, in Chapter 3, to the subject of classification.

Chapter 3

Classification

The core of the prison system

In this chapter we mobilise the discourse matrix, developed in the previous chapter, to understand the changing nature of the classification of adult, male, long-term prisoners at the start of their sentence. Classification is not only of considerable importance for individual prisoners, for establishments and for the prison service as a whole, it is also of substantial theoretical interest. In their pioneering work *Primitive Classification*, Durkheim and Mauss (1963) argue that systems of classification cannot be derived from the innate characteristics of individuals but are completely social. Although this conclusion was derived from an analysis of what they called 'primitive societies', it is implicit in their study that it holds good for complex contemporary societies as well.

Recognising that Durkheim and Mauss's views have been subject to critical attention,[1] we have nevertheless found it useful to utilise two recent developments of their ideas. The first of these is the social anthropology of Mary Douglas. In *Implicit Meanings*, to take just one example, Douglas (1975:296) claims that:

> My wish has always been to take seriously Durkheim's idea that the properties of classification systems derive from, and are indeed properties of, the social systems in which they are used.

Drawing on a wide range of anthropological evidence (much of which stems from her own primary research), Douglas concludes that classification systems reflect the nature of the social systems that contain and structure them. In our case, this prompts us to consider the relationship between the systems of classification encountered in the Scottish prison system and the social organisation of the prison system in which they are found. We are led to expect that the characteristics of the classification system will in some way reflect those of the prison system as a whole. Of course, there is the possibility that the two may be out of step although such situations are inherently unstable.

Drawing on the work of Durkheim and Mauss, Douglas formulates a set of five empirical questions which can be asked of any classification system. These are: 'How fuzzy are the boundaries of the categories?'; 'How well insulated are the meanings they enclose?'; 'How many categories are there?'; 'Are the principles relating them to each other systematic?'; 'If there is a system of thought, how stable is it?' (ibid.:296). In the course of our analysis of classification in the Scottish prison system we have addressed similar questions to the classification of long-term prisoners.

However, we have also been concerned with the changing nature of classification. This is an issue which has been addressed by David Bloor (1982), who also adapts Durkheim and Mauss's views, locating them within a perspective derived from Mary Hesse's network theory (Hesse 1974). For Bloor, as for Hesse, systems of classification are not necessarily static. Because systems of classification always in some way simplify the world (otherwise, of course, they would be the world) space is opened for reclassification (Bloor 1982:278). Classifications can be out of step with society and vice versa but, when this is so, there is invariably a tension which can lead to change. Bloor's approach overcomes the rather 'static' slant in Durkheim and Mauss and in Douglas's work which is, of course, primarily the result of their focus on relatively unchanging societies. Bloor illustrates his thesis with several examples, the most important of which is Robert Boyle's development of the corpuscular theory of matter in the context of English society disturbed by the Puritan revolution and the development of radical sects such as the Diggers and Levellers. Boyle was concerned with the increasing social turbulence. In response to the idea that people could take over and determine their own lives, he believed that their behaviour should be restricted and controlled. This may explain why, in his science, Boyle argued for a mechanical philosophy, which entailed a view of matter as 'inanimate and irrational', against beliefs in an 'animated and intelligent universe' (Bloor 1982:286).

The writings of Durkheim and Mauss, Douglas and Bloor focus on the relationship between systems of classification and the social systems of which they form a part. Each of them maintains that classification systems will, in general, reflect the characteristics of social systems. It follows from this that by focusing on systems of classification, it should be possible to identify problems in the wider social system. Moreover, since classification systems do not always reflect the characteristics of social systems, it is important to ascertain whether they are in step with each other and, if not, whether the system of classification is leading or lagging behind the social system. Rapid changes in the social system can have profound effects on the system of classification just as imposed changes in the system of classification can have profound implications for the social system. It is thus very important to examine movement and change in the two systems, to analyse their implications for each other and to give special attention to the anomalous case. As Douglas (1975:226–7) says,

> When there is non-fit, there is choice. The classification can either be clamped down more firmly, and the misfit removed in the name of purity, or the classification can be softened. . .Some social structures can tolerate anomaly and deal with it constructively, while others are rigid in their classifications. This difference is probably the most important subject on which sociological research can focus.

It can be asked, for example, to what extent anomalies are dealt with systematically and whether the system can cope with these difficulties while remaining true to its own principles.

These analytic considerations provide a general context for our study of penal classification suggesting a general approach and pointing to a set of questions and issues which can be addressed to the classification of long-term prisoners.

The final point we wish to emphasise in this introductory discussion of classification is the historical importance of classification in Scottish prisons and its centrality in contemporary debates about the future direction of the Scottish Prison Service. The emphasis, in the nineteenth century, on reform and subsequently, in the twentieth century, on rehabilitation (described in Chapter 2 above) reflected a belief in the efficacy of the prison to bring about change in those who were given custodial sentences. It also gave rise to a whole list of categorical distinctions which reflected the highly differentiated social organisation of the prison system and prevailing views concerning prison regimes and those who should be subject to them. Most, but not all, of these categorical distinctions, can be expressed in terms of simple polarities: male/female, on remand/under sentence, adult/young offenders, short-term/

long-term, first offender/recidivist, trainable/non-trainable. One of the few, more elaborate systems of classification is the four-fold system of security categorisation, ranging from those whose escape must be prevented at all costs (Category A) to those for whom no physical security is necessary (Category D) which was introduced in accordance with the recommendations of the *Mountbatten Report on Prison Escapes and Security* (Home Office 1966). This determines the degree of security under which prisoners are held and thus, *inter alia*, the prison to which they are assigned and the work party to which they are allocated. Given that our concern is primarily with adult, male, long-term prisoners, the classifications which are of particular concern to us are those which are used to distinguish first offenders from recidivists and prisoners who are deemed to be 'trainable' from those who are held to be 'non-trainable', and to allocate all prisoners to one of the four security categories.

Classification was an important issue throughout the period of our study. For example, in 1987 HM Chief Inspector of Prisons for Scotland (HMCIP(S)) expressed disquiet

> regarding the inadequate systems for classifying long-term prisoners (LTPs) after sentence, and the lack of a clear plan for them linked to progression toward more open conditions. Often the location of LTPs appears to be arbitrary, the result of temporary problems or well-intentioned 'trade-offs' between Governors. We see a need for an ordered system, with initial assessment and classification at a suitable centre within but separate from a main prison.
>
> (HMCIP(S) 1987a:para. 3.3)

He recommended that

> All long-term prisoners should attend an assessment centre after sentence, where a plan can be developed for their progression and where educational and other needs can be identified. In the case of prisoners sentenced to five years or over, there should be an annual review of their progress in which they should participate.
>
> (Ibid.:para. 11.2)

This theme was taken up in several of the policy documents which were subsequently produced by the Scottish Prison Service, discussed more fully in Chapter 9 below.

In this chapter we attempt to describe the implications of some important developments in the prison system which took place in 1987 for the classification of long-term prisoners. These developments resulted from a combination of internal and external pressures on the prison system. The internal pressures represented a series of struggles between some of the most important groups of social actors (described in Chapter 1 above) which culminated in the spate of violent, hostage-taking incidents, while the external pressures were a consequence of the seemingly unrelenting increase in the size of the prison population. However, before considering the effects of these developments on the system of classification, it is important to describe the characteristics of the classification system as it existed prior to 1987. We shall begin our discussion at this point, then address the nature of the pressures which resulted in a changed role for classification before finally characterising classification as it subsequently emerged.

INITIAL CLASSIFICATION – PRE 1987

Prison (Scotland) Standing Orders (SHHD n.d.:Section C, Classification of Male Prisoners, para. 1(2)) provide for the existence of a National Classification Centre in Edinburgh Prison – to which all adult, male prisoners serving sentences over eighteen months (except those in Barlinnie who were to remain there) should be transferred 'immediately after appellant period' for an assessment period of two weeks.

Standing Orders state that:

> on the day following admission, prisoners will be interviewed by a panel (Assistant Governor, Psychologist and Welfare Officer) to discuss the purpose of the classification unit and to ascertain any problems which the prisoner may have.
>
> (SHHD n.d.:Section C, Appendix 1, para. 1(2))

This panel interview is to be followed by a set of tests and then a series of 'individual interviews by the Assistant Governor, Psychologist, Welfare Officer, and Industrial Manager during the week following admission' (ibid.).

Standing Orders also state that the National Classification Centre will allocate prisoners as follows:

1 First offender class. . .to Edinburgh Prison with, where appropriate, a recommendation for open conditions.

2 Ordinary class prisoners capable of and willing to undergo trade training to Perth Prison.
3 Ordinary class prisoners not within Class (ii) above to Peterhead Prison.
4 Ordinary class prisoners not within Class (ii) above to Aberdeen Prison where it is considered advantageous that they should be sent directly. [It is pointed out that vacancies for Aberdeen are normally filled from the oldest prisoners at Peterhead.]
5 Known trouble-makers, non-co-operatives etc. who would be a disturbing influence in other establishments to the Inverness Unit.

(SHHD n.d.:Section C, para. 4)

It is clear that Standing Orders envisage a fairly extensive period of testing and interviewing by various professionals, to assess the correct 'prison of classification' for the prisoners. Since the suitability of the prisoner for 'training' was of particular importance, the classification process would have been located in Cell 4 of our matrix, i.e. at the confluence of professional and rehabilitative concerns had it actually taken such a form. However, it would appear that such an assessment procedure period has never existed in this form. The National Classification Centre was never established, and classification of long-term prisoners has taken place on occasions in Aberdeen, Inverness and Perth as well as regularly in Edinburgh and Barlinnie.

The National Classification Board (NCB) actually operated in the following way. In Edinburgh, the prisoners who had already completed their induction tests[2] were called in individually, their warrants were briefly scrutinised[3] and they were then interviewed by the Deputy Governor (or, if he was unavailable, the Training Governor) who acted as chairman of the Board, the Industrial Manager (or one of his deputies) and a social worker. The Social Work Unit at Edinburgh Prison used the Board as a convenient place to interview long-term prisoners on admission and, in two out of the three meetings we observed in Edinburgh, the social worker played little or no part in the actual decision-making processes of the Board. One social worker (S1) explained that when he first joined the Social Work Unit, social workers used to see every long-term prisoner before the Board met and produce a lengthy report for the Board. However, since 'this was ignored in the decision about where the prisoner served his sentence', and since there were many other demands on the Social Work Unit's resources they had 'stepped back from that'. The senior social worker who had done this had done very little else. In any case, the social worker's involvement had raised expectations for the prisoner about what could be done for him. When the senior social worker left the Unit, it had been agreed that there was not a lot of point in going on with the procedure. Thus the Social Work Unit had withdrawn from the process of assessment at the start of the prisoner's sentence because 'in terms of classification, assessment wasn't worth anything'. S1 explained his continued presence at meetings of the Board as follows:

> The main reason I use the Classification Board is that I can't find anywhere else in the prison to interview newly sentenced prisoners.

In spite of these difficulties, S1 was strongly of the view that 'more weight should be given to social factors in classification' than was the case.

The interviews carried out at the NCB were fairly brisk and normally quite short (five minutes was a very long interview), but, of course, the length of the interview varied depending on who was carrying it out as well as the character and response of the prisoner. Some interviewers, for example, would use the interview to have a chat with the prisoner or to ask specific questions about his situation. This was particularly common with first offenders who would not have known the system as well as those who had been in and out of it several times (see further below). When all the prisoners had been interviewed, the members of the Board (including the induction officer who serviced the Board and quite often answered specific queries) sat together and decided which prison to allocate the inmate to. They always dealt with initial classifications first and only then went on to consider young offenders and recommendations for reclassification. Decisions were reached fairly briskly and, while there was sometimes a brief discussion and Board members often passed comment on the prisoners and their classification, systemic or fundamental disagreement was rare. At the conclusion of this meeting, the decisions of the Board were entered on a sheet which was then sent to Casework Branch in HQ for formal ratification. The decisions made by the Board were never challenged, though the Chairperson of the Board was occasionally asked for clarification of a particular decision which appeared unusual. Such queries were normally dealt with quickly and again without serious disagreement.

The operation of the Board at Barlinnie differed in a number of respects. The chairperson was the Deputy or Training Governor from Edinburgh Prison, the Industrial Manager was from Barlinnie and no social worker was ever present. All the prisoners took induction tests immediately before the meeting of the Board, in the room that was used for the interviews, and then sat around at the back of the room until called for interview. Groups of prisoners were taken back to their halls at intervals by the discipline officers who were present at the back of the room during the classification process.

The NCB used two main principles to classify prisoners. First, it established whether the prisoner was a first offender or not. It is important to point out that the meaning of the term a 'first offender' in Scottish prison parlance is not necessarily what the general public would understand by this term. The term 'first offender' is used to refer to someone who has not served a sentence in an adult prison in the last ten years and is therefore applied to prisoners who have served long sentences in the more distant past as well as those who have more recently completed a sentence in a Young Offenders' Institution (YOI). First offenders would be sent to Edinburgh, but for others, i.e. for recidivists, the choice was between Perth and Peterhead or Aberdeen. Here, the second principle, 'trainability', came into play. The NCB would decide whether a prisoner was trainable or not, by considering his likely response to the regime in a training prison. Trainable prisoners would be sent to Perth, those under 35 years of age who were not trainable would be allocated to Peterhead, those over 35 to Aberdeen.

In Table 3.1, we present a summary of data relating to meetings of the National Classification Board between January 1985 and June 1987.[4] A few points are worth noting. After meeting weekly in Edinburgh in 1985, the NCB settled into a pattern of meeting approximately once every two weeks in Edinburgh and Barlinnie and of hearing ten to fifteen cases a time. The chairmanship of the Board was shared by the Deputy Governor of Edinburgh and a number of Assistant Governors and, in addition to dealing with long-term offenders at the beginning of their sentence, when the Board met in Edinburgh it also dealt with the cases of inmates from YOIs who had reached the age of 21 and a small number of requests

Table 3.1 Data relating to meetings of the National Classification Board, January 1985–June 1987

Period	*1.85–6.85*	*7.85–12.85*	*1.86–6.86*	*7.86–12.86*	*1.87–6.87*
Edinburgh					
number of meetings	24	24	12	13	9
number of chairmen	5	3	5	5	4
number of cases	190	165	159	125	128
of which					
number of YOs	41	25	25	18	11
reclassifications	9	–	6	5	10
Barlinnie					
number of meetings	15	18	17	14	14
number of chairmen	4	4	3	4	3
number of cases	214	262	242	196	208
of which					
number of YOs	–	–	–	–	–
reclassification	–	2	–	–	–

for reclassification. In these cases, the prisoner was not present and decisions were reached on the basis of recommendations put to the Board by the YOI or prison in which the prisoner was being held. Table 3.2 records the decisions reached by the Board between January 1985 and June 1987. We wish now to point to some key aspects of these decisions. Once again, a few points are worth noting. The decisions reported in Table 3.2 include a few mixed classifications, e.g. Edinburgh/Penninghame, Perth/Shotts and Peterhead/Aberdeen but, in such cases, we have classified the outcome in terms of the prisoner's ultimate destination. Thus, in terms of the provisions in Standing Orders (see above) it is remarkable that, over a period of two and a half years, only thirty prisoners (1.6 per cent of the total) were recommended for Penninghame, i.e. for open conditions. Most prisoners were classified for one of three establishments: 652 to Edinburgh (35.1 per cent), 473 to Perth (25.4 per cent) and 423 to Dumfries (22.8 per cent). A significant number (115, 6.2 per cent) of the total were classified for Peterhead and smaller numbers for Shotts and Aberdeen.

We observed five meetings of the National Classification Board prior to the implementation of Grand Design in May 1987 (see below), three in Edinburgh and two at Barlinnie. On each occasion, we extracted data from prisoners' warrants, sat in on interviews carried out by the governor who chaired the Board and

Table 3.2 Decisions of National Classification Board, January 1985–June 1987

Location/date	*Prison of classification**									
*Classification**	*1*	*2*	*3*	*4*	*5*	*6*	*7*	*8*	*9*	*Total*
Edinburgh										
1.85–6.85	4	29	87	6	45	16	2	1	–	190
7.85–12.85	2	30	78	1	46	5	3	–	–	165
1.86–6.86	–	27	69	4	42	15	1	–	1	159
7.86–12.86	2	20	54	1	28	14	5	1	–	125
1.87–6.87	1	14	51	5	38	3	13	3	–	128
Barlinnie										
1.85–6.85	5	53	64	3	56	15	18	–	–	214
7.85–12.85	4	77	84	1	63	19	13	–	1	262
1.86–6.86	3	86	77	1	52	8	15	–	–	242
7.86–12.86	2	59	57	4	43	13	18	–	–	196
1.87–6.87	–	28	31	4	60	7	65**	–	11***	206
Total										
Number	23	423	652	30	473	115	153	5	13	1,887
Percentage	1.2	22.4	34.7	1.6	25.1	6.1	8.1	0.3	0.7	100

Notes: * 1 = Aberdeen, 2 = Dumfries, 3 = Edinburgh, 4 = Penninghame, 5 = Perth, 6 = Peterhead, 7 = Shotts, 8 = Remain in YOI, 9 = Others. (Prior to the implementation of Grand Design in May 1987, Dumfries was a prison (see below). Thereafter it became a YOI.)

** Includes twenty-seven prisoners classified for Shotts after the opening of Phase 2 and the implementation of Grand Design in May 1987.

*** Includes ten prisoners classified for Glenochil. Prior to the implementation of Grand Design in May 1987, Glenochil was a YOI. Thereafter it became a prison.

the industrial manager, and observed the deliberations of the Board. The account which follows is based on those observations and on interviews with members of the Board.

The decisions reached by the National Classification Board at five meetings we observed at this point are summarised in Table 3.3.

Table 3.3 Disposals at five pre-Grand Design meetings of the National Classification Board, 1986 and early 1987

Prison of classification	*First classification*	*YOs*	*Reclassification*
Dumfries	1	1	–
Edinburgh	10	1	–
Perth	19	1	–
Peterhead	2	1	2
Shotts	15	–	–
Mixed*	2	–	–
Remain in YOI	–	1	–
Other (Barlinnie)	1	–	–
Total	50	5	2

Note: * Includes Perth/Shotts and Shotts/Perth.

Several aspects of Table 3.3 call for further explanation, the first being the use of Shotts Prison. All but one of the fifteen Shotts classifications were made at Barlinnie, in the course of two Board meetings. At the first, an Assistant Governor from Shotts attended in order to select prisoners who were thought to be suitable for the type of work available there (in the laundry which then provided almost the only form of employment).[5] It was explained to us that Shotts did contract work for hospitals and that syringes and other potential drug-taking equipment could find their way into the laundry. This meant in practice that those convicted of drugs offences or having a history of drug use were not classified for Shotts. By the second meeting of the Board we attended at Barlinnie in May 1987, the Board was already anticipating the opening of Phase II in June 1987. In the main, those serving relatively shorter sentences were being sent to Shotts, though the distinction between those allocated to Shotts or Perth was not clear-cut. One prisoner was classified for Dumfries, which was still accepting 'Perth-type' prisoners serving sentences from eighteen months to three years. The allocation to Barlinnie was of a prisoner who had already done nine months of an eighteen months plus fifty-one day sentence. The fifty-one days had brought him into the remit of the NCB. However, it was thought that he might as well stay in Barlinnie since he was appealing the fifty-one day sentence and said he was 'relatively happy' there.

The largest number of recidivists were classified to Perth in the first instance. Of the classifications to Peterhead, one was an inmate who was classified to the Peterhead Protection Unit (a multiple rapist), the second was a 25-year-old offender serving three years for theft, who came from Fraserburgh and argued to the Board that, because of his family ties and the fact that he was to be married soon, he wished to serve his sentence in Peterhead (he actually went to Peterhead, but was subsequently, in spite of his age, transferred to Aberdeen). This prisoner appeared to be well liked by the members of the Board, despite being described as an 'incorrigible rogue' and an 'old lag with young shoulders', and the Board, albeit rather reluctantly, gave him his wish. This reluctance to direct prisoners to Peterhead at the beginning of a sentence is also confirmed by the statistics in Table 3.1.

The nature of the classification interviews illustrates the concerns and mode of operation of the NCB at this stage and we shall therefore describe these interviews in more detail, beginning with the governors. Four main topic areas were covered. Of course, govèrnors did not conform rigidly to a set formula – some would cover all of these areas (albeit briefly within the time available), others only two or three. Some interviews would involve a fair amount of detail and discussion, others very little. The first stage of an interview would normally consist of a series of questions which would confirm the factual details contained in the prisoner's warrant.

The prisoner would almost always be asked how long his sentence was, whether he was appealing, whether he had served previous terms of imprisonment, what these had been for and where they had been served. Sometimes the prisoner would be asked about his current and previous offences. A prisoner might be asked if he had taken drugs or whether he had had difficulty in coming off drugs when he was brought into prison (if he had been convicted of a drugs offence), or he might be asked more about the circumstances of his offence – whether he had been drinking and what exactly happened.

The second set of questions revolved around the prisoner's current imprisonment. He might be asked what he wanted to do in prison, i.e. whether there was any particular work or course of training that he would like to do, whether he understood the parole system, and whether he understood that he could appeal against conviction or sentence – this would normally follow on from a question in the initial part of the interview about whether he was appealing. Further, the prisoner might be asked if he was already working or if he was 'behind his door', which was often the case with those convicted of sex offences. These sorts of offenders would often be advised of the strategy which they should adopt to deal with the jibes and taunts of other inmates. If a prisoner was on 'protection' and the reason for this was not clear (and perhaps even if it was) he might be asked to explain why he had requested this. Additionally, the prisoner might be asked if he was facing any outstanding charges. The exploration of this area would often also include general questions about how the prisoner was finding prison and whether there were any particular problems relating to his imprisonment. A first offender, again, might be asked how he was finding his first experience of imprisonment. Finally, he might be asked where he would like to serve his sentence. However, at this stage there was actually very little scope for choice on the part of the prisoner.

The third main area of questioning concerned the prisoner's personal and family life. Topics covered here included the location of the prisoner's home, whether his family was keeping up contact and, especially, whether he was receiving visits. Again, these issues could be particularly pertinent for those convicted of sexual offences. The final area covered in the governor interviews concerned the kind of work (if any) that the prisoner had done outside the prison and whether he had any particular skills which might be of use in prison and which could influence his employment in prison. However, this issue was dealt with at greater length by the industrial manager.

Some prisoners also asked questions of the governor, though normally they adopted a very passive role in the interview. Most of their questions arose in areas of discussion initiated by the governor, though they were normally provided with an opportunity to raise questions of their own at the end of the interview. During the interviews we observed, prisoners raised three kinds of issue. First, if they were concerned about the difficulty of visiting for relatives, they would often have specific queries, for example, about how far Perth was from Glasgow. The governor's response to this sort of inquiry would normally be helpful and he would explain about

SACRO buses and the like. Visiting arrangements were often raised by prisoners from England who had little familiarity with the geography of Scotland.

The second main area brought up by prisoners concerned training and education. Issues brought up here were not always dealt with so helpfully, and while information was certainly not concealed, governors were clearly less well informed about such matters than about geography and travelling arrangements. This is an issue to which we shall return when we consider the later meetings of the Board.

The third issue raised by prisoners concerned the possibility of altering the classification made by the Board. The governor would explain that this could be done through the petition system (see Chapter 6 below).[6] If this was not understood by the prisoner it would be explained to him. Something that was not explained to the prisoner was that any petition he submitted on this topic would then be passed to the Chairman of the Board for comment – though this is not to imply that any such petition would necessarily be unsuccessful.

This brings us to the fourth aspect of the prison interview: the passing of information to the prisoner. This could sometimes follow a question to the prisoner, e.g. whether he understood the appeal system. If he did not, it would briefly be explained to him. Other areas which we heard explained included the imminent changes to the prison system, in particular, the proposed changes in use of Glenochil and the opening of Shotts Phase II, and the fact that the prisoner might not reach the prison for which he had been classified because of these changes. This was especially the case with prisoners who were classified to Perth.[7] We also heard the parole and petition systems explained. In conclusion, while these interviews were short, a good deal of information was imparted or elicited through them. However, the brevity of these interviews should be stressed, especially those carried out towards the end of the Board. Furthermore, the results of the induction tests were never mentioned and appeared not to influence the Board's deliberations.

The interviews carried out by the industrial manager (IM) reproduced those carried out by the governor in many respects, though there were some significant differences of emphasis. Like the governor, the industrial manager confirmed the details of the prisoner's warrant, asking whether the prisoner was facing any outstanding charges and whether he was appealing. Those convicted of drugs offences would be asked about their involvement with drugs. Industrial managers also questioned the prisoners about their current sentence, asking them (especially sex offenders) if they were having any trouble with their sentences, if they wanted to learn things during the course of their sentence and sometimes (one particular IM did this a great deal) how they thought they had got on in the induction tests. This might be followed up by a general statement about the prisoner's performance in the tests. The IM placed more emphasis on the inmate's previous prison sentences than the governors did (though, as we have stated, the governors did check and refer to this) and this formed the third main area of questioning. The IM would often ask where the prisoner had served a previous sentence and what work he had done in previous establishments. This led into the fifth main area, that of the prisoner's personal circumstances and his situation outside prison. The prisoner might be asked when he had left school and about the work he had done outside prison.

The prisoners again played a subordinate role in the interview, raising similar issues with the IM to those they raised with the governor. However, as might be expected, prisoners often wished to discuss work opportunities more in these interviews, though topics like the proximity of a prison for visiting purposes and the possibility of going to another prison also came up. Again, information and advice were passed to the prisoner. Areas which we heard explained included: the imminent changes in the prison system, especially the future use of Shotts and Glenochil; the role of the National Classification Board; the Rehabilitation of Offenders Act; and how sex offenders should attempt to cope with their sentences and deal with other offenders. In this connection, the use of the print/bookbinding shop in Edinburgh (where many sex offenders worked) was often explained.[8] Further, again in Edinburgh, allocation of work was often explained to those who would begin their sentence there.

The governor and the IM would both make a recommendation as to where the prisoner should serve his sentence. However, the IM would usually see the prisoner after the governor and could easily have been influenced by what had already been recommended. Indeed, one IM explained to us that he would very often follow the governor's recommendation. Another clarified a governor's recommendation with him during the course of a Board, as the governor appeared to be operating on somewhat different principles than the IM. The potential for disagreement was thus reduced but this does not mean that it was completely eliminated. This is illustrated in Table 3.4.

Table 3.4 Recommendations and outcomes in twenty-seven initial classification cases at pre-Grand Design meetings of the National Classification Board

Case No.	*Governor's recommendations*	*Industrial manager's recommendations*	*Outcome*
1	Perth/Shotts	Perth	Perth/Shotts
2	Perth	Perth	Perth
3	Edinburgh	Edinburgh	Edinburgh
4	Edinburgh	Edinburgh	Edinburgh
5	Perth	Perth	Perth
6	Perth	Perth	Perth
7	Peterhead	Peterhead	Peterhead
8	Edinburgh	Edinburgh	Edinburgh
9	Edinburgh	Edinburgh	Edinburgh
10	Edinburgh	Edinburgh*	Edinburgh
11	Perth	Peterhead**	Perth
12	Perth	Perth	Perth
13	Perth	Perth	Perth
14	Shotts	Shotts	Shotts***
15	Shotts	Shotts	Shotts
16	Perth	Perth	Perth
17	Shotts	Perth	Shotts
18	Perth	Shotts/Glenochil	Shotts
19	Shotts	Perth/Shotts	Perth/Shotts
20	Shotts	Shotts	Shotts
21	Shotts	Shotts	Shotts
22	Shotts	Shotts	Shotts
23	Perth	Perth	Perth
24	Shotts	Shotts	Shotts
25	Shotts	Shotts	Shotts
26	Perth	Perth	Perth
27	Peterhead (PU)†	Peterhead (PU)	Peterhead (PU)

Notes: * IM had initially told the prisoner that 'by rights' he should go to Perth, but he agreed with the governor in this case.

** IM had initially recommended Edinburgh, thinking that the prisoner was a first offender; when informed to the contrary he altered his recommendation to Peterhead.

*** An exceptional classification to Shotts. The prisoner had been 'co-operating' with the police and was to be separated from his co-accused who had been classified to Perth.

† PU = Protection Unit.

Out of the twenty-seven initial classifications we examined in detail, the governor and the industrial manager agreed on twenty-two occasions, leaving five cases to be resolved through discussion. In the first of these cases (Case 1), the governor had told the prisoner who was serving four years for Assault and Breach of the Peace that his correct prison of classification was Perth. In reply the prisoner said that he and his wife had a young child and that visiting in Perth would be a problem as they lived in Glasgow. In response to this the governor had asked if the prisoner had ever taken drugs. The prisoner had not and the governor said that he would think about a joint recommendation for Perth/Shotts. In effect, because there was a waiting list for Perth and vacancies at Shotts, this meant that the prisoner would go straight to Shotts. He also explained that the prisoner could petition to be located elsewhere. The governor subsequently commented to us that the inmate's marital situation and the fact that he seemed to be an 'honest' prisoner made him 'a good bet for Shotts'. The IM, who had put the prisoner down for Perth, readily concurred with the governor's recommendation.

In the case of the second disagreement (Case 11), the IM did not look at the prisoner's record before the interview. He asked the prisoner if he had served any previous prison sentences, to which the prisoner replied that he had not. At this point the IM told him that, as a first offender, he would be classified to Edinburgh. After the interview, it was brought to the IM's attention that the prisoner had in fact served several prison sentences, at which point the IM called the prisoner back and asked why he had concealed this information. The prisoner replied that he had misunderstood the question and explained that he had served all his previous sentences in England and had not served any sentences in Scotland before. The IM clearly did not believe this explanation and told the prisoner that, because of his record, he would be recommending Peterhead. At the meeting of the Board, the governor, who had 'correctly' put the prisoner down for Perth, asked the IM if the fact that 'the prisoner had lied to him had influenced his recommendation'. The IM replied that it had not, but that he did not feel strongly about Peterhead and was assuming that the prisoner would end up in England anyway. The prisoner was then classified to Perth.

In the third case (Case 17), the governor had recommended Shotts. On reading the prisoner's file, the IM expressed surprise at this, saying that he thought that the prisoner should go to a training establishment and that Perth would be more suitable as it had more training facilities. The prisoner was very unhappy about this as he felt that Shotts would be far more convenient for visits. However, the IM stuck to his guns, commenting after the interview that he did not think that Shotts had anything to offer the long-term prisoner. At the Board meeting itself, the IM commented that he did not think that anyone serving a six-year sentence should be sent to Shotts immediately. At this point, the governor explained the changing role of Shotts, stating that it could now take prisoners with any length of sentence. The governor also mentioned the prisoner's home address. The IM then dropped his objections and a Shotts classification was agreed.

The fourth case of disagreement (Case 18) concerned a prisoner who was serving consecutive sentences of eighteen months and three months, having been sentenced on 17 November 1986 and 22 April 1987. (This board took place in mid-May 1987.) The governor informed the prisoner that his prison of classification ought to be Perth, but wondered if it was really worth sending him there. He stated that, since the NCB could not recommend that he stay in his current prison (Barlinnie), he would have to be classified for Perth, but told him that he could petition to stay where he was. After the interview the governor commented that the prisoner would probably stay in his current establishment, but that this would depend on his behaviour. When it came to his turn, the IM thought that the governor was not really being consistent in recommending Perth and that the prisoner was a 'real Shotts type'. In any case, he thought that if they recommended Perth the prisoner would never get there (because of the length of the waiting list). The IM consequently recommended Shotts/Glenochil. At the full meeting of the Board, the governor argued that the Board had no remit for classifying to Glenochil, but said that he would be happy for the prisoner to go to Shotts. The IM concurred.

In the final case (Case 19), the governor had recommended Shotts, although he was concerned that the prisoner was categorised as a 'strict escapee' and encouraged the prisoner to divest himself of this label. The IM thought that because of this the prisoner ought to go to Perth first and consequently classified him as Perth/Shotts. The governor agreed to this in the Board meeting.

It is clear, therefore, that there was little scope for individualised decision-making at this point in time. Only two characteristics of the prisoner had to be established: whether he was a first offender or a recidivist and whether he was trainable or not trainable.

Although there was little scope for disagreement over the meaning of the first pair of terms, it might be thought that there could be scope for debate over the meaning of the second pair. However, those responsible for classification seemed to have a shared understanding of what these terms meant. This was well expressed by one IM involved in classification (I1) when he explained that:

> It was fairly straightforward; I assessed from my knowledge of the prisoner and from my information if he was an arsehole or if he wasnae an arsehole.

As we have seen, the classifiers rarely disagreed and their disagreements often reflected some misunderstanding, e.g. about which type of prisoner could be allocated to a non-mainstream prison (Shotts), or confusion, e.g. a prisoner answering a question in such a way as to lead a classifier to regard him as a first offender when he was actually a recidivist, rather than a real difference of opinion and were quickly (in a matter of seconds) overcome.

At this point, the Board used a simple set of rules to distinguish between first offenders and recidivists and a shared set of commonsense understandings to distinguish prisoners who were trainable from those who were not. Both these distinctions reflected a residual commitment to rehabilitation.

For many years, it had been the practice of the Board to automatically deem 'untrainable' any prisoner who refused to take the induction tests.[9] However, as we have seen, there was some residual scope for classifiers to draw on their experience in judging the individual prisoner. 'Professional' knowledge and expertise were also used in the passing of information to the prisoner in the interview. Thus, the activities of the Board represented a confluence of bureaucratic and, to a much lesser extent, professional forms of discourse with those of a rather muted version of rehabilitation: that is a version of rehabilitation centred on the idea of training where the role of professionals (like psychologists, social workers and teachers) in directing the programme of change for the prisoner was played down. In terms of our discourse matrix, the activities of the NCB at this time were primarily those characterised by Cell 1 which represented a confluence of bureaucratic and rehabilitation discourses, although the Board also exhibited some features represented by Cell 4 which represented a confluence of professional and rehabilitation discourses. It will be recalled that a reading of Standing Orders suggested that the activities of the NCB should have been those characterised by Cell 4. However, the dominant role played by Headquarters staff had resulted in a substantial measure of displacement towards Cell 1.

CHANGES IN 1987

During 1987 the position of the NCB became increasingly anachronistic. Two sets of forces combined to make the NCB almost irrelevant. First, there were practical and institutional pressures. Overcrowding, changes in the nature of the prison population, in particular the marked increase in the number of sex and drug offenders, and the spate of hostage-taking incidents threw classification into crisis. Prisoners were being classified to certain prisons, e.g. Perth, in the full knowledge that it was unlikely that they would reach there for a long time, if at all. Likewise, prisoners were being classified to the Peterhead Protection Unit when it was clear that, on the basis of the plans then current, it might take years before a space became available.

Our analysis of prison careers (for more detail see Chapter 4 below) indicates that, whereas 57.9 per cent of those sentenced in 1984 had reached their prison of classification within six months of being sentenced, by 1986 the proportion had fallen to 19.8 per cent. The increases in the numbers sentenced for drugs and sex offences over this period can be seen in Table 3.5. Among those

Table 3.5 Changing composition of long-term prisoners over the period 1981–6 – numbers in sample and percentages of those sentenced in the year(s) in question

Offence	*Year of sentence*			
	1981–3	*1984*	*1985*	*1986*
Homicide	18 (58.1)	11 (28.9)	12 (14.5)	7 (6.3)
Crimes of violence	26 (83.9)	32 (84.2)	68 (81.9)	65 (58.6)
Sexual offences	4 (12.9)	3 (7.9)	7 (8.4)	28 (25.2)
Housebreaking and theft	3 (9.7)	2 (5.3)	18 (21.7)	17 (15.3)
Crimes of dishonesty	4 (12.9)	4 (10.5)	21 (25.3)	17 (15.3)
Drugs offences	2 (6.5)	10 (26.3)	19 (22.9)	24 (21.6)
Miscellaneous	16 (51.6)	13 (34.2)	27 (32.5)	37 (33.3)

in prison in 1987, 21.6 per cent of those sentenced in 1986 had a drugs offence listed, while 25.2 per cent had a sex offence listed. These proportions compared with 6.5 per cent and 12.9 per cent of those sentenced in 1981–3.

Although the classification system made sense in its own terms and perhaps in relation to the relatively stable system that had existed hitherto, it moved increasingly out of line with operational considerations as other factors seriously curtailed the room for manoeuvre. One response of the Scottish Prison Service to these sorts of pressures was to transfer some of the spare capacity which existed in Young Offenders' Institutions to the overcrowded adult long-term system. Under Grand Design as the reorganisation was known, two prisons, Dumfries and Greenock (which had only recently reopened as a prison for adult LTPs), became Young Offenders' Institutions (YOIs), while two YOIs, Glenochil and Noranside, became adult long-term prisons.[10] This, and the opening of Shotts Phase II, altered the situation considerably and greatly relieved the overcrowding referred to above.[11] Henceforth all adult, male, long-term prisoners would normally begin their sentence at one of three new 'core' establishments: Shotts, Glenochil or Perth. The role of Edinburgh was left undefined although there was already talk of it becoming a 'progression' prison taking upgraded prisoners from one of the core establishments.

Grand Design was described by one governor (G16) as an administrative exercise, which 'was formulated by HQ with very little input from the field' and by another (G14) as a 'mathematical exercise which was very useful at the time. . .purely done to provide spaces. . .although all it did was shuffle people around'. Other governors argued that Grand Design had profound effects, in particular on a new establishment like Shotts. A governor at this establishment (G6) was vitriolic in his attack on the scheme. He said

> We assumed – and we were led to believe – that Shotts would be the senior training establishment. . .but before we opened, Grand Design came along and I sometimes feel we play the role that was previously enacted by Peterhead. We have everything and anything in here.

For this governor, 'grand disaster' was a better title than Grand Design.

> We saw our role – as containing the lifers and long-termers for

> five to six years during which time we would give them a basic education. The short-termers we saw as feeding quickly into Dungavel or Penninghame. Under Grand Design, we ended up with anybody other prisons could get rid of.

For this governor, the majority of prisoners felt in 'their terms conned, that they had been persuaded to leave their little niches' in Peterhead, Perth and Edinburgh for Shotts. He continued:

> People that would previously have been classified – rightly or wrongly – for Peterhead are now coming to Glenochil, Perth and Shotts. . .There is no middle ground now, in the old days, Edinburgh was at the top, Peterhead was the bottom, Perth was in-between. Now at Perth, Glenochil, Shotts, we pay lip service to them all being equal – we are trying to work the same broad policy.

For a civil servant (A2), one of the problems with Grand Design was the lack of 'co-operation from governors who didn't want to give it a chance'. For others the problems of Grand Design had more to do with the speed of implementation. G4 maintained, for example, that under the pressure of numbers of long-termers, 'Ministers got a bit anxious' and that bits of Grand Design were 'forced on us by pressure of numbers. . .[the Director] panicked and said to [the Minister]. . .that he had started Grand Design – they wanted it to happen quickly'.

During 1987, in tandem with Grand Design, the Scottish Prison Service came increasingly under the sway of a normalising strategy. In addition to the practical and institutional pressures on the NCB, ideological pressures further undercut its rationale. The language of 'training' and 'progression' was challenged by that of normalisation and 'parity of regimes'. The initial thinking through of this strategy is contained in *Custody and Care* (SPS 1988a), discussed in Chapter 9 below.

These two developments fed into each other: 'parity of regimes' caused a good deal of controversy within the prison service itself. For administrators, this was an attempt to try 'to bring some national ordering of priorities and policy objectives' (A2). This involved the adoption of a systemic point of view. A2 argued that governors must learn to co-operate, 'parity of regimes is – in a sense – about policing governors'. For A2, parity could not be left to governors as they were trained to run prisons, not trained to run a service or trained in teamwork, as civil servants were.

A series of meetings between administrators and governors to discuss the parity of regimes issue took place during 1987. However, G4 argued that while governors took part in the parity discussions, they did so with some reluctance. They always wanted parity based on their own establishment, on their own terms: 'a number of governors had been most obstructive and had not wanted to surrender anything'. Other governors explained that the problems with the parity of regimes policy were due to the fact that 'governors are individuals' (G12).

However, many governors were sympathetic to the principle of parity and accepted the need to ensure that regimes in comparable establishments were similar. For example, in a discussion of Glenochil, G18 maintained that 'within reason it should be the same as other comparable institutions. . .within reasonable limits . . .[prisoners]. . .should have the same things. . .[and] the four main prisons should be roughly the same'. G17 stressed that 'we should try and achieve parity of regimes' and G11 maintained 'we would like to think that we are operating parity'. There was, further, a clear recognition of the need to compare the regimes at the two open prisons (Penninghame and Noranside, which had previously been an open YOI) and to make clear the differences between them and the semi-open prison at Dungavel. Thus, while the strict policy of 'parity of regimes' ran into difficulties, it was clear that a new form of discourse was increasingly coming to the fore.

Classifiers were thinking along the same lines. As one governor involved in classification (G12) told us

> Trainable or non-trainable are out of date concepts because, in actual fact, if you analyse what we have called training in the past, I think it is a misnomer. We have provided work opportunities and the opportunity for people to learn one or two skills. There has been little attempt at training in social skills or even in training people for release. We have done it on some occasions and in some prisons, but not for the mass. So training in that respect was really a misnomer. What I think we ought to be providing is a system where we make opportunities available because it is then up to the individual to avail himself of these opportunities.

The combination of practical pressures, on the one hand, and ideological pressures, on the other, threw the NCB into crisis. While the format of the Board remained essentially the same, by late 1987 its rationale had ceased to exist. This was recognised by a number of governors. As G19 observed,

> we are identifying the move out of the treatment and training model (and our present classification system is treatment and training based) into a justice and opportunities model, which requires an entirely different classification system.

The demise of a treatment and training model based on the discourse of rehabilitation was described in Chapter 2 above. Its replacement by a new model based on opportunity and responsibility is analysed in more detail in Chapter 9 below.

INITIAL CLASSIFICATION – POST-1987

The response to these pressures and changes was pragmatic. As one interviewee (G12) explained, 'we are changing the classification system to meet the needs of the moment as we go along'. Classifiers tried, as far as possible, to meet the choices that prisoners expressed for a particular prison. These were often made on the basis of geographical location, rather than on knowledge of the nature of individual prisons. Furthermore, classifiers made judgments about security matters, expressing concern that Glenochil might not be as secure as the other 'mainstream' prisons.

The National Classification Board continued to sit in much the same way as it had done previously. In Table 3.6, we present a summary of data relating to meetings of the Board between July 1987 and December 1988. The somewhat smaller number of cases processed by the Board in the second half of 1987 was probably a consequence of the spate of violent disturbances during this period which led to the curtailment of a good deal of 'normal business'.

The format of the Board did not change except that the IM tended not to make such a clear-cut recommendation to the Board. Again we shall examine the structure of the interviews. However, this will not detain us very long as they were very similar to those carried out before Grand Design. The governor would scan the information in the warrant and often ask follow-up questions relating to current and past imprisonment. The prisoner's domestic circumstances would be examined and in particular his home address or home area would be confirmed. The governor would make sure that the prisoner understood the function of the Board

Table 3.6 Data relating to meetings of the National Classification Board, July 1987–December 1988

Period	*7.87–12.87*	*1.88–6.88*	*7.88–12.88*
Edinburgh			
number of meetings	12	14	16
number of chairmen	5	3	5
number of cases	123	182	162
of which			
number of YOs	37	47	34
reclassifications	5	3	5
Barlinnie			
number of meetings	13	15	14
number of chairmen	4	3	5
number of cases	178	216	266
of which			
number of YOs	–	–	–
reclassifications	–	4	5

and the working of the parole system. He would also be asked if he had any problems. The main difference in the governor's interviews was the stress placed on asking the prisoner where he would like to serve his sentence. It was explained that the choice was between three institutions, though prisoners often asked (several repeatedly) if they could be sent to open conditions. In all cases that we observed, bar one, the response to this was negative. This led to some complaints from two English prisoners who had served their previous sentences in England in less secure conditions. The system for upgrading was also often explained to the prisoners, leading some of them to ask when they would be likely to be able to return to Edinburgh. In the circumstances, since Edinburgh's role in the system was still undecided at this stage, no clear indication could be given. Prisoners often asked how long it would be before they were transferred and if they could stay in their current prison for a while longer. They also asked about the work and education opportunities at their 'prison of classification', but governors and IMs did not always possess up-to-date information on these matters. This would not have mattered under the old system, but was now of crucial importance.

The new approach to classification led to much more discussion of travel arrangements and opportunities for visits. However, one of the governors we observed in this period took much longer over his interviews than others, which may have been because he was happy to discuss such issues as geography and the reorganisation of the prison system at quite substantial length with prisoners. The explanation of the progression system in Scottish prisons entailed a consideration of the nature of open prisons and the possibility of getting to them. One governor in particular often discussed this and explained why it was not possible to send a particular prisoner to open conditions immediately.

The interviews carried out by the IM tended to be much briefer than those we observed during our first round of research. This may have been because they were carried out by more junior staff.[12] The IM tended to concentrate more on the identification of the work that the prisoner had previously done in prison as well as that done outside. Thus there was a clear focus on any skills that the prisoner possessed.

Table 3.7 records the decisions reached by the Board between July 1987 and December 1988. A comparison with Table 3.2, and with the decisions of the National Classification Board prior to Grand Design, points to a number of changes. Most prisoners were classified to three establishments, although these were not the same ones as before. 439 were classified for Shotts (39.0 per cent), 309 to Glenochil (27.4 per cent) and 177 to Perth (15.7 per cent). Although Edinburgh ceased to be a prison of classification in the second half of 1987, prisoners were still classified to Edinburgh in substantial numbers during 1988. Far fewer prisoners were classified to Peterhead (1.6 per cent compared with 6.2 per cent) and, of those who were, most were either classified for the Protection Unit or were reclassifications. However, it remained the case that very few prisoners were classified for open conditions (1.9 per cent compared with 1.6 per cent before Grand Design).

The classifications of the newly sentenced prisoners at four Boards we observed at this point are summarised in Table 3.8. Once again several points in the table call for explanation, in particular the role of Edinburgh Prison. The three Edinburgh classifications all came at the final Board we attended in Edinburgh Prison. Two of those selected were 'traditional' Edinburgh types (i.e. first offenders) while the other had previously served only one term of imprisonment (three months in 1985 under the Civic Government Act). 'Officially', however, Edinburgh was no longer a prison of classification and the Board therefore should not have allocated any prisoners to Edinburgh. However, it was explained that the

Table 3.7 Decisions of the National Classification Board, July 1987–December 1988

Location and dates	*Prison of classification**								
of NCB meetings	*1*	*2*	*3*	*4*	*5*	*6*	*7*	*8*	*Total*
Edinburgh									
7.87–12.87	2	45	8	18	2	41	5	2	123
1.88–6.88	42	48	4	33	1	47	6	1	182
7.88–12.88	62	22	–	23	2	49	3	1	162
Barlinnie									
7.87–12.87	1	88	3	13	6	66	–	1	178
1.88–6.88	10	54	3	19	5	120	–	2	213
7.88–12.88	21	52	3	71	3	116	–	–	266
Total									
Number	138	309	21	177	19	439	14	7	1,124
Percentage	12.3	27.5	1.9	15.7	1.7	39.1	1.2	0.6	100

Note: * 1 = Edinburgh, 2 = Glenochil, 3 = Penninghame, 4 = Perth, 5 = Peterhead, 6 = Shotts, 7 = Remain in YOI, 8 = Others.

Table 3.8 Disposals at four post-Grand Design meetings of the National Classification Board, early 1988

Prison of classification	*First classifications*	*YOs*	*Reclassification*
Edinburgh	3	1	–
Glenochil	23	3	2
Penninghame	1	–	–
Perth	8	–	–
Shotts	13	–	–
Total	48	4	2

three prisoners were selected because of the fall in numbers in Edinburgh, this being caused, in part, by the fact that upgradings were not coming through from Glenochil, Perth or Shotts. This was a clear change from the first Board we observed after the implementation of Grand Design when several prisoners were told that they could not stay in Edinburgh. Although Edinburgh's place in the system was still undecided, it is clear that those responsible for classification had decided that something had to be done about its use. This was at least partly due to the fact that they were concerned to remedy the problems of their own establishment (the NCB was always chaired by a governor from Edinburgh). Further, there was one classification to Penninghame. This was a 'first offender' (with one suspended sentence for theft in 1980 and several fines in his record) serving thirty-six months, who had been convicted of reset, theft, theft by housebreaking, and offences under the Police (Scotland) Act, who fulfilled the criteria for an immediate transfer to Penninghame.[13] It was unusual because this particular prisoner was not a typical white-collar criminal. Although the criteria would appear to have fitted substantially more prisoners than the number to which they were applied, those who were given an initial classification for Penninghame had almost all been convicted of white-collar crimes, e.g. fraud and embezzlement.

Disagreement between the classifiers was even more uncommon than before, as there was now even less to disagree about. Discussion at the full Board was even more perfunctory than it had been before Grand Design. Furthermore, prisoners were quite often upset at interview. They were being asked to make a choice between establishments on the basis of little background information. Some said that they would like to go to open conditions and were irritated when it was explained that this would only be possible for a tiny number. A summary of requests, governors' recommendations and decisions is contained in Table 3.9.

Table 3.9 summarises the data on initial classifications at three post-Grand Design meetings of the National Classification Boards which we attended. In general, the governor's recommendation was transformed into the decision, though there was scope for discussion (see Cases 1–3). The most salient feature of Table 3.9, however, is the content of the prisoner's request column. We should emphasise that the table 'tidies up' what the prisoners were saying. Many prisoners were immediately offered the choice between Shotts, Glenochil and Perth and some expressed a preference with some reluctance. When offered a 'free choice', a significant number had no clear preference and had to be prodded to express a view. Even then, many wanted to go or stay somewhere outside the options available. This suggests to us that 'choice' does not describe at all convincingly the exercise engaged in by the prisoners (cf. Bottoms and McLean 1976). We have already referred to some of the new principles which were introduced into the classification system. Security considerations, as reflected in length of sentence, were said to be important. At this stage we do not wish to enter into a detailed consideration of the evaluation of security risk. However there seemed to be little systematic allocation of prisoners serving shorter sentences to Glenochil where the need for high security is usually less.

DISCOURSE, POWER AND CLASSIFICATION

The changes in the role of the National Classification Board and in the nature and significance of initial classification can be explained in terms of what we have referred to as discursive struggle (see Chapter 2 above). As we pointed out earlier in this chapter, until 1987, classification could be identified with Cell 1 and, to a lesser extent, Cell 4 in our discourse matrix (see Figure 2.5 on p.46). However, the increasing demands of normalisation discourse and the attempt to move the prison system in this direction shattered the rationale and practice of the NCB. A prison system moving in the direction of normalisation had no use for a system of classification based on distinctions between first offenders and recidivists and between prisoners who were deemed to be trainable and those who were not. Not only was the muted form of rehabilitation undercut by normalisation, the combination of bureaucratic and professional

Table 3.9 Requests, recommendations and outcomes in thirty-six initial classification cases from three of the National Classification Board post-Grand Design meetings

Case no.	*Prisoner's request*	*Governor's recommendation*	*Decision*
1	Open conditions	Shotts/Glenochil	Glenochil
2	Shotts	Shotts/Glenochil	Shotts
3	Anywhere	Glenochil/Shotts	Shotts
4	Glenochil	Glenochil	Glenochil
5	Shotts (unless open conditions)	Shotts	Shotts
6	Shotts (after asking about open conditions)	Shotts	Shotts
7	Penninghame, then Glenochil	Glenochil	Glenochil
8	Glenochil (but might prefer Perth)	Glenochil	Glenochil
9	Shotts	Shotts	Glenochil
10	Glenochil	Glenochil	Glenochil
11	Shotts	Shotts	Shotts
12	Shotts	Shotts	Shotts
13	Not clear	Shotts	Shotts
14	Not clear	Perth	Perth
15	'No idea'	Shotts	Shotts
16	Edinburgh, then Perth	Perth	Perth
17	Glenochil	Glenochil	Glenochil
18	Glenochil	Glenochil	Glenochil
19	Glenochil	Glenochil	Glenochil
20	Not clear	Glenochil	Glenochil
21	Shotts	Perth	Perth
22	Glenochil	Glenochil	Glenochil
23	Perth	Perth	Perth
24	Glenochil	Glenochil	Glenochil
25	Perth	Perth	Perth
26	Perth	Perth	Perth
27	Open, then refused to make choice	Edinburgh	Edinburgh
28	Edinburgh	Glenochil	Glenochil
29	Glenochil	Glenochil	Glenochil
30	Glenochil	Glenochil	Glenochil
31	Shotts	Shotts	Shotts
32	Edinburgh	Edinburgh	Edinburgh
33	Edinburgh, but would accept Glenochil	Edinburgh	Edinburgh
34	Perth/Shotts	Shotts	Perth
35	'No idea', then Glenochil	Possibly Edinburgh	Glenochil
36	Glenochil	Glenochil	Glenochil

discourses was undercut by a very weak form of juridical discourse. Subject to security considerations and the availability of places, this enabled adult, male, long-term prisoners to choose in which of three prisons they wished to start their sentence, and went some way towards establishing the prisoner's right to choose. From 1987 onwards, the activities of the Board were primarily those characterised by Cell 2 of our matrix (a confluence of bureaucratic and normalisation discourse), although the Board also exhibited some features characteristic of Cell 8 (a confluence of legal and normalisation discourse).

These moves across the discourse matrix reflect changes in the power relations among the principal actors in the Scottish prison system. The seemingly relentless increase in the size of the prison population and, in particular, the rapid increase in the number of adult, male, long-term prisoners contributed to the spate of violent hostage-taking incidents and brought the system to a state of near paralysis. The effect of this, at least in the short run, was greatly to enhance the centralising power of Headquarters as against that of individual establishments and, in relation to classification, to reduce still further the power of the National Classification Board and of the prison governors and industrial managers who sat on the Board. Since, by this time, HQ was increasingly strongly committed to a strategy of normalisation, this, in turn, led to the partial enfranchisement of prisoners. Whether this would have happened if the violent hostage-taking incidents had not taken place must be an open question.

Classification occurs at the beginning of the prisoner's sentence and, in Chapter 4, we examine its implications for the prisoner's career and assess the extent to which the decisions of the National Classification Board were undermined by subsequent decisions made by prison governors and Headquarters staff.

Chapter 4

Transfers and careers

Reinforcing classification

We argued in the previous chapter that classification is important because it reflects the core concerns of the particular social system in which it operates, and consequently that the classification of adult, male, long-term prisoners is an activity of central importance for the Scottish prison system. Moreover, we demonstrated a high degree of concern over the operation of the classification system voiced by prison governors as well as administrators at Headquarters. We suggested that, before Grand Design, classification discourse represented a confluence of bureaucratic and rehabilitation discourses and occupied Cell 1 of our discourse matrix (see Figure 2.5 on p.46). Subsequently, as normalisation took over, it occupied Cells 2 and 8. In coming to these conclusions, we argued that the bureaucratic discourse of the centre held sway over classification despite the actual operationalisation of decision-making by professionals and the, albeit limited, scope for professional judgment. In this chapter we develop these themes.

In particular, we focus on the extent to which initial classification decisions determined the subsequent prison career of the adult, male, long-term prisoner. We begin with a brief outline of some of the more salient social characteristics of the prison population. This is important as it produces a clear picture of a social group which is often characterised in a stereotypical way. We then examine the nature of the 'debate' concerning the transfers of prisoners between establishments which was taking place at the time of our research and was one of the topics on which prison governors most frequently voiced their concern with the action of staff at Headquarters. We also consider the actual careers of prisoners in some detail. Our prime focus here is on the extent to which subsequent decisions and actions *diluted* the decision made at the National Classification Board (NCB). For example, if our data showed that Edinburgh Prison contained a majority of recidivist prisoners, it would be possible to maintain that significant dilution of the initial classification decision had taken place, and that classification at the NCB was of only relatively marginal importance. To anticipate our conclusions on this matter, we shall demonstrate that much less of this dilution took place than we actually expected, suggesting a rather secure hold on the management of prisoners' careers by Headquarters. We finish the chapter by backing up this judgment with an analysis of the prison careers of life-sentence prisoners, whose sentences are even more tightly controlled by Headquarters.

BACKGROUND CHARACTERISTICS OF THE LONG-TERM PRISON POPULATION

Our discussion of prisoners' mobility and their prison careers in this chapter is based upon two quantitative data sets. We refer to these as transfer data and careers data.[1]

A majority (53.3 per cent and 55.8 per cent) of prisoners in both samples (for whom this information was available) came from four cities (Aberdeen, Dundee, Edinburgh and Glasgow). Likewise a majority (54.5 per cent and 55.8 per cent) came from Strathclyde Region. These proportions are broadly in line with the distribution of the Scottish population.

Over half (50.6 per cent and 56.6 per cent) of our samples had been convicted of more than one charge, with crimes of violence being the largest category of crime overall (37.8 per cent and 21.9 per cent). When all offences committed are considered, it became clear that the majority of long-term prisoners in our sample had been convicted of crimes of violence and that significant minorities had been convicted, either on their own or in combination, of homicide, sexual offences, housebreaking and theft, crimes of dishonesty and drugs offences. The distribution of crimes and offences committed for both samples is shown in Table 4.1. These crimes and offences resulted in sentences as shown in Table 4.2.

The careers data provide information on previous offences and sentences. About 60 per cent of the sample were serving sentences of five years or more while 20 per cent were lifers. Most of the sample had previously served a non-custodial sentence (only 13.6 per cent had not); and a majority had served a sentence

Table 4.1 Crimes and offences resulting in sentences of imprisonment (transfer data and careers data)

	(*Transfer data*)			(*Careers data*)		
Composite category	*No.*	*% of 5,307 crimes and offences*	*% of 2,758 prisoners*	*No.*	*% of 835 crimes and offences*	*% of 429 prisoners*
Homicide	388	7.3	14.1	95	11.4	22.1
Crimes of violence	2,008	37.8	72.8	275	32.9	64.1
Sexual offences	306	5.8	11.1	78	9.3	18.2
Housebreaking/theft	571	10.8	20.7	75	9.0	17.5
Crimes of dishonesty	625	11.8	22.7	77	9.2	17.9
Drugs offences	526	9.9	19.1	71	8.5	16.6
Miscellaneous	883	16.6	32.0	164	19.6	38.2
Information available on crimes and offences	5,307	100.0	192.5	835	100.0	194.6
Missing data	718			1		
Information available on prisoners	2,758			429		

Note: * The classification of crimes and offences used by the Scottish Home and Health Department contains over 300 categories. These were grouped first into twenty-nine categories and then into the seven composite categories used here.

Table 4.2 Length of sentence imposed (transfer data and careers data)

	(Transfer data)		*(Careers data)*	
Length of sentence	*Number*	*%*	*Number*	*%*
18 months–less than 3 years	624	19.1	55	12.8
3 years – less than 5 years	842	25.8	103	24.0
5 years – less than 10 years	1,182	36.2	142	33.0
19 years or more	248	7.6	51	11.9
Life or equivalent	370	11.3	78	18.2
Information available	3,266	100.0	429	100.0
Missing data	210		0	
Total	3,476		429	

in a Young Offenders' Institution (although 48.2 per cent had not); 53.8 per cent had not previously served a short-term prison sentence (under eighteen months); and 75.5 per cent had not served a previous long-term prison sentence. Indeed only 14.0 per cent had served more than three short-term sentences and only 1.2 per cent more than three long-term sentences.

As might be expected, prisoners in the sample had previously been charged with a variety of offences, the most common being in the relatively minor categories of forgery, reset and embezzlement, but housebreaking, and breach of the peace also figured prominently. This is consistent with the account of sentences previously served given above, as the prisoners would not have been sentenced to long periods for such offences.

From these figures, a preliminary picture of adult, male, long-term prisoners emerges. These prisoners came, in the main, from the cities and, in particular, from the West of Scotland; they had been convicted of crimes of violence, most commonly serious assault, and most of them were serving sentences of five years or more. Most of them had a criminal background (in the sense of having previously been convicted of crime) but this was of a relatively petty nature and although most of them had previously served a custodial sentence, very few had had repeated spells of long-term imprisonment. This is in spite of the fact that the

Table 4.3 Prisoners' ages (careers data)

Age at date of data collection	*Number*	*%*	*Cumulative %*
21–23	45	10.5	10.5
24–26	70	16.3	26.8
27–29	88	20.5	47.3
30–32	57	13.3	60.6
33–35	34	7.9	68.5
36+	135	31.5	100.0
Total	429	100.0	100.0

majority were old enough to have served one or more previous long-term sentences.

The age range of the sample is given in Table 4.3. As can be seen just under half (47.3 per cent) of the sample was under 30 years of age. However, a significant minority (31.5 per cent) was over 35.

Our careers data were collected during 1987 and early 1988 and almost three-quarters (73.0 per cent) of the sample had begun their sentence since the beginning of 1985. More than half the sample (53.6 per cent) had begun their sentence since the beginning of 1986. Thus, the picture that emerges is of a long-term prison population which had not spent a very long time in prison; 76.6 per cent had served less than three years and 44.9 per cent had served less than eighteen months. Leaving aside the lifers in the sample, 82.7 per cent had less than three years left to serve and 56.4 per cent less than eighteen months. Allowing for remission, 53.0 per cent of the sample had an 'Earliest Date of Liberation' (EDL) before the end of 1989. Although eighteen months to serve may seem like a very long time for prisoners and observers (particularly if they are committed to reducing the length of prison sentences), it goes against the stereotypical view of the long-term prisoner as a prisoner engaged in a long sentence of, say, ten years or more. Our data suggest that the long-term prison population in Scotland is relatively transient, and that it is *not* made up of offenders who have been convicted of a series of serious offences, leading to repeated long-term sentences.

TRANSFERS OF PRISONERS

Because of the importance of classification for the prison system, we began our examination of the management of adult, male, long-term prisoners in Scotland with an extended examination of this topic in Chapter 3. However, it is clearly important to examine the extent to which classification decisions *actually* affect the subsequent career of the long-term prisoner. If prisoners were being transferred from one prison to another in a way that led to a different distribution from that envisaged by the decisions of the NCB, then there would be evidence that the consequences were being *diluted*. At the time of our research, Headquarters had attempted to take explicit control over the transfer of prisoners between establishments, and there was much discussion of this issue among prison governors.

Governors were very keen to discuss the issue of transfers with us. Indeed, it was one of the issues about which they clearly felt very strongly. Many of them made references to their professionalism – they claimed to understand what prisoners were up to and to know when prisoners were ready for a move. Likewise, they claimed to understand their establishments and to know when it was advisable in the interests of 'good order and discipline' for a prisoner to be moved to another prison and when prisoners from elsewhere could be accommodated without too much difficulty. In their view, 'governor-to-governor' transfers had worked well – they had helped to make it possible for every prisoner to find a niche somewhere (even in Peterhead) and enabled governors to deal with problems as and when they arose. Thus, according to G10, Aberdeen used to take prisoners from a number of establishments and a certain amount of 'horsetrading' had gone on, especially with Peterhead. 'The Governor would ring up and explain that he had a problem. In return for taking a prisoner from Peterhead, I might ask Peterhead to take one of ours.' Likewise, G12 explained:

> The Governor of Perth would phone the Governor at Peterhead saying 'We've got a bad lad'. The Governor at Peterhead would say 'We've got quite a good lad' and they would arrange a swap.

He was of the opinion that 'governors were professional enough to make a judgment as to whether a particular prisoner was suited to a particular prison'. G2 told us that he had 'got rid of people' in this way 'five or six times a year' and explained that he would rather do this than keep them out of circulation (on Rule 36).[2] Although he realised that this 'ghost train facility' put a big responsibility on governors and had to be used sparingly, he felt that it was absolutely essential.

Most governors were very resentful that Headquarters had effectively put a stop to this practice. As they saw it, 'Headquarters' staff could not possibly know what they knew about individual prisoners or about establishments and, as a result, they often got it wrong'. Even having to go through Headquarters created problems because it took so long to get a decision. They argued that this was not only inconsistent with the need, on occasion, for a quick decision but could also have a detrimental effect on the relationships between prisoners and prison staff. Thus, for example, G18 complained about the length of time it took Headquarters to agree a transfer to semi-open or open conditions, pointing out that 'governors know the prisoners best' and claiming that 'procrastination leads to governors looking bad in the eyes of the prisoners'.

Although they resented the direct involvement of Headquarters, most governors accepted that Headquarters needed to know what was going on and many would have welcomed clearer guidelines. According to G12, the decision by Headquarters to take control of transfers 'was a direct consequence of the Peterhead incident when they [Headquarters] were a wee bit shocked to find out exactly where prisoners were in the system at the time'. G12 maintained that a large number of Peterhead prisoners were actually in Edinburgh on 'accumulated visits' or for a trial but thought that, by insisting that governors had to seek approval for every transfer, 'Headquarters had used a sledgehammer to crack a nut'. Of course, Headquarters did not see it that way. Their concern was with the prison system as a whole and they argued that what was in the interests of individual prisoners or of individual establishments was not necessarily in the interests of the whole system. While governors emphasised their need to exercise (professional) discretion in order to respond to problems as and when they arose, Headquarters' staff stressed the importance of applying (bureaucratic) rules and guidelines in order to achieve greater consistency and fairness. As A7 explained, 'we aim for consistency. . .but it is very difficult. . .given the difficulties of dealing with different governors'. He stressed the interrelationship between fairness and consistency, claiming that

> we aim for fairness first of all. We aim to see that what is done complies with natural justice as much as anything. We aim to ensure that someone is not treated vastly differently in one establishment than he would be in another one.

In terms of our discourse matrix, governors' transfer discourse clearly exemplifies the professional forms of discourse found in the second row of the matrix. To the extent that 'upgradings' were frequently justified by reference to rehabilitation discourse while 'downgradings' usually invoked the discourse of control, governors' transfer discourse can be located in Cells 4 and 6 of our discourse matrix. Any potential purchase for such a discourse was called into question and eventually undermined by two separate sets of problems which emerged during 1986 and 1987. As we pointed out in Chapter 3, overcrowding, which led to Grand Design, and the series of hostage-taking incidents, which was seen to require the decanting of many of the prisoners who were held in those establishments that were under siege, gave the centre (Headquarters) an opportunity to assert its control over the periphery (individual establishments). Bureaucratic forms of transfer discourse which are associated with administrators at Headquarters and can be located in the first row of our discourse matrix displaced the professional forms of transfer discourse associated with prison governors.

This attempt by the centre to assert its control over the periphery created a good deal of opposition. As Headquarters came under the sway of normalisation discourse, individual establishments, in particular the mainstream establishments, came to hold a much more heterogeneous population of prisoners than had previously been the case. At the same time, the hostage-taking incidents led to large groups of prisoners being moved from one prison to another for operational reasons. Both these developments increased the pressures on establishments. Thus, central control led to greater demands for institutional autonomy, and the emergence of bureaucratic forms of transfer discourse (associated with Cell 1 and, to an even greater extent, Cell 3 in the discourse matrix) produced, as a reaction, a vocal expression of the professional forms of transfer discourse (associated with Cells 4 and 6 of the matrix).

It seems clear that transfers were a contentious issue: governors perceived their professional discretion and authority to be under attack and believed that this was one of the main causes of institutional unrest, whereas civil servants believed that the activities of governors who arranged transfers without the knowledge and approval of Headquarters had actually led to the unrest and therefore needed to be curtailed. Somewhat paradoxically, the spate of serious disturbances was attributed to too much professional discretion by the bureaucrats and to not enough by the professionals. Unfortunately, our transfer data, which were collected over a period of rapid change, do not allow us to assess the truth of these claims. However, our careers data are more helpful in this regard. We now use them to consider the extent to which the transfers of long-term prisoners had 'diluted' the decisions of the National Classification Board.

CAREERS

The prisons of classification are set out in Table 4.4. The core classification prisons are represented in a clear fashion here. Under the classification system as it operated prior to 1987, it would be expected that the overwhelming majority of prisoners would have been classified for Edinburgh, Perth or Peterhead. Under the developing system of classification from 1987 onwards, Glenochil and Shotts assumed greater importance.

Table 4.4 Prison of classification (careers data)

*Prison of classification**	*No. of prisoners*	*%***
Aberdeen	9	2.7
Edinburgh	88	26.0
Dumfries	11	3.2
Glenochil	24	7.1
Penninghame	1	0.3
Perth	118	34.8
Peterhead	55	16.2
Shotts	17	5.0
Others	16	4.7
Information available	339	100.0
Missing data	90	.
Total	429	

Notes: * Hybrid classifications of the form Prison 1/Prison 2 were always included with Prison 2 since it implied that Prison 1 was a provisional classification and that the prisoner was intended to move to Prison 2 when circumstances allowed.

** Percentage figures based on 339 cases for which information is available.

The nature of the offence committed did not determine the prison of classification in any very obvious way. This is not surprising as members of the National Classification Board did not take it into account (see Chapter 3 above). However, those convicted of crimes of violence were less likely to go to Edinburgh than to one of the other prisons, while Edinburgh took more of those who had been convicted of homicide. Those with less serious offences were more likely to be classified outside the main classification prisons. In general, those sentenced to the longest periods of imprisonment were more likely to be classified for Peterhead. For example, of those sentenced to ten years or more, 32.8 per cent of prisoners in our sample were classified to Peterhead compared with 13.6 per cent to Perth and 5.7 per cent to Edinburgh. By comparison, of those sentenced to less than five years, 29.5 per cent were classified to Edinburgh, 24.5 per cent to Perth and 10.4 per cent to Peterhead.

The prior number of offences was clearly reflected in the prison of classification decision. Of the eighty-eight prisoners in the sample classified for Edinburgh, eighty-five (96.6 per cent) had not previously served a long-term sentence. This compared with seventy-eight out of 118 (66.1 per cent) prisoners classified for Perth and twenty-six out of fifty-five (47.3 per cent) of those classified for Peterhead. The figure for Peterhead, in particular, is rather surprising. However, 54.6 per cent of prisoners classified for Peterhead had previously served one or more long-term sentences, the proportions for Edinburgh and Perth being 3.4 per cent and 27.1 per cent respectively. Thus, serious long-term recidivists were almost equally likely to be classified for Perth or Peterhead. What is more surprising is that 29.8 per cent of those classified for Peterhead had not previously served a short-term sentence, 35.7 per cent had not previously served a young-offender sentence and 13.2 per cent had not previously served a non-custodial sentence. Conversely 12.2 per cent of prisoners classified for Edinburgh had previously served a short-term sentence, 16.0 per cent had served a young-offenders sentence and 77.4 per cent had served a non-custodial sentence. It is clear, as we have pointed out in Chapter 3, that many of those who were treated as first offenders by the Scottish Prison Service and classified for Edinburgh would not have been regarded as first offenders by the general public. It is also clear that some of those who were classified for Peterhead did not appear to be serious long-term recidivists.

As we have suggested, it is important to ascertain whether initial classification actually determined the prison at which the sentence was served. Analysis shows that the largest group in each prison consisted of those who had been classified to that prison, i.e. in

Edinburgh 61.7 per cent of the population had been classified there, in Perth 81.0 per cent, in Peterhead 59.6 per cent, in Glenochil 29.6 per cent and in Shotts 27.8 per cent. The lower figures for the last two prisons are explained by the fact that they had only recently become prisons of classification. Further, of those who had been classified to Edinburgh, 33.0 per cent were still there and few had been downgraded to Perth (3.4 per cent) or Peterhead (3.4 per cent). For those who had been classified to Perth, 28.8 per cent were still there, and the next largest group were those who had been upgraded to Dungavel (15.3 per cent). Turning to the figures for Peterhead, 50.9 per cent of those classified to that prison were still there while a similar percentage (14.5 per cent) had been upgraded to Dungavel. Of those classified to Glenochil, 66.7 per cent were still there and of those classified to Shotts, 58.8 per cent, were still there. Thus, at the most general level, it is clear that the prison of classification *did* have an effect on where the prisoner served his sentence and on the structure of the population at the main prisons – especially, it should be said, when the function of the prison within the prison system was relatively stable.

Table 4.5 shows that there were wide variations in the proportion of prisoners at the different prisons who had previously served a custodial sentence of one kind or another.

Table 4.5 Previous custodial sentences (careers data)

Prison	*% of prisoners who have previously served a custodial sentence*
Barlinnie	92.9*
Perth	84.0
Peterhead	80.0
Noranside	74.1
Aberdeen	70.6
Dungavel	70.2
Shotts	70.0
Glenochil	64.6
Edinburgh	39.2
Penninghame	30.4

Note: * Based on a very small sample (n=14). For details, see note 1 (p.252). As a local prison, Barlinnie should not hold any long-term prisoners. Prior to Grand Design large numbers of long-term prisoners were held in Barlinnie awaiting transfer to other prisons but, at the time of data collection (Spring 1988), the number of long-term prisoners in Barlinnie was very small.

Two prisons (Edinburgh and Penninghame) were very different from the rest in that minorities of prisoners there compared with clear majorities elsewhere had previous experience of custody. We can take this analysis further by comparing those who are held in the three 'traditional' classification prisons with those who were classified for these prisons.

Table 4.6 Backgrounds of prisoners classified for and held at different prisons (careers data)

	No previous sentence (%)		*Previous sentence (%)*	
	Classified	*Held*	*Classified*	*Held*
Edinburgh				
previous YO	84.0	69.4	16.0	30.6
previous short-term	87.8	77.6	12.2	22.4
previous long-term	96.4	86.0	3.6	14.0
Perth				
previous YO	28.1	27.5	71.9	72.5
previous short-term	40.2	45.8	59.8	54.2
previous long-term	72.9	89.6	27.1	10.4
Peterhead				
previous YO	35.7	32.4	64.3	67.6
previous short-term	29.8	46.8	70.2	53.2
previous long-term	45.6	62.5	54.4	37.5

Table 4.6 throws up some interesting comparisons. If the figures for those who had not previously served a prison sentence are considered first, it is possible to see some of the differences between classification decisions and actual populations. For example, 96.4 per cent of those classified for Edinburgh had not previously served a long-term prison sentence, whereas the proportion of those who were held in Edinburgh who had not previously served a long-term prison sentence was 86 per cent, still high but showing some dilution of the first offender status of the prison. The same pattern holds for prisoners who had previously served short-term or young-offender sentences. For those who had served long-term sentences before, there were similar changes in the other direction. Of those classified for Perth, 27.1 per cent had previously served one or more long-term custodial sentences, but only 10.4 per cent of the actual prison population had done so. For Peterhead, 54.5 per cent of

those classified for the prison had previously served a long-term sentence, but this was reduced to 37.5 per cent in the actual prison population. Thus, some 'dilution' of the principles which are applied at classification took place subsequently.

Despite this evidence of some dilution of classification decisions, they were still important determinants of the populations held in the different prisons. In the analysis of classification set out in Chapter 3, we argued that the activities of the pre-Grand Design National Classification Board represented a confluence of bureaucratic and, to a lesser extent, professional discourses with a muted discourse of rehabilitation. Post-Grand Design, this residual commitment to rehabilitation was displaced by the ascendancy of normalisation while the weak form of professionalism was simultaneously undermined by a limited form of legality which enabled prisoners to choose, subject to security considerations and the availability of places, in which of three establishments they wished to serve their sentences. It follows that, before and after Grand Design, the distribution of long-term prisoners was structured by the interplay between means and ends discourses. Although, as we pointed out above, there was a good deal of bargaining between individual governors and conflict with Headquarters over the transfer of prisoners between establishments, it is clear that initial classification mapped out the terrain on which subsequent transfers took place.

The position we have been outlining in this chapter suggests that Headquarters significantly constrained the scope of operation of the governors. This develops the argument of Chapter 3 which suggested that the centrally-determined categories were operationalised by professionals in the NCB. Further evidence of the power of Headquarters can be found in the arrangements for dealing with life-sentence prisoners, and it is to this group that we now turn.

LIFE-SENTENCE PRISONERS

Headquarters is much more closely involved in decisions concerning life-sentence prisoners than in decisions involving prisoners serving determinate sentences. A group of officials in the lifers' section of casework branch at Headquarters has administrative responsibility for all the key decisions concerning, for example, transfers between establishments and, in particular, to semi-open and open conditions, security categorisation, outside placements, parole and related matters. Thus, decision-making for lifers is much more centralised than for other long-term prisoners and this would suggest that the powers of governors, and other staff at establishment level, in respect of lifers, are even more constrained by Headquarters than their powers in respect of other long-term prisoners.

The lifers in our sample[3] were predominantly young when they were sentenced (average age 23 years and 6 months) and becoming progressively younger, they were overwhelmingly single, unskilled and unqualified. They came disproportionately from Glasgow and the West of Scotland; most of them had previously been in some sort of trouble but, for many of them, this was their first serious experience of incarceration, most of them had been convicted of murder and nothing else and only a small proportion had been recalled after being paroled on a life licence.

Like other long-term prisoners, lifers are classified at the National Classification Board. We found evidence of three main lifer routes based on this initial classification and the subsequent regulation of the lifer's prison career.

1 For first offenders, and other ex-young offenders with good prison records who were given 'first offender' status, a start at Edinburgh (the prison of classification for this group), progression through the different halls in Edinburgh, followed by a move to the open prison at Penninghame (or, since 1987, to the second open prison at Noranside) and from there to one of the Training for Freedom (TFF) hostels at Aberdeen, Edinburgh or Perth Prisons.
2 For 'trainable recidivists', a start at Perth (the prison of classification for this group), followed after some time by a move to the semi-open prison at Dungavel or to one of the more 'relaxed' halls at Edinburgh, and from there to Penninghame and TFF.
3 For 'non-trainable recidivists', a start at Peterhead or Aberdeen (the prisons of classification for this group) followed, after a testing time at Peterhead, by a move to Perth and then through the 'trainable recidivist' route described above.

Although some lifers were downgraded (from Edinburgh or Perth to Peterhead and from semi-open or open conditions back to closed conditions), this was most likely for prisoners on the third route and least likely for prisoners on the first route.

Initial classification was of great significance for lifers. Prisoners with an Edinburgh classification were most likely to progress smoothly through the system – compared with other lifers, they spent shorter periods of time in high security (Category B) conditions, were less likely to be subject to control measures, spent time in fewer establishments, had fewer parole reviews and served shorter periods in prison. Conversely, prisoners with a Peterhead or Aberdeen classification were most likely to create problems for the prison authorities – they spent longer periods of time in high security (Category B) conditions, were more likely to be regarded as escape risks and to be placed on Rule 36, were transferred more frequently, had most parole reviews and served longer sentences.[4]

We have suggested so far that lifers' careers are much more centrally controlled than those of other long-term prisoners. However, it is important in addition to recognise the important role of the Parole Board in the lifer's career. A life-sentence prisoner is liable to be detained in prison for the rest of his life. However, the Secretary of State for Scotland (and, likewise, the Home Secretary in England and Wales) has the power to release him or her on licence if this is recommended by the Parole Board. The procedure is a complicated one and the various stages are set out in Figure 4.1.

After a life-sentence prisoner has been detained for a period, his case will be considered by the Preliminary Review Committee (PRC) with a view to recommending a date for the first formal review of his suitability for release on licence. The prisoner does not need to instigate this process and his case is considered, normally after he has served about four years in custody, regardless of his views. The PRC is chaired by an Under-Secretary in the Scottish Home and Health Department (SHHD), and its members include a High Court judge (who is also a member of the Parole Board), two other members of the Parole Board (by convention the Chairman and a psychiatrist) and a retired prison governor. The views of the judiciary are not sought at this stage but the report prepared by the trial judge at the end of the trial and any recommendation as to the minimum period the offender should serve in custody will be available to the PRC.

The PRC's recommendation as to the date on which the case should be referred to a Local Review Committee (LRC) is submitted to the Secretary of State. Each establishment holding prisoners who are eligible for release on licence has its own LRC comprising the governor (or his deputy), a number of social workers and

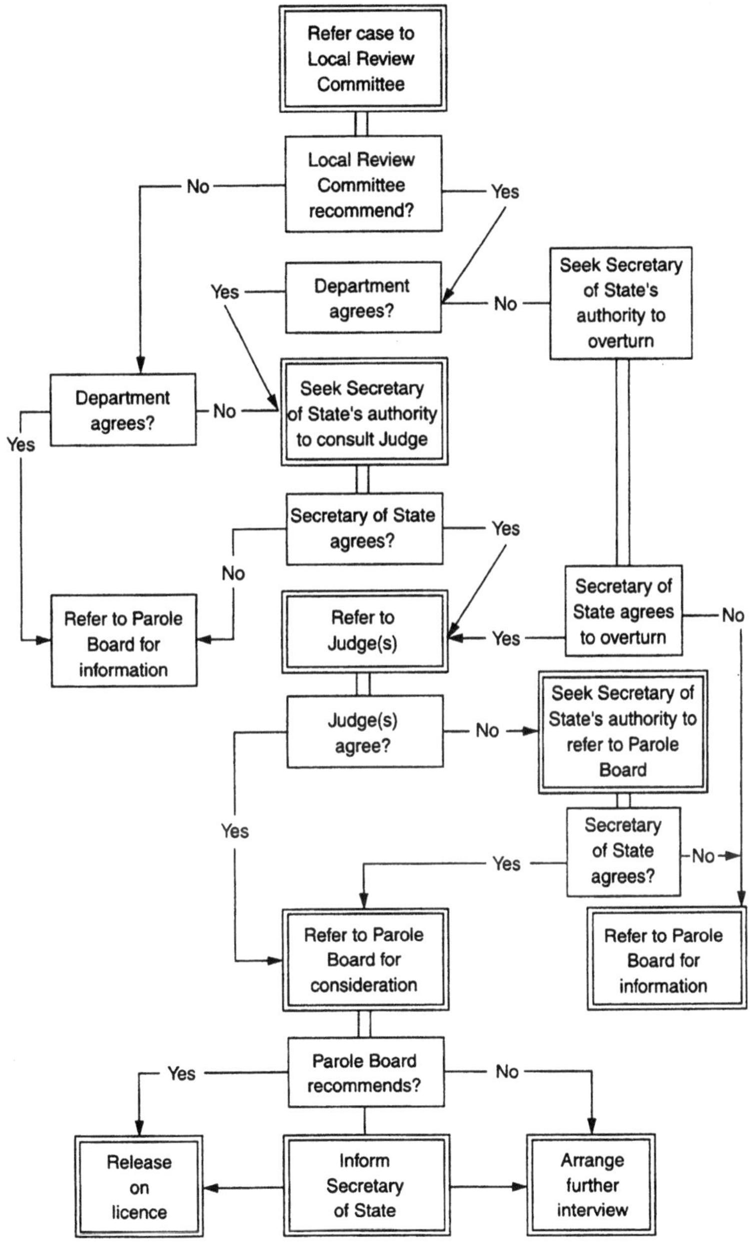

Figure 4.1 Referral of life-sentence cases to the Parole Board

independent members appointed by the Secretary of State. Prior to the LRC meeting, a single member of the LRC interviews the prisoner to assist him in presenting his case.

If the LRC does not recommend release, or if the SHHD view is that a positive LRC recommendation for release is not appropriate, the case is referred to the Parole Board for information with a proposal for a later review. If the LRC recommendation is in favour of release but the SHHD view is that the case is a particularly complex one (particularly if there are doubts about the public safety aspects) the case may be referred to the Parole Board for preliminary assessment before reference to the Secretary of State who will then have an informal indication of the position the Board is likely to take.

If, in due course, the LRC recommends the grant of a provisional release date and SHHD concurs, the Secretary of State will then authorise reference to the Lord Justice General and the trial judge (if available) and (subject to reference back to the Secretary of State if the two judges disagree) to the Parole Board. If the Secretary of State does not authorise consultation, the case is referred to the Parole Board for information with a proposal for a later review.

If the outcome of consultations is a favourable recommendation from the Parole Board, the prisoner will then be granted a provisional date for his release on licence. This will almost invariably be subject to the satisfactory completion of a pre-release programme, which normally lasts twelve to eighteen months and may involve progression through semi-open conditions, open conditions and outside employment under the Training for Freedom (TFF) scheme.

Between May 1980 and June 1987 the PRC met seventeen times and considered the cases of 350 life-sentence prisoners. The outcomes are set out in Table 4.7. Of the 350 reviews, 288 (82.3 per cent) were first reviews, 54 (15.4 per cent) second reviews, seven (2.0 per cent) third reviews and one (0.3 per cent) a fourth review. Overall, approximately 70 per cent were successful in that they were referred to the Local Review Committee while 30 per cent were recommended for further consideration by the PRC at a later date. It is of particular interest that the 70:30 split was virtually the same for first, second and third reviews.

The PRC not only decides whether to refer the case to the LRC or to consider it again before doing so, but also specifies when these events should take place. The stages in the lifers' careers at which these events took place are set out in Table 4.8. The mean time for

Table 4.7 Preliminary Review Committee decisions, May 1980–June 1987

	Cases		*Refer to LRC*		*Refer back to PRC*	
	No.	*%*	*No.*	*%*	*No.*	*%*
1st Review	288	82.3	202	70.1	86	29.9
2nd Review	54	15.4	37	68.5	17	31.5
3rd Review	7	2.0	5	71.4	2	28.6
4th Review	1	0.3	0	0.0	1	100.0
Total	350	100.0	244	69.7	106	30.3

Table 4.8 Timing of PRC and LRC decisions

	Cases		*Time**		
	No.	*%*	*Shortest*	*Longest*	*Mean*
PRC (350)					
1st Review	288	82.3	4.0	4.8	4.3
2nd Review	54	15.4	6.8	8.4	7.6
3rd Review	7	2.0	–	–	10.0
4th Review	1	0.3	–	–	11.9
LRC (244)					
After 1st PRC	202	82.8	6.0	8.4	7.3
After 2nd PRC	37	15.2	8.5	9.8	9.0
After 3rd PRC	5	2.0	–	–	11.0
After 4th PRC	0	0.0	–	–	–
Reconsideration (106)					
After 1st PRC	86	81.1	6.3	7.6	7.2
After 2nd PRC	17	16.0	10.2	11.4	10.1
After 3rd PRC	2	1.9	–	–	15.0
After 4th PRC	1	0.9	–	–	16.9

Note: * All times in years and months, i.e. 11.9 = 11 years 9 months.

the first PRC was four years three months (range four years to four years eight months). For cases that were referred to the LRC, this took place after seven years three months (range six years to eight years four months) and for cases which the PRC wished to reconsider, this took place at much the same time (mean seven years two months, range six years three months to seven years six months). Thereafter cases were reconsidered every two to three years. Although there was some variation in the treatment of individual cases, Headquarters control ensured that this was kept within limits.

On average, LRCs recommended parole in about 60 per cent of the cases they considered. However, if one excludes the cases that were deferred because the LRC failed to reach a decision, the figure rises to about 85 per cent. This caused considerable backlogs at Headquarters, where up to ninety lifers cases were under review at any one time. A9 took up the problems with the Chairperson of the Parole Board as follows:

> I explained that the very high proportion of favourable LRC recommendations (56 out of 64 in June) was central to the backlog situation and added that the feeling in the Department was that LRCs tended to be over-generous in their assessment of the suitability of life sentence prisoners for early release. I said that there might be an advantage in the Department writing to LRCs to direct their attention to the issues it was expected that they would address in considering cases – in particular, the quality of the inmate's behaviour and response, the need for adequate and appropriate testing before reaching a judgment on suitability for release, the inmate's likely response to supervision, and the nature of the crime. Discussion focused on the latter point, with the PRC's role being questioned on the basis that there were arguments in favour of not referring cases to the LRC if early release was not in prospect.

Two features of this intervention are worth noting. First, it demonstrates that Headquarters directly attempted to influence the extent of local discretion of the LRCs, illustrating the degree to which civil servants wanted to constrain the activities of these local bodies. Second, there is a clear exemplification of the strength of rehabilitation discourse associated with parole in the references to the inmate's response to imprisonment and likely receptiveness to supervision.

The parole process is extremely complex and prisoners who were recommended for parole by the LRC had to jump a number of further hurdles before being released on licence. The further stages are set out in Figure 4.2. Where a case was rejected by Headquarters (and merely referred to the Parole Board for information) or rejected by the Parole Board, it would eventually go back to the governor (the first point in the process set out in Figure 4.2) for the review to begin again.[5]

1 Letter to the Governor requesting initiation of review
2 Receipt of dossier
3 Submission to the Secretary of State (with recommended programme for release)
4 Refer case to the judiciary
5 Refer case to the Parole Board
6 Arrange interview with Parole Board member
7 Refer case to the Parole Board
8 Submission to the Secretary of State
9 Notification of decision to prisoner
10 Receipt of progress report on Penninghame phase
11 Receipt of progress report on Training for Freedom (TFF) phase
12 Submission to the Secretary of State

Figure 4.2 Procedure for reviewing parole applications from life-sentence prisoners following a favourable recommendation by the LRC

There were clear policy guidelines on lifers, and decisions relating to them were made in a separate branch at Headquarters as we have already noted. The branch was headed by a Principal (A9) and consisted of two Higher Executive Officers (HEO: A10 and A11), two Executive Officers (EO: A12 and A13), one Administrative Officer (AO: A14) and one Administrative Assistant (AA: A15). The EOs, the AO and the AA shared one office, while the other members of the branch were located nearby but in separate offices. A good deal of routine casework was carried out by the less senior members of the branch, involving a substantial amount of record-keeping on lifers in the prison system as well as those who had been released on life licence. We have nothing to say on this aspect of the branch's work. Rather we wish to point to two areas of decision-making which exemplify the role of Headquarters: the staging of the sentence; and the use of 'outside' work and educational placements.

The concept of a 'staged' sentence underlay and informed Headquarters' decision-making for life-sentence prisoners. Lifers branch put a great deal of effort into ensuring that the parole review process began at the correct point in the prisoner's sentence, and proceeded at an appropriate pace. Once a decision that the lifer should be released on licence had been taken, a 'programme' was worked out. This normally lasted for between eighteen months and two years and would, in accordance with the three ideal types set out earlier in this chapter, involve the prisoner moving from Edinburgh or Dungavel to Penninghame and thence to Training for Freedom and release. This idea of staging also affects the other area of decision-making considered below.

The decision to place a lifer in the community for work or educational reasons was the biggest single area of contention between lifers branch and governors in establishments. All such placements for lifers at Dungavel who did not have a release date required Headquarters approval (though interestingly Special Escorted Leaves carried out by prison officers did not). A12 explained that most of these were accepted but that Headquarters might refuse 'in controversial cases', where, for example, a prisoner was considered to be a security risk. Requests might also be refused early in a lifer's sentence where Headquarters felt that it was 'too soon to judge whether the prisoner was suitable'. Particular resentment was created by what were perceived to be delays and prevarication at Headquarters which prevented lifers from being able to enrol in courses at local colleges. Decisions about educational placements were regarded as 'particularly difficult' since all of them usually had to be dealt with at the same time, i.e. at the beginning of the college year.

The main responsibility for all decisions concerning outside placements lay with the Principal in the branch, although at the time of our research, the Minister wished to examine the procedures in this area and there was a freeze on all new placements. The procedures caused considerable concern to those working in establishments, indeed it was an aspect of casework which those dealing with lifers were very keen to discuss. One governor (G8) argued that the centre wanted

> to make decisions with regard to placements, [this]. . .takes a long time to arrange and Headquarters are not so happy about lifers going out without a provisional release date, though there is nothing formal written down – so that adds to the complication.

These procedures caused a good deal of frustration – another governor (G14) complained that he regularly had to wait three months for the Department to reply to applications for placements, after prisoners had been sent to the prison with the recommendation 'that they be further tested. We then have to write to ask permission for this further testing'.

Governors felt that civil servants used their own logic to structure the lifer's career and shielded themselves behind Ministerial accountability, e.g. G16 maintained that Headquarters based its decisions on the length of time the lifer had served and whether he had a PRC date, claiming that this was 'absolute and utter nonsense – they apply civil service logic, bureaucracy'. He argued that Headquarters wanted control at the centre, assuming all of the authority without taking any of the responsibility for the prisoner. In his view, civil servants would argue that the Minister did not like something, without ever actually putting it to him. G16 gave an example of what he saw as the difficulties here, saying that the prison had a lifer well into his sentence who had a three day per week outside placement. His employer wanted him to work one extra hour for one evening per week. The response of Headquarters was that this would have to be referred to the Minister as it was too serious a matter for the Principal to make a decision on. But as it was too insignificant to put to the Minister on its own, it would have to wait until other issues had accumulated. G16 stated that he had gone ahead and allowed the extra hour.

G25 claimed that, when there were disagreements over lifers, the civil servant would often say that 'they know the Secretary of State's policy better'. G8 made a similar point, saying that

> To satisfy the top of the tree, the centre want to try and control it, but they cannot really do it because it is the governor's direct decision – having said that they will try and influence it. I can understand their dilemma in that they feel they have to answer to the politicians, but. . .do the politicians really want to know in the first place?

G8 argued that much of this work could have been carried out in establishments, pointing out that 'I'm under a political master as well'.

It would appear that lifers' discourse, i.e. official discourse about life-sentence prisoners, is best understood as a compromise between a greater degree of central control over local decision-making than is encountered with prisoners serving determinate sentences and a clearer accommodation by establishments to these centralising forces than is the case with determinate sentence prisoners.

The centralising forces referred to above are exemplified by the staging of lifers' careers and by the parole process, in particular by the role of the Preliminary Review Committee (PRC), by Headquarter's control over the decisions of Local Review Committees (LRC) and by the recommendations of the Parole Board. Staging is evident in many separate domains which include allocations to work, changes in security categorisation, transfers between establishments and the granting of escorted home leaves on which we have data, but which we do not discuss in this chapter.

The underlying rationale, and thus the dominant form of ends discourse (see Figure 2.2 on p.41), was clearly that of rehabilitation. Initial classification, particularly for those who were sentenced to life imprisonment as adults, was of considerable significance in that it influenced the routes taken through the prison system, the number of establishments in which the prisoner served time and, most importantly, the period served in prison. Subsequently, the lifers' response to imprisonment was a major consideration in decisions concerning transfers between establishments, particularly transfers to semi-open and open conditions, security upgradings, work allocation and escorted home leaves. But rehabilitation was even more evident in decisions relating to parole which, more than any other type of decision-making, embodied the rehabilitative principle.

Although rehabilitation was clearly the dominant form of ends discourse, traces of other ends discourses could also be detected. The only identifiable evidence of normalisation lay in the influence of the trial judge, and thus of sentencing considerations, over the parole process. Although explicit control measures, such as the use of Rule 36, were rarely invoked, control considerations were evident in some transfers, in security downgradings and in estimating the degree of danger involved in releasing the prisoner on a life licence. However, normalisation and control discourse are, in the case of lifers, of much lesser importance than rehabilitation discourse.

Several sets of actors serve as carriers for rehabilitation discourse. We have already referred to the degree of central control over local decision-making and the important roles played by Headquarters staff and by the Parole Board. Although most of the recommendations in individual cases are made by prison staff and by what we have previously referred to as prison professionals and membership of the Parole Board includes a number of professionals,[6] the determining set of considerations and the dominant form of discourse are clearly bureaucratic rather than professional. This is very well illustrated by initial classification and by the staging of lifers' careers since, in both cases, professional judgments are subordinated to bureaucratic constraints. Legal discourse is only to be found in muted form through the involvement of the Lord Justice General and the trial judge in the assessment of applications for parole.

In terms of our discourse matrix (see Figure 2.5 on p.46) the dominant form of lifers' discourse can be located in Cell 1 with a secondary variant in Cell 2. This reflects the degree of central control over lifers' careers which is likely to continue for as long as life remains the mandatory sentence for murder and the duration of life sentences is determined administratively.[7]

DISCOURSE, POWER AND PRISONERS' CAREERS

In this chapter we have developed the themes introduced and initially expounded in Chapter 3. In analysing the transfers of long-termers around the system and their prison careers, we have reached the conclusion that the system was operating along the lines set for it by the NCB. The careers of long-term prisoners were, in the main, structured by the discursive combination represented by Cell 1 of our matrix. As with initial classification, the scope for professional decision-making was relatively limited. This is not necessarily the result that we would have expected given the volume of argument around the issue of transfers. However, we did expect the careers of lifers to be centrally managed and this indeed proved to be the case. In this context, it is worth noting that the confluence between Parole Board and Headquarters effectively structures the career of the life-sentence prisoner. This supports the points made in Chapter 1 about the importance of the Parole Board with the proviso explained above that Headquarters actually plays the dominant role. Further, in relation to life-sentence prisoners, it is important to note that the concept of staging which is so important at Headquarters is also followed at a local level in the prison.

It seems clear that the combination of bureaucratic and rehabilitation discourses was particularly powerful in that it had effectively hegemonised the Scottish prison system. Governors' professional discourse was weak in that it was unable to offer a systemically focused discourse with which to combat that of the powerful bureaucratic centre. The transition to a normalising discourse by the bureaucracy, in response both to external social changes and to internal unrest, marginalised governors even more, in that it left them little room for decision-making, e.g. about transfers.

In this chapter and the previous one, we have demonstrated the relative weakness of governors' professional discourse. We continue this theme in Chapter 5, by examining the impact of prison governors and other prison professionals, in particular teachers and social workers, on prison regimes.

Chapter 5

Regimes

The power of the governors and the marginalisation of other professionals

In the last two chapters we examined the relationships between the power-holders identified in Chapter 1 and the ends and means discourses described in Chapter 2 and explored a number of different areas of decision-making which are of central importance to the Scottish Prison Services (SPS), in particular initial classification and transfers between establishments, which together structure the prisoner's career. We attempted to demonstrate that the SPS has been the site of a power struggle between groups of actors acting as the bearers of different ends and means discourses and that decision-making can be understood in terms of the interplay between discourse and power.

In this chapter we turn our attention to the analysis of prison regimes, focusing on the roles played by governors and three groups of prison professionals, i.e. industrial managers, education officers and social workers. We use this term 'regime' to refer to the various components of prison life which structure the experience of imprisonment or, as Wozniak and McAllister (1991:2–3) put it 'the total experience of prisoners and staff living and working in the defined environment of the prison'. Utilising the analytic framework developed in the first two chapters of this book, we examine, first, the nature of the regimes which are to be found in establishments holding adult, male, long-term prisoners in Scotland, and consider, second, the place of work as a central component of the prison regime. Drawing on data derived from the observation of Local Induction Boards (at which prisoners are assigned to work parties) and from interviews, in particular with industrial managers, we pay particular attention to the allocation of work to prisoners. Third, we look at the place of education within the prison regime and the role of the education officer, and, fourth, we examine the position of social work in the prison.

PENAL REGIMES

Writing on penal regimes, as on other aspects of imprisonment, has tended to be either very general or very specific. By general, we refer to the tendency to relate the nature of penal regimes to social, political or economic forces in society or to the needs of capitalism. Thus, for example, Rusche and Kirchheimer (1968) argue that the modern prison is, among other things, 'a way of training new labour reserves' (ibid.:63) and that the designers and administrators of nineteenth-century prison regimes 'endeavoured to train prisoners into an unconditional submission to authority' (ibid.:107). One of the problems with this sort of approach (for a general critique see Garland 1990:105–10) is the way in which it tends to generalise about all prison regimes at a particular point in time. A similar criticism can be made of case-studies of a single prison. Here, we refer to the tendency to generalise from a supposedly typical regime. An example of this can be found in the work of Scraton, Sim and Skidmore (1991) where, in spite of its rather unique position, Peterhead is taken to represent the conditions of imprisonment for all prisoners in Scotland. In contrast to such approaches, we are neither concerned with the overall nature of penal regimes nor with the regime in a single prison, but rather with variations in regimes between and within different prisons and how they reflect different configurations of power and discourse. Thus, we examine the structure of regimes across the prison system as a whole.

As Foucault (1979) and others have argued, the organisation of the day in the modern prison takes a particular form. In one of the most well-known passages in *Discipline and Punish*, Foucault (1979:3–7) compares the torture of Damiens the regicide with the rules for the regime drawn up by Leon Faucher 'for the House of young prisoners in Paris', and argues that this reflects a shift in the discourse of punishment. The regime of early-to-rise, meals, work, education and bed, identified by Foucault, is still a familiar one and forms the bedrock of the contemporary prison regime. The regime at Peterhead Prison in the late 1980s illustrates this:

06.00	Cells are unlocked but there is no onus on the prisoner to get up; breakfast is optional and formally the day starts at 09.00 when prisoners must make themselves available for work;
09.00–09.15	Inmates are mustered and counted and then organised into pre-selected work parties and escorted to the worksheds;
11.30	Inmates return to their halls for lunch in their cells, except for 'C' Hall inmates who eat together;
13.00–14.00	Exercise in the yard if the weather is fair and dry or in the halls if inclement. Exercise is a statutory daily requirement but is very much an informal activity at Peterhead with inmates kicking a ball about the yard or jogging or sitting around in groups chatting. Occasionally during this period, when the weather precludes outside exercise, videos are shown;
14.00–14.15	Muster in the yard, prisoners are counted and returned to the worksheds in parties;
16.30	Return from worksheds for evening meal in the halls;
17.00–18.15	Lock-up while staff are at their meal;
18.15–20.45	Recreation each weekday evening with one night per week, prior to start of recreation, for shower and bathing. During recreation period there are various options open to inmates, including the choice not to go. Cell doors are open and free association is permitted in the halls;
20.45–21.00	Supper, usually a mug of tea and a bun;
21.00	Lock-up;
22.15–22.45	Lights out.

At weekends the programme is much reduced. Recreation inside and outside is available. Prisoners may receive visits in the mornings though most take place between 14.00 and 16.00. Lock-up on both days is at 17.00.

Figure 5.1 Regime at Peterhead, 1986
Source: HMCIP(S) (1987b:18–19)

Although many prison regimes conform to this model, it is important to consider variations in regimes between and within establishments. In the rest of this section we explore these variations, drawing in part on regime data collected on our visits to prisons.

To begin with it is important to note that it is quite erroneous to describe any prison in terms of a single regime. The account of the Peterhead regime ignores the fact that, by 1987, Peterhead was, in effect, a penal complex rather than a unitary establishment. At this time it consisted of the following accommodation:

A Hall: a 'restricted' regime, offering limited recreation and exercise for a small number of prisoners. (Capacity: 16; held: 12.) High staff–prisoner ratio (10:3).

B Hall: total 'lockdown' facility, inmates held under Rule 36.[1] Also held a maximum of sixteen prisoners.

C Hall: a 'protection unit' for the Scottish Prison Service, taking sex offenders, informers and those who had got into difficulties with other prisoners. Operates like a 'normal' penal regime. (Capacity: 50; held: 49.)

10-cell unit: another 'lockdown' facility, inmates held under Rule 36.

Separate cells: a further 'lockdown' facility, normally used for punishments.

B Hall Annex: for short-term prisoners from Aberdeen Prison who were allocated the 'service jobs' at Peterhead.[2] (Capacity: 26.)

In theory there was no mixing between these different units which functioned as virtually autonomous units. Consequently, it makes very little sense to refer to a 'Peterhead regime'. Of course, given its particular role, it might be argued that Peterhead was exceptional in this regard. However, a similar argument can be made about other prisons, even though there may be more contact between the different halls and facilities than there was at Peterhead. This was certainly the case in the older, well-established prisons like Perth and Edinburgh. Perth consisted of four main halls (as well as a separate Training for Freedom hostel) (HMCIP(S) 1985a and regime data):

A Hall: around seventy cells in double or treble occupancy with an additional sixteen single cells and a dormitory. Used mainly for short-termers but with some long-termers. (Capacity: 169.)

C Hall: single cells although some were being used as doubles; also contained a dormitory. At the time of our research the top-floor gallery was out of use. The hall held a mixture of prisoners, the ground floor held those on punishment or under observation, the first-floor gallery those on remand and the third-floor gallery long-term prisoners. (Capacity: 153.)

D Hall: single cells and three dormitories. Accommodated those long-termers who had progressed from C Hall. (Capacity: 129.)

E Hall: single accommodation plus two dormitories. Accommodated long-termers who had progressed from D Hall. (Capacity: 81.)

Some of the problems of treating Perth as a single prison with a single regime can be seen from this simple description of the four main halls. This was also the case with Edinburgh which, at the time of our research, comprised the following accommodation:

B Hall: three galleries, each with twenty-eight cells, some occupied by two prisoners; sex offenders and prisoners on protection were located on the ground floor and would often be doubled up.

C Hall: three galleries, each with twenty-four cells; all inmates in single accommodation except those working in the kitchens who were doubled up. At the time of our research this hall was said to be a 'melting pot' and contained fifty Peterhead prisoners who had been moved to Edinburgh after a riot at Peterhead.

Forth Hall: three galleries, each with twenty-eight cells. All in single accommodation. Nine of the cells had their own toilet facilities, and were allocated to those who had been longest in the hall, if they so wished.

Pentland Hall: twenty-five cells, all single accommodation, nine cells had their own washbasins.

It is clear that many prisons contain specialised facilities. This would require some modification of the idea of a single prison regime, even if there was an intention to operate all the different units in the same way. However, this is not the case as halls and facilities are often arranged in hierarchies reflecting the idea of progression which is closely associated with rehabilitation discourse. We wish now to explore these patterns of progression in more detail.

The idea of progression

Examples of progression operated across the prison system as a whole, producing a hierarchy of establishments and, within individual prisons, producing a hierarchy of halls and facilities. The prisons could be ranked as in Figure 5.2. The ranking of establishments set out in Figure 5.2 is a composite of the different

Prison	Characteristics	Status
Penninghame Noranside (after 1987)	open	High
Dungavel Edinburgh	semi-open trainable first offenders; transfers (Forth and Pentland Halls)	
Dumfries (before 1987) Greenock (before 1987)	Medium-term sentences (Dumfries) and transfers	
Perth Glenochil (after 1987) Shotts (after 1987)	trainable recidivists, post-sentence inmates	
Peterhead Aberdeen	secure, untrainable recidivists, control problems	Low

Figure 5.2 Progressive hierarchy of prisons, 1987

hierarchies which existed before and after Grand Design (see Chapter 3 above). The former, which was more differentiated than the latter, was structured by rehabilitation discourse while the latter was influenced by the discourse of normalisation.

In Chapter 4 we identified three ideal-type careers for life-sentence prisoners, i.e. for 'first offenders', 'trainable recidivists' and 'non-trainable recidivists'. The progression system, based on hierarchies between and within establishments, was clearly intended to facilitate the elaboration of these ideal types for all long-term prisoners. Hence, the first offender would have been expected to begin his sentence at Edinburgh, progress through its halls and then move to Dungavel or (more likely) directly to Penninghame. The 'trainable recidivist' would begin his sentence at Perth, progress through its halls, and then move to Dungavel and, from there, to Penninghame. The 'non-trainable recidivist' would begin his sentence at Peterhead and then join to the 'trainable recidivist' route.

By 1987, however, there were a number of problems with this model. First, other prisons, e.g. Glenochil and Shotts, were brought into the long-term system and, although they contained very different facilities, were given very similar roles to perform. Thus, Shotts was meant to play a similar role to Perth and prisoners were expected to move on from there to Dungavel. However, Shotts is a new prison with single-cell accommodation and integral sanitation for all inmates while Dungavel can only offer shared dormitory accommodation. Many of our interviewees told us that prisoners were reluctant for this reason to move to Dungavel and only agreed to move because they thought it would help with parole and because of the Special Escorted Leave (SEL) scheme which meant that home visits would be possible.[3] According to G8:

> Prisoners don't like the dormitory conditions at Dungavel – for a man who has been sixteen years in single cell accommodation to find himself in a dormitory situation is not particularly welcoming and this tends to discourage prisoners from applying. Dungavel is supposed to mean progression for the prisoner and a move towards re-entering society. Unfortunately, prisoners often see a move to Dungavel as regression rather than progression and we have to convince them that it is in their best interests to move to Dungavel.

However, because SELs are also available to prisoners in Pentland Hall at Edinburgh, moving to Dungavel is a particularly unattractive option for those at the top of the progression system in Edinburgh. In this respect the progressive hierarchy contained a number of inconsistencies.

Second, the influence of normalisation discourse and the new emphasis on 'parity of regimes' also confused the system. A key element involved abandoning the distinctions between 'trainable' and 'non-trainable' prisoners and between 'first offenders' and 'recidivists' and allowing prisoners to choose between three broadly similar prisons of classification. Under Grand Design, Glenochil and Shotts were meant to perform a similar role to Perth, and to operate as 'core' or 'mainstream' establishments for the long-term prisoner. However, as we have already pointed out, Perth consisted of a variety of halls arranged in a progression system. By contrast, all the halls at Shotts and Glenochil were intended to be similar and there was no system of progression within these two prisons. However, although the Governor of Glenochil (G3) said he was not a 'carrot and stick man' and was 'not a believer in progression within a single establishment',[4] the Governor of Shotts (G6) was a keen advocate of progression and wanted 'to introduce an admissions hall followed by a system of progression through the other halls in Shotts'. While G3 regarded progression within a prison as 'a time-wasting process of reports and Committees' and thought that 'although it may be alright for YOs, it was not suitable for adults',[5] G6 thought that 'prisoners preferred it and regarded non-progression as a "dead end"'. His views were similar to those of the Governor of Perth (G2) who wanted to retain progression both because 'the whole culture of Perth is based on it' and because 'prisoners see their sentence in blocks'.

Headquarters tried hard to encourage these three establishments, and likewise others, e.g. the two open prisons (Noranside and Penninghame), to move towards greater 'parity of regimes' but progress was slow. There were a number of reasons for this. First, governors tended to focus on the needs of their own establishment (see Figure 2.4 on p.46). They resented the loss of autonomy that this policy entailed and found it hard to focus on the needs of the system as a whole. Headquarters were certainly aware of these problems. As A2 explained:

> Parity of regimes is, in a sense, about policing governors. Policy cannot be left to them – they are trained to run prisons, not to run a service. But, although Headquarters can direct and influence, it cannot exercise day-to-day supervision or control over them. They must learn to co-operate.

Second, there were so many differences between prisons in terms of the available accommodation, the nature and extent of privileges, and the inmate population. The variations in 'privileges' which existed in different prisons (e.g. could pictures be stuck on walls as opposed to only on noticeboards?, how many paperback books were allowed to an individual prisoner at one time?) were considerable. They reflected local tradition and, to a certain extent, the views and practices of hall staff. Privileges of this nature may sound trivial but they are of enormous importance to prisoners. Thus the problems of levelling down (rather than levelling up) would have been considerable. This, combined with the struggle between Headquarters and establishments, and thus between bureaucratic and control discourse, left the future pattern of regimes wide open.

PRISON WORK

The regimes described in the previous section reflect the importance of work in the prison routine. In the literature on imprisonment, a good deal of attention has been paid to the place of work in prison. This is particularly so with writing from a Marxist perspective which frequently emphasises the centrality of prison work and examines the connections between it and the economic and ideological needs of capitalism. Thus, following Rusche and Kirchheimer (1968), Melossi and Pavarini (1981) argue that the sorts of work discipline that are a part of prison life, involving the regulation of the working day, function to discipline a proletarian workforce by instilling factory-based values of manual labour, obedience and docile behaviour.

Such concerns have informed some of the more detailed studies of the place of work in prison, most of which have adopted an historical approach to the subject. Although the political economy approach associated with Marxism is not always accepted, much of this work has sought to 'debunk' the rhetoric surrounding the aims of imprisonment (especially rehabilitation) by showing that behind these aims lies an attempt to impose forms of regulation and discipline which meet the needs of the labour market. Thus, Conley (1980) insists that it is important to consider the nature of prison industries and, more generally, prison work as topics in their own right, rather than seeing them as 'subservient to the punitive and rehabilitative goals of penal systems (ibid.:257), while Dobash et al. (1986) point to the importance of work in the experience of imprisonment for women, although this is often played down in the construction of a therapeutic model of women's imprisonment.

Dobash (1983:3) has also maintained that 'there has been little or no systematic analysis of labour and its relationship to various forms of discipline within. . .the Scottish Prison System'. In this section we take this omission seriously, although we consider labour in relation to a number of other facets of imprisonment in addition to discipline. This involves examining the work that is available in Scotland's prisons and the processes by which prisoners are allocated to different work parties.

Types of prison work in Scotland

The pattern of employment in Scottish prisons is shown in Table 5.1. According to these figures, which are for the whole of the prison system and therefore include both women and short-term prisoners,[6] around 75 per cent of the prison population were in 'effective employment'. If prisoners on remand (who are not required to work) are excluded, it is clear that around 90 per cent of sentenced prisoners were in 'effective employment'. Since the figures suggest that the remainder were not working for good reasons,[7] it would appear that there are few breaches of the Prison Rules which specify that 'unless excused by the Medical Officer on medical grounds, every prisoner shall be employed on useful work' (Rule 55(1) of the Prison (Scotland) Rules 1952).

The figures show that between 50–60 per cent of those in 'effective employment' were employed in manufacturing.[8] There was some variation in what was being manufactured, which ranged from panel furniture to shoes, but the figures conceal a high degree of concentration of output. The largest of the manufacturing categories were woodworking, textiles and miscellaneous. In the case of textiles, the largest number of prisoners was employed in 'heavy textiles' summarised as 'mailbag making, kitbags etc'; the miscellaneous category included 'mailbag repairs, cardboard boxes, rough joiners, and simple assemblies'. The next largest overall category were those employed in 'domestic' work. This category includes the jobs that are needed to keep the prison running. The largest of the domestic categories were those that involved working in the kitchens. There is, then, a large service sector, providing about 30 per cent of employment in prisons. In addition, a certain amount of the manufacturing that goes on in Scottish prisons is for internal use, e.g. making prison officers' uniforms and prison clothing. All the other categories of employment involve rather small numbers. In spite of the large number of vocational training (VT) courses (see below), less than 100 prisoners were on a training course at any one time. Forms of employment were distributed across the system, though not necessarily in a clear progression (i.e. with the 'best' employment at the 'best' prison). This can be seen if the availability of work at the main long-term prisons is considered.

At Peterhead the four main industries were 'tailoring/textiles, woodwork, ropework and the production of nets' and, in addition,

Table 5.1 Employment in Scottish prisons, 1986–7 and 1988–9

	1986–7			*1988–9*		
	No.	*% of pop.*	*% of eff.emp.*	*No.*	*% of pop.*	*% of eff.emp.*
Average daily population	4,219			3,779		
Effectively employed	3,202	75.9		2,880	76.2	
Manufacturing	1,861	44.1	58.1	1,549	41.0	53.8
Farms and gardens (F&G)	136	3.2	4.2	163	4.3	5.6
Training	80	1.9	2.5	88	2.3	3.1
Works	134	3.2	4.2	109	2.9	3.8
Domestic	940	22.3	29.4	909	24.1	31.6
Outside employment	51	1.2	1.6	62	1.6	2.2
Not effectively employed	1,017	24.1		899	23.8	

Source: Scottish Home and Health Department 1989b and 1990a

there was a small laundry (HMCIP(S) 1987b:23). At Aberdeen, manufacturing was concentrated on the production of nets (originally for the fishing industry but more recently for a variety of customers) and knitwear.

Perth offered employment for joiners, cobblers and tailors as well as vocational training in painting and decorating and in bricklaying. Shotts had textiles and a laundry and had recently acquired bookbinding and printing from Edinburgh (see below). In addition, it offered vocational training in engineering, painting and decorating, joinery and hairdressing. At the time of our research, the industrial manager at Shotts was hoping to add vocational training (VT) courses in car mechanics and in bricklaying. Glenochil had wood assembly, engineering, upholstery and textiles. It also had a fairly large number of VT courses: bricklaying, painting and decorating, radio and television repairs, domestic appliance repairs and hairdressing. This extensive range of VT courses reflected Glenochil's previous role as a Young Offenders' Institution. Edinburgh offered the widest variety of employment, including farming and gardening, metal fabrication and engineering, paint finishing, wood machinery and assembly and heavy textiles, as well as VT courses in upholstery, welding and hairdressing.

The less secure prisons provided narrower ranges of work. Dungavel had a wood panel shop and textiles. It had once been famous throughout the Scottish prison system for its luggage manufacture, but as he pointed out there was no luggage party there anymore 'as it is impossible to compete price-wise with the Taiwanese'. He also maintained that this closure was 'unfortunate' as the luggage shop had been popular with the prisoners – it was more 'macho' than many other types of work. When the manufacture of luggage ceased, prisoners at Dungavel had made mailbags for a while. I6 expressed the view that this was totally wrong for Dungavel, stating, however, that it 'was horrific, but it was work'. Moreover, he was 'still not a great believer in textiles for a place like Dungavel'. At Penninghame most of the work was in the grounds and gardens of the prison itself, which are extensive. There was also a poultry unit and VT courses in bricklaying and cookery.

The types of work which are available at each prison and indeed the actual articles produced result from decisions made at the centre. An industrial manager (I3) explained that outside contracts are obtained by the 'marketing and sales section' at Headquarters. These are then filtered through 'production and control' to make sure that the Prison Service has the 'capacity and capability' to do the job. However, individual prisons could take on local contracts, doing special 'one-off' jobs, e.g. manufacturing a garden seat. On behalf of the governor, I3 could in theory accept or reject the work offered by Headquarters. In practice, this was very much a matter of routine since, although there could be some negotiation about the exact details of a contract, there was normally little disagreement. The inquiry to the prison from Headquarters about work came on a 'tender enquiry form'.

Although the official in charge of prison industries at Headquarters (A3) stressed that finding suitable work was a two-way process between Headquarters and establishments, the allocation of a particular type of work to a given prison was clearly determined at Headquarters. On occasion this could be very controversial. One instance of this was the decision to move the printing and bookbinding shop from Edinburgh to the newly expanded Shotts Prison. This shop at Edinburgh had been the main place of employment for the sex offenders at the prison and staff at Edinburgh believed that it was an important part of the process of encouraging these prisoners to come out 'from behind the door of their cells'. A3 explained that the 'Prison Service Management Group (PSMG) could take a wider view' on such matters than some of those working in prisons and that the move of this shop to Shotts 'was decided in the context of Grand Design'. Grand Design meant a reduction in the number of long-term prisoners at Edinburgh while Shotts did not have enough good-quality industrial work. Furthermore, according to A3, it would not have been possible to open a second bookbinding and printing shop at Shotts as this would not have been countenanced by the Scottish Trades Union Congress (STUC).

Before developing some general issues arising out of this account of work in Scottish prisons we now turn to consider how prisoners are allocated to work.

Allocation to work

Every prison in Scotland has what is generally known as a Local Induction Board (LIB) which makes decisions about allocating prisoners to work on arrival at the prison, reallocating prisoners from one type of work to another, and upgrading or downgrading prisoners' security categorisation. In addition, LIBs in closed establishments make recommendations for transfer to semi-open and open conditions while those in open prisons decide whether to recommend accepting a prisoner from closed conditions. We focus here on the process of allocating prisoners to work.

We observed the LIB in action in Perth, Aberdeen (since it dealt only with short-term prisoners we have excluded this data), Penninghame, Dungavel, Glenochil and Noranside during 1987–8. In addition, we attended the LIB in Edinburgh on four separate occasions in 1987. As shown in Table 5.2, this resulted in the observation of sixty-six cases in all, thirty initial allocations to work (45 per cent) and thirty-six reallocations from one work party to another (55 per cent). LIBs, in the main, consist of three people:

Table 5.2 Allocation and reallocation to work: cases observed at Local Induction Boards, 1987–8

Prison	*Allocations*	*Reallocations*	*Total*
Edinburgh	14	19	33
Perth	1	6	7
Glenochil	11	5	16
Dungavel	4	2	6
Penninghame	0	3	3
Noranside	0	1	1
Total	30	36	66

a governor (before Fresh Start, this would usually be the Training Governor or his/her deputy, after Fresh Start the Functional Manager – Regimes or his/her deputy);[9] the Industrial Manager or his/her deputy; and the Chief Officer (or Divisional Chief Officer). The intention clearly is to bring together, in one decision-making body, representatives of the key areas of prison management, i.e. overall administration with particular reference to the notion of training represented by the Governor, work represented by the Industrial Manager and discipline (or control) represented by the Chief Officer (a role somewhat akin to the Regimental Sergeant Major in the Army). However, once the Board actually meets these distinctions appear to be of little significance as discussion ranges across a wide variety of issues.

With some small local variations, the operation of the LIB also tends to follow a general pattern. The LIB has information on the work currently available at the prison, i.e. the number of vacancies in the different work parties. It also has information on the individual prisoner and, in many cases, recommendations from those in charge of relevant work parties and general comments about the prisoner from hall staff.

The Board briefly discusses each prisoner's request or the individual circumstances of each prisoner's case before he is called for interview. The form of this interview varies, depending both on the tradition of the prison and on the personalities of those comprising the Board. At some of the 'core' closed establishments, e.g. Perth and Edinburgh, there was an almost military air to the proceedings. The prisoner was encouraged to stand up straight during the course of the interview while the Board sat at a table in front of him. At the open and semi-open establishments there was an attempt to foster a more relaxed atmosphere. For example, the prisoner would be asked to sit at the same table as the Board.

The atmosphere of the LIB was greatly affected by the personality of the governor who chaired the Board and was usually the most important figure. At one prison, the chairman managed to provoke nearly all the prisoners who came before the Board. In one memorable interview, this resulted in a prisoner storming out yelling that the governor should 'fuck off'. Interestingly, we observed the same prisoner coming 'on request' to his hall governor the next morning to discuss his problems with the governor in charge of the LIB. Other chairpersons went out of their way to listen to prisoners, establish a rapport with them and, if possible, to help them. For example, in December 1987, we observed an LIB at a closed prison where some of the prisoners who had taken part in the rooftop protest at Peterhead in November 1986 were allocated work. In one case, the governor explained that he had known a particular prisoner since his YO days, that he was an habitual criminal (indeed when asked what he did 'outside', the prisoner replied that 'he broke into shops') but was really quite 'harmless', and proceeded to address him by his first name all through the interview. Another prisoner, again before the Board to be allocated to work, raised a problem he was having arranging a visit by his wife to the prison, at which point the governor telephoned the Social Work Unit to see what could be done to help. After the Board the governor in question (G18) commented that he liked to explain procedures as fully as possible and try to avert conflict. He reasoned that allocating a prisoner to a job he did not want would only lead to trouble in the future if the prisoner refused to work, though he maintained that it was not always possible to give every prisoner the job they wanted.

Interviews were normally short (no more than five minutes) and wide-ranging, covering a variety of topics which often strayed beyond the immediate concerns of the decision to allocate work. Members of the Board would often fire questions at the prisoner in fairly rapid succession. A prisoner might be asked about his experience of work in the prison or in previous prisons. If the prisoner had received a 'bad' report from the officer in charge of his work party, he might be asked to comment on it. However the officer's point of view invariably held sway. The prisoner would be asked why he wanted to change party. A variety of reasons might be given, which members of the Board would interpret for themselves after the interview had finished. For example, a prisoner who wanted to move from a job in a hall pantry stated that he wanted 'a change' and accepted a place on the vocational training course in bricklaying. After the interview the LIB considered why the prisoner had asked for a move from the 'best job in the jail' and concluded that he might be 'under pressure' from other prisoners.

How the prisoner related to staff would be fed into the discussion of allocation to work. Before one interview, at an open prison, the Chief Officer commented that the prisoner did not seem to be very partial to the prison staff and that he had 'a chip on his shoulder'. The Chief Officer brought this up in the interview, asking the prisoner why he ignored him. The prisoner replied that as an ex-policeman, he could not be seen to be speaking to prison officers very much. He had been very careful about this in closed conditions. After the interview, the Chief Officer commented that the prisoner had given a 'reasonable explanation' of why he tended to ignore staff, and in general the Board seemed happier with the prisoner after the interview than it had been before. It acceded to his request for a change of work party.

The prisoner's relations with other prisoners could come into the discussion as would his general attitude and behaviour. All sorts of comments would be made along these lines. The 'macho' appearance of a prisoner or his 'inadequacy' might be mentioned.

Sometimes there were local policies which impinged on the decision (but which could be overruled). For example, institutions had differing policies on how long a prisoner should have worked in one party before he could request a transfer for another one.

Furthermore, the Governor-in-Charge might have a policy of not wanting life-sentence prisoners or very long-term prisoners at the start of sentence to be employed on 'menial' cleaning jobs, and such policies would be taken into account.

The allocation of prisoners to work decided at the LIBs we observed are summarised in Table 5.3. In keeping with the figures detailed in Table 5.1 earlier, the largest number of allocations and reallocations was to manufacturing (thirty-one or 48 per cent) followed by domestic jobs (sixteen or 25 per cent). These categories were followed by training (seven or 11 per cent). In this case the numbers are much higher than the comparable figures in Table 5.1 above. This may be due to chance but may also be due to the fact that long-term prisoners are more likely to be allocated to a vocational training (VT) course. A number of important points arise from Table 5.3. There seemed to be a preference for allocating those new to a prison to a manufacturing job in the first instance, irrespective of the type of work they had previously been doing. This could mean that a prisoner could go from a responsible job at a closed prison, e.g. reception passman, to a manufacturing job on 'progression' to an open or semi-open prison. This is largely due to the fact that work was allocated to prisons without paying due regard to the overall regime or to the place of the prison in the progression system. Jobs like working on farms, in gardens, or in the works party tended to be given to those already in the prison. In an important sense, these jobs were 'earned', often by the prisoner having his security categorisation upgraded from 'B' to 'C' or by having reached a position of trust with members of staff. Places on VT courses and the 'best' domestic jobs, i.e. those with some cachet in the prison rather than the more mundane hall-cleaning jobs, also tended to be allocated in this fashion.

LIB decisions concerning allocation to work are grounded in the professional discourse associated with prison governors (identified in Chapter 2 above). Although the decision made may be constrained by some rules of thumb, for example, about how long a prisoner should have spent in a certain work party before asking for a transfer or whether long-term prisoners should take on more menial jobs, there was much scope for the mobilisation of individualised judgment on the part of the decision-makers. Within the framework of centrally organised allocation of work to prisons, the allocation of work to prisoners involved little policy guidance from

Table 5.3 Allocations and reallocations to work: outcomes in observed cases

Prison	*Manuf.*		*F & G*		*Training*		*Works*		*Domestic*		*Deferred*		*Total*	
	A	*RA*	*A*	*RA*	*A*	*RA*	*A*	*RA*	*A*	*RA*	*A*	*RA*	*A*	*RA*
Edinburgh	10	6	0	5	0	0	0	1	3	5	1	1	14	18
Perth	1	4							0	1	0	1	1	6
Glenochil	4	1			2	3			5	1			11	5
Dungavel	4	0							0	1	0	1	4	2
Penninghame					0	2					0	1	0	3
Noranside	0	1											0	1
Total	19	12	0	5	2	5	0	1	8	8	1	4	30	35

Headquarters. Thus, bureaucratic discourse was very weak here. Furthermore, although prisoners' preferences for particular types of work were taken into account they had to be consistent with the operational needs of the prison as a whole. It follows that legal discourse was rather weak too.

Newly-arrived prisoners were often not asked to express a preference or were given a very restricted set of jobs to choose from, and the requests of those who sought a change in their work party were not always granted. This can be illustrated by referring to the patterns of requests and allocations in Tables 5.4 and 5.5. Among newly-arrived prisoners, eleven (out of thirty) did not express a preference, two were offered a very limited choice and eight were given a different job from the one they had requested. However, those who requested a change of work party did rather better. Five (out of thirty-six) made an open-ended request and, of the remainder, five were refused and twenty-three were granted (three were deferred). Only one prisoner had to remain in his present work party. The precise form of professional discourse adopted depended on the individual case. In some cases, training was important and the decision-making process reflected a confluence of professional and rehabilitation discourses. As such, it can be represented by Cell 4 in our discourse matrix (see Figure 2.5 on p.46 above). However, it should be pointed out that decisions to allocate to vocational training did not necessarily take place in the context of an assessment of how the prisoner's sentence was progressing. In other cases, good order and discipline were at the heart of the decision-making process and a control logic came into play. Here the decision-making process reflected a combination of rehabilitation and control discourse which can be represented by Cell 6 in the matrix. Although some prisoners were allocated the jobs they had asked for, normalisation discourse was relatively weak in this context; little attention was paid to what was happening in other prisons and the skills that the prisoner had used outside (if they existed) were only occasionally mentioned.

Prison work: themes and issues

We concluded the previous section by arguing that the decision-making involved in the allocation of prisoners to particular forms of work took place at the confluence between professional, control and rehabilitation discourses, i.e. in Cells 4 and 6 of our discourse

Table 5.4 Allocation to work: expressed preferences and LIB decisions

Prison	*Case*	*Preference (if any)*	*Decision*
Edinburgh	1	'Something mentally stimulating'	Printshop
	2	Joiners	Joiners
	3	Not asked (previously in cookhouses)	Cookhouse
	4	Not asked (previously in mailbags)	Mailbags
	5	Not asked (previously on pass)	Corridor pass
	6	From printshop to gardens	Deferred (to discuss with governor i/c)
	7	Not asked (sex offender)	Printshop
	8	Given choice between engineers and light textiles (chose latter)	Light textiles
	9	Not asked (engineering background)	Engineers
	10	Not asked ('experienced with tools')	Engineers
	11	Not asked	Printshop
	12	Not asked (previously in engineers)	Engineers
	13	Not asked	Textile audit
	14	Textiles or braille unit	Hairdresser
Perth	15	Not sewing machines	Sewing machines
Glenochil	16	'Not in sheds' (previously in cooks and works)	Cooks, pool meanwhile
	17	Not asked (previously in cooks)	Cooks, pool meanwhile
	18	Not asked ('welder to trade')	Engineers
	19	B Hall pass (has C & G in upholstery)	Upholstery shop
	20	Kitchen	Cooks, pool meanwhile
	21	VT course (previously in engineers)	Engineers
	22	Cooks	Cooks, pool meanwhile
	23	D Hall pass	D Hall pass
	24	'Avoid the shed'	VT painting/decorating
	25	Cooks (or pass)	Engineers
	26	Painting and decorating	VT hairdressing
Dungavel	27	Given choice between textiles/woodshop, preferred textiles	Textiles
	28	Pass	Textiles
	29	Painting	Woodshop
	30	'Clean work'	Textiles

Table 5.5 Work reallocations: expressed preferences and LIB decisions

Prison	*Case*	*Request*	*Decision*
Edinburgh	1	Salvage to hall pass	Engineers
	2	Printshop to textiles	Textiles
	3	Textiles to kitchens	Deferred (for psychiatric report)
	4	Stores to library pass	Library pass
	5	Painters to stores (job vacated by 4)	Stores
	6	Gardens to stores (job vacated by 4)	Gardens
	7	Engineers to C Dorm pass	C Dorm pass
	8	Printshop to pantry	Pantry
	9	Engineers to gardens	Gardens
	10	From laundry	Mailbags
	11	Printshop to Pentland Hall storeroom	Printshop
	12	To the cookhouse	Listed for cookhouse
	13	Textile audit to works	Listed for works
	14	Education to gardens	Gardens
	15	Textile audit to works or gardens	Gardens
	16	Induction pass to hall pass	Hall pass
	17	Printshop to textile audit	Listed for textile audit
	18	Engineers to gardens	Listed for gardens
	19	Cooks to salvage	Salvage
Perth	20	Cobblers to laundry	Listed for laundry
	21	Laundry to 'dust-free' job	Deferred (for medical)
	22	From textiles	Tailors
	23	From sewing machines (textiles)	Pass (textiles)
	24	To works	Listed for cobblers
	25	From gate pass	Sewing machines (textiles)
Glenochil	26	To VT domestic appliances	VT domestic appliances
	27	Pool to VT bricklaying	VT bricklaying
	28	B Hall pantry to outside job	VT bricklaying
	29	Cooks to stores	Stores
	30	VT course to hall pass	Pool
Dungavel	31	Textiles to TV room pass	TV room pass
	32	To TV room pass	Stay in current work
Penninghame	33	VT bricklaying	VT bricklaying
	34	VT bricklaying	VT bricklaying
	35	Grounds to works	Deferred (for interview with IM)
Noranside	36	From farm	Textiles

matrix. It can be argued, more generally, that prison work can itself be located in these positions.

As we have already mentioned, the overall responsibility for work within each prison lies with the Industrial Manager who is responsible to the Governor (since Fresh Start, to the Functional Manager – Regimes). Despite the central allocation of work to prisons, the Governor and the Industrial Manager tended to control its organisation in the prison on the basis of their professional skills and the perceived needs and requirements of the prison in question. Professionalism was very much to the fore in this area.

Concerns with training were evident in prison work, but in a relatively muted form. Except in the case of lifers (see Chapter 4 above) there was little planning of training in the context of the prisoner's sentence and little consideration of the relationship of training to work opportunities or its place within the overall regime. As Legge (1978:11) has maintained 'whereas rehabilitation might demand that the prisoner's needs and his release plans in connection with work be taken into consideration when planning his allocation to work and training, the economic objectives of prison maintenance and income generation may take precedence'. Prison clearly does not provide many prisoners with a set of skills which they can subsequently employ in life on the outside.

Work plays an important part in control discourse. The processes of production are deskilled so that they can be performed in a routine manner by any inmate. Rather than training a prisoner to do a job the idea is to break the job down so that relatively little training is required. I3 was quite explicit in arguing that, 'to manufacture a lot of products we have to deskill [the production process] and make [the product] in component parts whenever possible. . .the idea is to deskill as far as possible'.

Wages varied across the system, with those doing similar jobs in different prisons receiving different rates of pay. This reflected a lack of central planning and caused problems when prisoners moved from one prison to another. I4 noted in this regard that he had to cope with 'sabotage and strikes, sit-downs and protests' because prisoners had been moved from a prison where they had been receiving higher rates of pay. Here too, normalisation, as reflected in the idea of parity of regimes, has had little influence. I6 bemoaned the role played by Headquarters, saying that it 'annoys me that HQ abrogated responsibility on this one'. He maintained that a Wages Committee had sat for two years but had only come up with the idea of setting an average per capita rate for each establishment, and he expressed the view that 'this is ludicrous because nearly every establishment will have its own wages system'. Thus, in most prisons, some jobs would be paid on a flat-rate basis, others would have opportunities for working overtime or paying bonuses, while a third group would be paid 'piece rates'. The average ranged from £3.72 per week in Glenochil to £4.59 per week in Penninghame but individual prisoners would receive more or less than this depending on the work they did and their performance.[10]

The wages paid were sometimes used to effect a significant element of control. I3 again commented that there was often a certain flexibility in pay and he would 'take cognisance of their [the prisoners'] response, in other words, their manners, how they generally behaved and their general attitude to work'. The 'bonus' element in the pay could be evaluated by the instructor in the shop. He maintained that 'you have got to be careful that you don't cause a riot over 10p' and that consequently he would expect instructors in the shops to use their 'common-sense' and be 'fair'.

The increasing dominance of work in the regime as a whole is also significant. As industrial managers were redesignated regime managers under the Fresh Start reorganisation, they assumed responsibility for education and physical training in the prison. I1 was enthusiastic about his potential role as a regime manager, he felt that there was a need to integrate work with education and physical training, but it was clear to him that work would lead the way to overcome the 'nonsense situation where the Physical Training Instructor was taking people away from workshops to go to PT – we cannae have that'. I2 made similar points about education, maintaining that, when most education had taken place on a part-time basis, it had disrupted production as prisoners had come and gone from the workshops. Education at this prison had now become a full-time 'work' party. However, education officers (see below) were concerned that this did not reflect the needs of prisoners who might have been more suited to part-time education for short spells, but reflected the dominant position of prison work. Thus, E1 maintained that education was 'tied up with survival at the moment' and that, compared with work, education was 'peripheral at the moment in prisons'. This issue is explored in more detail below.

PRISON EDUCATION

The nature and extent of educational provision varied across penal establishments in Scotland. A survey carried out by the Departmental Working Group on Prison Education in December 1983 (SHHD 1987a) revealed substantial variations in expenditure, staffing and the number and range of courses offered. Opportunities were much greater in some prisons, e.g. Edinburgh, than in others, e.g. Perth. As the Report of the Working Group comments, 'to a large extent, it is dependent on where an inmate serves his sentence whether or not reasonable educational facilities are available to him' (ibid.:12). It is clear that the place and scope of education in prison are related to the overall aims of imprisonment (as expressed in different ends discourses) and to its place in the overall regime. Hence, in the early and middle of the nineteenth century, great emphasis was placed on education and extensive resources were devoted to it. This declined during the early part of the twentieth century as rehabilitation became more intimately associated with industry. However, it increased again with the development of the borstal system and, more generally in the 1970s, when it reached its high point.

The uneven distribution of educational facilities across penal establishments, in association with local management decisions, produced an uneven distribution in the number and proportion of prisoners attending educational courses. For example, in 1987 Perth had eight prisoners in full-time education (with four on a waiting list), Glenochil (which had recently become an adult prison) had twenty-three prisoners in full-time education and Edinburgh had forty-five. There were similar variations in the numbers attending part-time courses.

A wide range of different types of courses was provided in the larger establishments, including remedial education, basic education, general interest courses, SCOTVEC modules, SCE, Higher and Open University courses as well as vocational training referred to above. Within the available resources, education officers, who are seconded to the SPS by local Further Education (FE) Colleges attempted to allocate prisoners to education according to their own particular needs. One education officer (E2) estimated that 80–90 per cent of long-term prisoners in Edinburgh came to the education unit at some point during their sentence.

Like many other areas of the Scottish prison system, education was perceived to be in a state of crisis in the late 1980s. As we have already noted, some industrial managers had begun to voice concern at the detrimental effects of part-time education on workshop routines and output and there were pressures from this quarter for education to become an alternative to 'work', i.e. for full-time education to become another work party, and for part-time education during the day to be phased out. Education officers took the view that, although this might suit the needs of prison industries (and indeed the regime as a whole) it would do little for many prisoners who would not be interested in or able to study on a full-time basis.

It was in this context that the Departmental Working Group on Prison Education was set up in March 1983. The Working Group, made up of administrators, governors, representatives of the SPOA, but with little representation from the Scottish Education Department[11] and none from (local) education authorities, argued explicitly for a 'justice model' approach to prison education, producing an explicit normalisation discourse. Deriving their position from the work of Morris (1974), the Working Group argued that 'the basic justification for providing educational facilities in penal establishments is that inmates should not be deprived of any opportunities which are available in the community outside, except insofar as this is an unavoidable consequence of imprisonment' (SHHD 1987a:para. 4.9). The group explicitly rejected a training or rehabilitation discourse and made a number of specific recommendations including amendments to the Prison Rules and Standing Orders to remove the statutory underpinning for the principle of rehabilitation and establish a statutory basis for the principle of normalisation. The Working Group also called for the appointment of a full-time Chief Education Officer to work at Headquarters in order to co-ordinate and give some direction to prison education.

While the Working Group was deliberating, a further problem was caused by the refurbishment of Greenock, the opening of Shotts and the changes in the roles of other establishments brought about by Grand Design. Because of the need to provide education at Greenock and Shotts and because no extra resources were available,[12] the budgets at some large institutions were reduced in 1987. The cut at Glenochil was from £138,000 to £108,000 per annum (22 per cent) and that at Edinburgh from £120,000 to £86,000 per annum (28 per cent). These decisions produced particularly severe problems for the education units at Glenochil and Edinburgh and a substantial lowering of morale.

The report of the Departmental Working Group was never published although it was eventually leaked to the press (Henderson 1987). It is impossible to give a definitive explanation for SHHD's reticence. However it was probably because of the explicit version of normalisation that the Report adopted. The version of normalisation that was being propounded at the time is clearly manifested in *Custody and Care* (SPS 1988a), which is discussed in detail in Chapter 9 below. This version of normalisation was a specifically bureaucratic one which played down the role of professionals and would have been antipathetic to the Working Group's attempt to promote the professionalism of education within the prison. The approach adopted in the Report was also out of step with the developing managerialism of the Scottish Prison Service (again see Chapter 9 below). Subsequent developments lend support to this explanation. A Chief Education Officer has not been appointed and education has been brought firmly under the control of the Deputy Director (Regime Services) at Headquarters and the Regime Manager (formally the Industrial Manager) and Grade 5 (Governor) – Regimes in establishments.

PRISON SOCIAL WORK

Social work was introduced to Scottish prisons comparatively recently. As Parsloe noted in her report on *Social Work Units in Scottish Prisons*, '[t]he first prison welfare officer was appointed to work in Barlinnie in 1959' (HMCIP(S) 1987d:3). Social work in Scottish prisons came under local government control in 1973 and, like education, is now the responsibility of the regional councils. Social workers are employed by the Regional Social Work Departments, though their posts are funded by the Prison Service. In 1984 there were 48.5 social work posts in Scotland's prisons, giving a ratio of social workers to prisoners of 1:98 (ibid.: Appendix C, Table II).

Parsloe drew a clear distinction between 'welfare' and 'social' work, maintaining that

> Welfare work is generally understood to mean the provision of advice and practical or material help given in response to a request from an individual or group.
>
> (Ibid.:4)

while

> Social work is distinguished by its philosophy and its approach to helping people with social or emotional problems. The philosophy stresses the value of each human being irrespective of age, sex, race, economic status or behaviour, their capacity for growth and change, their right to determine how to live their lives, at least as far as compatible with similar rights for others, and the fact that humans are social beings who can only develop and be understood through their interactions with each other. The approach to helping starts with an assessment of the individual or group with a social problem, and an agreed plan of what is to be done and how to do it is developed from the assessment.
>
> (Ibid.:5)

Social work in this sense comprised a small part of the work actually engaged in by prison social workers. As Parsloe maintained, prison social work tended to engage in responsive welfarism. There was little planned and structured intervention in accordance with a set of theoretical principles. Hence, while Parsloe was not as critical of prison social work as the logic of her report suggested that she could have been, her central recommendation was that 'a national framework for prison social work should be established' (ibid.:45).

Parsloe was unhappy with prison social work as it existed, but noted that prison governors were rather pleased with it. As she explained,

> Social work in prisons has a complex organisational structure. It is financed by one central government department but subject to the advice of another. At a local level social work staff are employed by the Regional Social Work Department and ultimately accountable to the Regional Social Work Committee through the Director of Social Work. However, they work within a prison where the governor has very wide authority to decide what can and cannot be done within the establishment. One might expect such a situation to lead to considerable discussion, if not actual conflict. However, there is little to suggest that this has been the case. Rather it seems that, until recently, prison social work has received little attention from social work management.
>
> (Ibid.:4)

Indeed,

> the governors were, almost without exception, strong in their praise of the social workers. They had no doubt that what the social workers did was what they wanted them to do and. . .they were clear that the social workers must continue to see those newly admitted, to provide reports and to deal with requests and referrals.
>
> (Ibid.:15)

These points lead us to conclude that the position of prison social work was one in which professional claims on the part of social workers were being subordinated to the concerns of those in control of the prison regime. As Parsloe suggested in her report,

> What must always be kept in mind, however, is the possibility that the price paid for the aforementioned working arrangements is a reluctance on the part of social workers and their managers to challenge or attempt to change the conditions which they may regard as damaging to the welfare of inmates.
>
> (Ibid.:35)

Social work in prison, despite the best efforts of the social workers themselves, was structured by a general concern for 'good order' in the prison.

This point of view was endorsed by many of the social workers we interviewed. S5, a 'singleton' social worker, described himself as 'purely and simply a welfare officer' who responded to requests and dealt with relatively minor immediate problems. Despite his obvious rapport with many of the prisoners in the prison, he recognised the existence of a prisoners' culture and suggested that 'we' are completely separate from it. S1, who worked in one of the large core prisons, explained that the social work unit was having problems finding space to carry out interviews with prisoners and the prison officers who accompanied them. Due to building work in the prison, a new fence was to be erected and the social work unit would no longer be inside the secure part of the prison. Hence, prisoners would not be allowed there. This would mean that the social work unit would be 'in the middle of a building site' and 'outside the wire'. Consequently, social workers were having to go to the halls to carry out interviews and 'having to negotiate with individual halls for a space and a time. . .they are interviewing in cells, store cupboards, in somebody else's office'. S1 offered the view that this is 'making us feel under-valued'. He had complained to both the Governor and the Divisional Director of Social Work but with few positive results. S1 continued

> Generally the prison doesn't see the problem because the service the prison is looking for from social workers is advice-giving, information-giving, message-passing, dealing with immediate practical problems. . .they don't want us to look beyond the problem. . .the previous Governor was not concerned with social work issues, he said at a meeting with me and the Divisional Director [of Social Work] that he was in the business of warehousing bodies for the courts.

He maintained that a major change of attitude in prison management was needed to ensure that social work had something to offer beyond message-passing and information-giving. 'The argument is that if this is what they want they could buy a better service from somewhere else than by employing social workers.' For S1, the place of social work in prisons was at a 'low ebb' and if the prison service only required a welfare service the social workers could be 'redeployed into the community' where they were much needed. S1 criticised governors, maintaining that there was no continuity of decisions from them, 'decisions are often taken on an individual basis and seem to bear little relation to previous decisions'. There was, he explained, a lack of consistency.

In April 1989, *Continuity Through Co-operation: A National Framework of Policy and Practical Guidance for Social Work in Scottish Penal Establishments* (Scottish Prison Service and Social Work Services Group 1989) was published. This long-awaited document set out proposals for social work in Scotland's prisons. These were explicitly linked to the general plans set out in *Custody and Care* (SPS 1988a) which is discussed more fully in Chapter 9. Community links are emphasised and the difference between the prison and other social settings played down. According to the document '[t]he fundamental purpose of social work in any setting is to help people to help themselves' (SPS and SWSG 1989:13). This is social work as seen through the lens of a centralising normalisation discourse and is clearly different from the more critical and independent conception advanced by Parsloe. In an illustrative section, the document considers the role of social work within the prison. 'Social work units have a particular contribution to make to the development of sentence planning, management plans and establishment prospectuses' (ibid.:17). With the additional proposal that many of the welfare aspects of social work could be taken on by prison officers (or dealt with by prisoners themselves over the telephone), the ground is prepared for social workers 'to undertake professional tasks' (ibid.:18). These professional tasks seem, though, to reflect the central strategy of those in charge of managing the Prison Service rather than any 'independent' social work theory.

DISCOURSE, POWER AND REGIMES

In this chapter we have examined the place of different groups of prison professionals through a discussion of prison regimes. Our argument is that prison regimes are structured by those in charge of establishments and that, in relation to regimes, the role of Headquarters is rather weak. A good example of this is the difficulty which Headquarters experienced in implementing 'parity of regimes'. Thus, in relation to regimes, governors and the professional discourse associated with them, are strong while officials, and the bureaucratic discourse which they espouse, are weak. The strength of the governors' position allows them to exercise a good deal of professional discretion and, in so doing, they are influenced by different ends discourses, i.e. by rehabilitation, normalisation and control. This affects the regimes they seek to develop and accounts, for example, for the different approaches to 'progression' adopted in different establishments. In terms of our discourse matrix (see Figure 2.5 on p.46), different forms of regime discourse occupy Cells 4, 5 and 6 of the matrix. Although officials at Headquarters are in a weak position *vis-à-vis* governors in establishments, they are in a much stronger position *vis-à-vis* other prison professionals. Thus, for example, they effectively determine the allocation of work to prisons. This explains the relative weakness of the industrial manager and the lack of fit between work and regimes. Education officers and social workers have traditionally lacked power and status within the prison and, in both cases, attempts have recently been made to enhance their professional standing. Although these attempts were strongly influenced by normalisation discourse, and as such must have been congenial to the management of the Scottish Prison Service, they both, in different ways, espoused a degree of independence that was clearly seen as threatening. Attempts have thus been made to integrate education and social work more effectively with the overall management of the service. In terms of our discourse matrix, the discourse associated with education officers and social workers reflects a confluence between professional and normalisation discourse and, as such, can be located in Cell 5 of the matrix. However, the weakness of each group of prison professionals means that, in each case, this is challenged by officials at Headquarters who espouse a composite bureaucratic–normalisation discourse located in Cell 2. We analyse recent attempts to resolve this discursive conflict in Chapter 9.

Chapter 6

Petitions to the Secretary of State

Handling requests and settling grievances?

In this chapter, we begin our analysis of accountability in the Scottish prison system. After examining three different models of accountability, we consider the special arguments for accountability in prisons and outline the various mechanisms for holding the prison system to account that exist in Scotland. We then provide a detailed account of the petition system and present a statistical analysis of the 3,371 petitions received in 1986. This is followed by a more detailed documentary analysis of three categories of petitions, namely those concerned with restoration of remission, security matters and transfers between establishments. We conclude with an assessment of the extent to which the petition system as it presently exists provides an effective mechanism of accountability. As in previous chapters, our account utilises the analytic framework outlined in Chapter 2 above and illustrates the interplay between discourse and power.

THE PRINCIPLE OF ACCOUNTABILITY

In a democratic society, great importance is attached to the principle that officials to whom powers have been delegated should be accountable for the ways in which they exercise these powers. In large and complex societies, it is very difficult to make officials directly accountable to the community for their actions and indirect forms of accountability are therefore much more common (Day and Klein 1987). A variety of mechanisms which mediate between powerful officials and the wider community has been developed and it is through these mechanisms that officials are held accountable for their actions.

Different forms of accountability are associated with different models of organisation and found in different organisational discourses. Hence, different mechanisms of accountability are found in the three means discourses which are encountered in the Scottish prison system (see Figure 2.4 on p.46). In bureaucratic discourse, accountability is internal and hierarchical. Individual decision-makers are held accountable to their superiors for their decisions and it is typically their superiors who are expected to check that bureaucratic rules, regulations and procedures have been properly applied. This chain of command leads upwards to the head of a bureaucratic organisation who may be held accountable to his/her political masters for the implementation of policy. Various forms of political accountability, e.g. to Parliament or to other representative bodies, may then ensure that decision-makers are accountable to the wider community. By contrast, in professional discourse, accountability is negotiated and interpersonal. Individuals are held accountable for their decisions to their peers who are charged with checking that professional standards have been properly adhered to. Finally, in legal discourse, accountability is external and independent. Decision-makers are held accountable to courts or tribunals which determine whether the law has been properly applied and ensure that the rights of those who are affected by the exercise of official powers have been respected. Where bureaucratic rules have not been applied, professional standards have not been adhered to, or the rights of subjects not respected in the first place, accountability is, in each case, the means of ensuring that these errors are corrected and that the initial decisions are reversed. The different forms of accountability found in the three means discourses encountered in the Scottish prison system are summarised in Figure 6.1.

Organisational discourse	Basis for accountability	Sources of accountability
bureaucracy	rules regulations	internal hierarchical
professionalism	standards of service	interpersonal negotiated
legality	rights of subjects	external independent

Figure 6.1 Different characteristics of accountability in different means discourses

In practice, because very few organisations conform to any of the models described above, and because most organisations are hybrids, different forms of accountability co-exist with each other. Thus, in any given context, including the Scottish prison system, staff may be simultaneously accountable to many different people in many different ways.

ACCOUNTABILITY IN PRISONS

The arguments for accountability apply to all officials to whom powers have been delegated and thus to all officials who exercise power over others. However, because of the special characteristics of prisons, they apply with particular force to prison officials (Justice 1983; Vagg et al. 1985). Prisons are closed and total institutions (Goffman 1968) in which individuals are usually held against their will through the exercise, *in extremis*, of coercive force. Prisoners are deprived of many of their liberties and subjected to close and detailed regulation by prison staff. They may be moved from one prison to another, upgraded and downgraded, subjected to punishment, such as loss of remission or loss of privileges, for offences against prison discipline and placed in cellular confinement. Their sanitation, exercise, clothing, visits and many other aspects of their daily lives are all highly regulated. This is, of course, not to imply that prisoners have no power or that prison staff are all-powerful. Whether, individually, through the exercise of 'censoriousness' (Mathiesen 1965) or, collectively, through socialisation into an oppositional inmate subculture (Clemmer 1958; Sykes 1958), prisoners clearly exercise a great deal of influence over prison staff. Nevertheless, the fact that prisoners are subject to such extensive official regulation, coupled with the fact that most of the decisions are taken *in camera* (Cohen and Taylor 1979) calls for a particularly strong and effective system of accountability.

In Scotland, most prisoners' requests and complaints are dealt with locally, i.e. within the establishment in which they are held, by prison officers, governor-grade staff or the governor in charge of the establishment. Under the Prison Rules, prisoners may, if they wish, complain to the Visiting Committee,[1] petition the Secretary of State for Scotland or ask to see an Officer of the Secretary of State, i.e. an official from Prison Service Headquarters on a visit to the establishment.[2] In addition, prisoners may complain to their Member of Parliament (MP) and approach the Parliamentary

Commissioner for Administration (PCA). Prisoners may obtain legal advice from a solicitor and may seek legal redress for their grievances by raising an action against prison staff or the prison authorities in the domestic courts. These actions may include applications for judicial review as well as civil actions for damages. Finally, prisoners may make an application to the European Commission on Human Rights, though this will not be considered unless domestic remedies have first been exhausted.

Each of the procedures outlined above is intended to provide a mechanism for handling grievances and for making officials accountable for their decisions. In addition, a different form of accountability is provided by the Prisons Inspectorate. Although it does not take up individual grievances, the Inspectorate visits each establishment on a regular basis and assesses its overall performance in a report to the Secretary of State. Thus, it provides a measure of institutional oversight which complements the various procedures for dealing with individual grievances. Finally, both the Director of the Scottish Prison Service and the Chief Inspector of Prisons for Scotland are required to produce Annual Reports which are published as Command Papers.

The strength and effectiveness of the various mechanisms for ensuring accountability are not easy to assess. Although the Inspectorate's reports on individual establishments are publicly available and are therefore open to public scrutiny, there is a paucity of publicly available information on the operation of grievance-handling procedures. The Annual Report of the Prison Service, *Prisons in Scotland* (e.g. SHHD 1990a) does not refer to them and neither it nor the annual summary of prison statistics published by the Scottish Home and Health Department (e.g. SHHD 1990b) contain any relevant statistics. The *Report for 1986 of Her Majesty's Chief Inspector of Prisons for Scotland* (HMCIP(S) 1987a) listed the available channels for dealing with complaints by prisoners and made a few observations (but no recommendations) about procedures in establishments. However, it likewise contained no statistics on the procedures for handling prisoners' grievances.

DIFFERENT MECHANISMS OF ACCOUNTABILITY

In order to assess the relative effectiveness of the various mechanisms of accountability it is necessary to consider each of them in more detail.

Governors' Requests

Rule 50(2) of the Prisons (Scotland) Rules 1952 (as amended) provides that 'The Governor shall, at a fixed time every day other than Sunday and public holidays, see all prisoners who have requested to see him.' Prisoners may ask to see the governor about any matter that is of concern to them, and the same procedure is used for all such requests. In practice, most establishments have devised a system in which requests are dealt with initially, for example, by a personal or group officer, then at a hall manager, then by functional manager and finally, and only if satisfaction has not already been achieved, by the governor-in-charge. Thus, governors' requests often consist of appeals against decisions taken by prison staff.

Relatively little is known about the incidence, substance, procedures or outcomes of governors' requests in Scotland. However, evidence from Ditchfield and Austin's (1986) study in England and Wales points to wide disparities in the number of recorded 'wing applications' and 'applications to duty governors' between different establishments and, although both types of applications would be treated as governors' requests in Scotland, it can be assumed that similar variations exist within the Scottish prison system. Ditchfield and Austin also revealed wide variations in the incidence of different subject matters which could not be fully explained in terms of differences in the characteristics of prisoners or in length of sentence and were assumed to reflect differences in local regimes and procedures. The Scottish Prison Service has recently questioned the acceptability of existing differences in regimes and procedures (SPS 1990a) and, although we did not investigate the area systematically, it can be assumed that these differences give rise to variations in the incidence and substance of governors' requests.

Complaints to Visiting Committees

Under Rule 194(1), prisoners who are dissatisfied with their treatment in prison may complain to the prison's Visiting Committee, which comprises lay members appointed by local authorities (in the case of adult establishments) or the Secretary of State (in the case of Young Offenders' Institutions). However, hearing complaints is only one of the functions of Visiting Committees which also have disciplinary, inspectorial and authorising powers (their duties include hearing and adjudicating on offences against prison discipline, visiting and inspecting establishments, and approving the governor's use of mechanical restraints and cellular confinement). The effectiveness of Visiting Committees as a mechanism for dealing with complaints from prisoners was assessed by McManus (1986) who observed fourteen hearings without the Visiting Committee finding in favour of the prisoner on a single occasion (ibid.:154). It is perhaps not surprising that McManus was left with an 'over-riding impression . . . of committee members' lack of knowledge of the Rules and Standing Orders and the implications of them for the running of an establishment' (ibid.:155). It is worth pointing out that, even if Visiting Committees had adopted a more independent stance, their role would only have been an indirect one since they cannot themselves take decisions but can only make recommendations to the Secretary of State. In practice, they would probably raise the matter informally with the governor before taking it further.

Petitions to the Secretary of State

Alternatively, prisoners who are dissatisfied with their treatment in prison may, under Rule 50(4), submit a written petition to the Secretary of State for Scotland. Petitions are processed by officials at Prison Service Headquarters in Edinburgh and carry the authority of the Secretary of State. Prisoners may petition about any subject and, in some cases, routine requests are transmitted to the Secretary of State through the petition procedure because the Secretary of State is the only person empowered to deal with the matter, e.g. restoration of remission or because it is customary to deal with matters in this way, e.g. compensation. In these cases, petitions constitute a mechanism for dealing with requests while in other cases they act as an appeal in which the prisoner tries to persuade the Secretary of State to set aside a local decision. Many prisoners use this procedure and, in recent years, the number of petitions to the Secretary of State for Scotland has increased substantially.[3] As can be seen from Table 6.1, the number of petitions from prisoners in Scotland almost doubled from 2,300 in 1985 to 4,557 in 1988.[4]

Table 6.1 Number of petitions received by the Scottish Prison Service, 1985–8

Year	*Number of petitions received*
1985	2,300
1986	3,351
1987	3,982
1988	4,557

Complaints to an officer of the Secretary of State visiting the prison

Under Prison Rule 50(1), a prisoner can ask to see 'an officer of the Secretary of State visiting the prison'. The term 'officer' is not defined in the Prison Rules but is generally taken to refer to an official from one of the casework branches at Prison Service Headquarters (see below). Since visits to establishments by officials from Headquarters are fairly infrequent, a prisoner might have to wait several weeks or even months before being able to submit his request or complaint in this way. Moreover, the official is unlikely to deal with the matter him/herself, this being dealt with much like an ordinary petition. What the prisoner would achieve by invoking this procedure is a personal interview. This may be very important to the prisoner but this procedure has little overall significance.

Letter to an MP

Prisoners are free to communicate with their MPs, although Standing Order Md5 makes it clear that a letter may be stopped if it includes a complaint which has not been raised through the prescribed procedures for remedying grievances. Normally the MP will forward the letter to the Minister, together with any observations he/she may have. This will be treated as a petition in the normal way, except that, as a 'green folder' case, it may be given priority and will be checked more carefully by senior officials and signed by the Minister. The method is not infrequently used by prisoners who may, as a result, receive more favoured treatment than would otherwise be the case.

Three of the procedures outlined above (governors' requests, petitions and speaking to an officer of the Secretary of State) reflect a bureaucratic form of accountability which is internal and hierarchical and what is, or ought to be, at issue is the correct application of policy. The other two procedures (complaint to the Visiting Committee or an MP) are clearly different in that they are both external to and independent from the Prison Service. They represent rather muted forms of political accountability. Visiting Committees and MPs are both free to publicise a prisoner's grievances, but neither has any powers to alter a decision and, in effect, both function as adjuncts to a bureaucratic mode of accountability. Of the five techniques, petitions are particularly significant because they are used so frequently and because, unlike governors' requests, they take the complaint outside the prison walls. The next mechanism involves a very different form of accountability.

The Prisons Inspectorate

The Inspectorate, which was established in 1981 following a recommendation in the *May Report* (Home Office 1979), comprises a Chief Inspector of Prisons for Scotland (appointed from outside the Scottish Prison Service), a Grade 1 and a Grade 3 prison governor (who are respectively Deputy Chief Inspector and Inspector), and a middle-ranking civil servant. The Inspectorate inspects each of the twenty penal establishments (but not the Headquarters of the Scottish Prison Service) and submits four to five reports per year to the Secretary of State for Scotland on the routine inspections it carries out. It has also carried out a number of thematic studies at the request of the Secretary of State, most recently on training (HMCIP(S) 1988a), on the chaplaincy service (HMCIP(S) 1989a) and on ethnic minorities (HMCIP(S) 1989b), and a special inquiry into the recent spate of prison disturbances (HMCIP(S) 1987b). In addition, it produces its own Annual Report (for example, HMCIP(S) 1990a).

The Inspectorate embodies a professional form of accountability which is interpersonal and negotiated and what is, or ought to be, at issue is the maintenance of acceptable standards of service. This is quite different from but complementary to the bureaucratic and political mechanisms of accountability outlined above.

Actions in the domestic courts

Prisoners may obtain legal advice from a solicitor and may seek legal redress for their grievances by raising an action against prison staff or the prison authorities in the domestic courts. These actions may, in theory, include actions of judicial review as well as civil actions for damages. In fact, there have only been two actions of judicial review involving prisoners in Scotland and both were rejected. In the first case (the *Thomson* case), the petitioner appealed against his transfer from Glenochil to Peterhead Prison, where he was immediately placed on Rule 36 (cellular confinement), and against the removal of his Category C security grading but, although no reasons were given, the court could find no grounds for interfering with the decision.

In the second case (the *Leech* case), the petitioner sought a declaration that Rule 74(4) of the Prison (Scotland) Rules, which allows the prison authorities to intercept and read correspondence between prisoners and their legal advisers was *ultra vires* and therefore unlawful on the grounds that this deprived them of their rights to legal advice, but the court rejected this argument on the grounds that, under Rule 76, prisoners were entitled to a confidential interview with their legal adviser. Considerably more actions of judicial review have been raised in England but, after a period of relative judicial activism in the early 1980s, the English courts appear to have returned to their traditional 'hands off' approach in cases involving prisoners (Richardson 1985). Although, in the *St Germain* case it was established that, despite their loss of liberty, prisoners retain certain rights which it is the duty of the courts to uphold and, in *Raymond v. Honey*, the court held that 'under English law, convicted prisoners, in spite of their imprisonment, retain all civil rights which are not taken away expressly or by necessary implication', the courts have failed to find many cases where the prison authorities have failed to uphold the general rights of prisoners. Moreover, the courts have also failed to identify any special rights which prisoners might enjoy as protection against the extensive discretion of the prison authorities.

Approach to the Parliamentary Commissioner for Administration (PCA)

Prisoners may approach the Parliamentary Commissioner for Administration, either directly or through their MP. If the approach is direct, the PCA will advise the prisoner to channel the complaint through his/her MP or, if this MP is not prepared to take it on, through an MP who is prepared to do so. The PCA's terms of reference limit investigations to complaints which allege injustice caused by maladministration and prevent investigation of grievances or complaints as such. Since these are what prisoners are typically concerned with, the PCA's role is rather limited and less than ten Scottish prisoners' cases have been investigated by the PCA.

Petition to the European Commission on Human Rights

Prisoners may also apply to the European Commission on Human Rights on the grounds that the prison authorities are in breach of the *European Convention on Human Rights.* In practice, the Commission requires prisoners to have exhausted the available measures of redress before it will accept the case for consideration. Thus it is very much a 'last resort' procedure. In spite of this, and the fact that the European Commission and Court take an extremely long time to review and decide on cases, at least fifteen Scottish cases have been submitted. None of them, including the recent *Boyle and Rice* cases, have been successful. However, prison conditions in Scotland have been affected as a result of ECHR cases brought by prisoners elsewhere. Of particular importance were the cases dealing with access to lawyers (the *Golder* case), restrictions on correspondence (the *Silver* case), and the conduct of disciplinary hearings (the case of *Campbell and Fell*).

In each of the three procedures outlined above, accountability is to an external authority whose status is independent of the prison authorities. The fact that, in the first case, the authority is that of a court, in the second (the PCA) that of administrative body and in the third (applications under the *European Convention on Human Rights*) that of a hybrid body is not particularly significant. What is significant is that all three procedures embody a juridical form of accountability. As such, they are quite different from but complementary to both the bureaucratic and the professional mechanisms of accountability referred to earlier.

From the above, it is clear that there are a variety of procedures for dealing with the grievances of disgruntled prisoners and for making prison officials accountable for their decisions. These procedures embody the different forms of accountability which are found in the three means discourses encountered in the Scottish prison system as summarised in Figure 6.1 above. In order to assess their effectiveness, we undertook a detailed examination of three procedures (petitions, the Inspectorate and applications to the

ECHR), each of which embodies a different form of accountability. We begin here with our analysis of the petition system. The Inspectorate is analysed in Chapter 7 and the ECHR in Chapter 8.

ANALYSING PETITION STATISTICS

In 1986, 3,351 petitions were submitted to the Secretary of State. There were considerable variations between different establishments. The largest number from one establishment was from Perth (531). However, per 100 prisoners, the highest rate was for Peterhead (235 per 100 prisoners). Adult establishments had higher rates than Young Offenders Institutions, those holding long-term prisoners had higher rates than those holding short-term prisoners, while those holding prisoners under sentence had higher rates than those holding prisoners on remand. Longriggend, a remand institution for young offenders, had the lowest rate of all (eight per 100 prisoners). The number of petitions and the petitioning rate for each establishment are set out in Table 6.2.

Table 6.2 Incidence of petitions in each establishment in 1986

Establishment	*Number of petitions*	*Average daily population*	*Rate per 100 prisoners*
Peterhead	427	182	235
Aberdeen	174	180	96
Perth	531	578	92
Shotts	54	60	90
Dumfries	127	144	88
Greenock	84	147	76[e]
Inverness	80	109	73
Noranside	49	74	66
Castle Huntly	63	103	61
Edinburgh	465	776	60
Glenochil	302	511	59
Polmont	217	378	57
Dungavel	64	135	47
Friarton	26	56	46
Barlinnie	500	1,270	39
Cornton Vale	72	188	38
Penninghame	23	69	33
Low Moss	70	345	20
Longriggend	23	280	8
Total	3,351	5,585	60

Note: e = estimate for twelve months (prison reopened in March 1986).

Most petitions raised only one issue but a few raised more than one. Thus the 3,351 petitions raised 3,485 issues. As can be seen from Table 6.3, the largest number of issues referred to restoration of remission (904 references, 25.9 per cent of the total) and six categories (out of fifty-five) accounted for 60.4 per cent of all the petitions.

Table 6.4, which groups petitions into composite categories, gives a better picture.

Table 6.3 Largest individual categories of petitions

Individual category	*Number of references*	*% of total (n = 3,485)*	*Cumulative %*
Restoration of remission	904	25.9	25.9
Transfers	458	13.1	39.0
Compensation	240	6.9	45.9
Medical	178	5.1	51.0
Out of Scotland	171	4.9	55.9
Home visits	155	4.4	60.3

Table 6.4 Distribution of petitions into composite categories

Composite category	*Number of individual categories in composite category*	*Number of references*	*% of total (n = 3,485)*
Restoration of remission	1	904	25.9
Classification/ transfer	6	758	21.8
Visits	6	319	9.2
Compensation	3	317	9.1
Conditions	8	257	7.4
Prison procedures	7	202	5.8
Medical	2	196	5.6
Privileges	6	142	4.1
Conviction/sentence/ legal action	3	120	3.4
Liberation/parole	3	79	2.3
Civil liberties	5	54	1.5
Security	2	18	0.5
Miscellaneous	4	119	3.4

Analysing the origin of petitions reveals that particular problems are clearly associated with different establishments. For example, restoration of remission was a particular issue at Friarton (which was a Detention Centre before it became an establishment for short-term prisoners in May 1986) and at three Young Offenders' Institutions, Glenochil (which also housed a Detention Centre), Noranside and Polomont; problems associated with classification and transfers came disproportionately from Barlinnie and Edinburgh (where, as we pointed out in chapter 3, the National Classification Board is based) and from Aberdeen, Inverness and Peterhead; visits and visiting arrangements were a particular problem in Dungavel, Greenock and, to a lesser extent, Shotts. These relationships can sometimes be explained in terms of the type of prisoner held in a particular establishment or its geographical location. However, such relationships may also be due to features of the prison regime. Although statistics on petitions are not routinely kept, let alone analysed, they could be used as a source of management information and as a means of identifying and dealing with management problems.

PROCESSING PETITIONS

Petitions were dealt with in the following way. After requesting a petition form, prisoners were free to put their own case in as much detail as they wished. There were no limits on the length of the petition or the number of matters which may be raised at any one time (although, as we have seen, the overwhelming majority of petitions raised only on issue). Under Rule 50(4), the prisoner had the choice of submitting the petition sealed or unsealed. If it was unsealed, it went first to one of the governor-grades in the prison who elicited the comments of prison staff, added his/her own recommendations and forwarded the petition to Headquarters. If it was sealed, it went first to headquarters where it was opened before being sent back to the prison for the governor in charge of the establishment to deal with. However, it was then dealt with as if it had been unsealed. Although sealing did prevent petitions from being tampered with or suppressed by prison staff at establishment level, it also caused some delay.[5]

At Headquarters, all new petitions were entered in thc petitions register and acknowledged by means of a postcard which was sent to the prisoner. Petitions were then divided into three categories which were dealt with by three sets of staff as follows:

1 Those relating to untried prisoners, young offenders and female offenders, and those concerning lost property and compensation.
2 Those from lifers, unless they concerned lost property and compensation.
3 Those from other adult prisoners, unless they concerned lost property and compensation.

We spent a good deal of time in the casework branch, observing the way in which petitions were dealt with and talking to the staff concerned. In the case of 'other adult prisoners', these comprised:

1 An Administrative Assistant (A16), who dealt with 'simple' cases, such as restoration of remission.
2 An Administrative Officer (A17), who dealt with requests for transfer out of Scotland, repatriation and accumulated visits in England.
3 Another Administrative Officer (A18), who dealt with most of the other matters in the first instance.

Petitions were dealt with in chronological order, although 'urgent' petitions were given priority – these included petitions from prisoners who were close to liberation and 'green folders' where the Minister's private office was involved. A18 would decide if the petition raised issues on which the advice of experts should be sought – examples here included matters relating to conviction and sentence, medical treatment and prison wages. In such cases, the petition was sent to other officials at Headquarters. A18 normally drafted the reply which then went to the Executive Officer (A19) or the Higher Executive Officer (A8) for approval and signature, although they did sometimes ask for replies to be redrafted. The roles of the EO (A19) and HEO (A8), and the Senior Executive Officer (A7) in charge of the branch, were thus largely supervisory in respect of petitions, although they did also give advice and take responsibility for some of the more 'difficult', 'sensitive' or 'urgent' cases. Thus, the SEO (A7) in charge made it clear that allegations of staff brutality, other allegations against officers, AIDS cases and cases involving segregation should be brought to his attention. He stated that:

> The really awkward ones comes to me and they tend not to be just routine petitions, they tend to be problem cases. . .People like X.

> X is sitting there on my desk because 'civil liberties people', the press and MPs have got interested and it all dovetails. These sort of cases, which often create management problems, tend to end up on my desk. In addition, I am responsible for the policy side of the work.

One of the AOs (A18) kept files of 'standard replies', organised alphabetically by topic, which could be used again and again and, whenever such a new reply was sent, it was kept for future reference. Although some standardised replies had been drafted, e.g. for responding to requests for compassionate leave, they were not used very often. Moreover, staff made few references to the Prison Rules or to Standing Orders but appeared to rely instead on a stock of accumulated knowledge and practice. As A18 explained:

> We deal with so many petitions and we therefore know what is reasonable and what is not.

This was accepted by A7, the SEO in charge of the branch, who explained that:

> There are certain things which are quite clearly covered by the Standing Orders and which [the staff] refer to. But I think they are well aware that if the Standing Orders are clearly out of date, you can't really refer to them. . . A lot of it is rule of thumb.

Prisoners and prison staff (including governors) also relied on a stock of accumulated knowledge and practice and, by and large, the discourse of petitions was one of 'common-sense' and 'everyday experience'.

Standing Order Mc7 lays down that replies to petitions should be read out to prisoners individually, i.e. not in the presence of other prisoners. Two copies of the reply are normally sent to the governor – one for the prison records and one for the prisoner. Our analysis of all the petitions submitted in 1986 indicated that, on average, prisoners had to wait thirty-four days for a reply. Of course, some had to wait considerably longer and 17.5 per cent of petitions took fifty days or more to deal with. Not surprisingly, there were substantial variations in the time taken to deal with different petitions. Relatively straightforward matters like restoration of remission were dealt with more quickly (mean time taken twenty-two days), transfers were fairly typical of all petitions (mean time taken thirty-three days), while security matters took rather longer (mean time taken forty-four days). Compensation cases took longest of all (mean time taken fifty-six days).

ASSESSING THE EFFECTIVENESS OF THE PETITION SYSTEM

In order to assess the extent to which petitions constitute an effective system of accountability, we focus on three areas: restoration of remission, security matters, and transfers. In so doing, we draw on a detailed analysis of a sample of petitions as well as observation and interviews in the branch.

Restoration of remission (ROR)

It will be recalled that this was the largest single category of petitions (904 petitions comprising 25.9 per cent of all references in 1986 were concerned with ROR). It was also regarded as one of the most straightforward matters and, for this reason, was handled by the AA (A16), the most junior member of the branch. According to Rule 47(1), 'any disciplinary award may be remitted or mitigated by the Secretary of State' but, in exercising this discretion, the governor's recommendations were almost invariably followed. The HEO (A8) maintained that 'often we are the mouthpiece for the establishment'. It was recognised that this resulted in considerable disparities between establishments and that some governors 'never seemed to grant ROR'. Nevertheless, the official view seemed to be that, as governors were free to impose loss of remission in the first place, so they should likewise be free to restore it if they wished. The only circumstances in which Headquarters actively intervened were where there was a disagreement between the governors of two establishments and where the request was made too long in advance of the prisoner's expected release date. Disagreements could arise where the governor of one prison had recommended ROR but the prisoner had been transferred to another prison and the governor there disagreed. In such cases, the view of the first governor was generally supported, on the grounds that he would have known the prisoner better. Where a petition was submitted three months or more before the prisoner's expected date of release, Headquarters would refuse to consider it, even if it was supported by the governor, on the grounds that it was too early, but would normally advise the prisoner to apply again nearer to his expected release date.

Security matters

Most of these petitions involved appeals against the imposition of 'strict' and 'modified' escapee status and the higher degree of surveillance this entails. Although they were relatively few in number (there were only seventeen such petitions in 1986), they raise issues of considerable importance because of the effect these statuses can have on a prisoner's quality of life. We looked in detail at eleven of these petitions. Prisoners complained that 'no reasons had been given' or that they had been given escapee status as a punishment or to intimidate them into making a statement about a fellow prisoner; they denied that they had ever tried to escape and complained about the consequences, e.g. an inability to sleep with the lights on, curtailment of access to education and normal privileges. Governors variously justified their decisions by pointing out that the prisoner had been charged with conspiracy to threaten witnesses and that 'it would be foolish to take any risks', and, several times, by referring to the length of the prisoner's sentence and the nature of the crimes for which the prisoner had been sentenced. Several governors also argued that 'a prisoner's security category is something for local management to decide' and claimed that 'security is not a matter for discussion with the prisoner'. This was the view which underlay the Secretary of State's response in every case. The reply given in many cases that 'matters of security rest with the governor... and the Secretary of State is not prepared to intervene on this occasion', can be taken to embody the Department's position on these matters. When asked about this sort of reply, the SEO (A7) replied:

> It is a fairly standard one . . . When you are talking about security, it is difficult to give details for security reasons. The one instance where we do tend to give reasons is when escapee status is imposed on the advice of the police. They [those working in the branch] should be saying that security categories are reviewed regularly and giving them some sort of hope . . . Governors are charged by law with keeping their prisoners and therefore it is their decision as to what degree of security they apply.

It is clear that Headquarters was extremely reluctant to challenge recommendations of governors where these were concerned with questions of security and that the petition system did not provide an effective means for prisoners to question governors' decisions relating to matters of security.

Transfers

Transfers were the second largest single category of petitions (458 petitions, comprising 13.1 per cent of all references in 1986 were concerned with transfers). This category included requests for transfers as well as appeals against transfers but, for convenience, we have run them together since they were dealt with in much the same way. We looked in detail at thirty-six requests and twenty-two appeals, i.e. at fifty-eight petitions in all. The outcomes are set out in Table 6.5. Since, in all but five of the cases, the decision followed

Table 6.5 Relationship between recommendations and outcomes in transfer petitions

Governor's recommendation	*Number of petitions*	*Outcome*
yes	17	yes 13, no 4*
no	33	no 32, yes 1
none	2	under consideration
unnecessary/ overtaken by events	6	unnecessary/overtaken by events
Total	58	[36 requests, 22 appeals]

Note: * Includes three cases of governor disagreement (see below).

the governor's recommendation, we can concentrate on these five cases. In three cases the prisoners' request was supported by the governor of the holding establishment, but opposed by the governor of the potential receiving establishment, in the first case because the prison did not hold prisoners serving sentences of that length; in the second because there was no room in the prison; and, in the third case, because psychiatric tests showed the prisoner to be unsuitable for that particular establishment. In another case the governor gave some support to the prisoner's request for a transfer while admitting that it was a weak case. However, a social work report suggested that the prisoner's real reason for wanting a transfer (to be near his girlfriend) was not the stated reason (to be near his wife and children) and Headquarters turned down the request. Finally, a long-term prisoner appealed against a decision to transfer him to Perth (his prison of classification) on the grounds that he had previously been assaulted by another prisoner in that prison. He asked to be allocated to Shotts instead but, although he had been 'badly slashed' in Edinburgh and was actually in the prison hospital there at the time, his request was not supported by his assistant governor, who referred to his 'poor reputation in Edinburgh' or by the Chairman of the National Classification Board. However, in this case, it is clear that Headquarters was anxious to avoid the risk of another incident. The prisoner was reclassified as suitable for Shotts but warned that 'his conduct and industry must be maintained, otherwise he will be transferred to Perth'. Thus, in the five cases where the governor's recommendations were not followed, only one led to a successful outcome for the prisoner. However, in addition to this case, it should be noted that, in thirteen other cases, the governor supported the petition and the governor's recommendation was followed by Headquarters.

Governors' own recommendations frequently made reference to the prisoner's behaviour. Thus, governors often wrote things like 'recent good behaviour has been noted' in support of a request or an appeal and '[prisoner] has not earned the right to such a move' to explain lack of support. Thus, we came across much evidence for what McNeill (1988) has referred to as 'sweeties for the good boys'. It is clear that, by and large, governors' recommendations were supported by Headquarters and that they effectively determined the outcome of the petition. Only if the governors' recommendations conflicted with operational practice or if the veracity of the prisoner's case was called into question, or if there was evidence to suggest that the prisoner might be at risk of serious injury was a governor's recommendation ever overruled. However, reasons for refusal were rarely given. Thus, replies of the type 'Please inform the prisoner in reply to his petition dated. . .that, after careful consideration, his request for a transfer to. . .is refused' were standard.[6]

It is clear that, at least in the three areas we have looked at, petitions did not constitute a particularly effective system of accountability. Of course, the very existence of petitions almost certainly makes the prison system more responsive to the circumstances and preferences of individual prisoners in that it forces governors to make and justify recommendations on the wide range of issues that prisoners raise in their petitions. In a number of the cases we looked at, particularly those relating to restoration of remission and transfers to other establishments, prisoners were able to secure the support of governors and, as a result, their petitions were granted. But, as a means of checking the ways in which prison staff exercise their power, petitions provided very inadequate protection for prisoners against abuses of that power.

DISCOURSE, POWER AND THE PETITION SYSTEM

There are two general reasons for the shortcomings we have just outlined. When discussing the principle of accountability, we argued that different forms of accountability are associated with different models of organisation and encountered in different organisational discourses. As such, petitions are located in bureaucratic discourse in which individual decision-makers are held accountable for their decisions to their superiors. Governors are appointed by and answerable to the Secretary of State and it follows that prisoners should be able to petition the Secretary of State and that governors should be accountable to the Secretary of State, albeit through Headquarters, for their decisions. However, the reality is very different. The power relationship between the governor who recommends a course of action and the official who considers the governor's recommendation in response to the prisoner's petition is not the traditional one of subordinate to superior but is exactly the opposite. In these circumstances, it is hardly surprising that so few decisions get reversed. Faced with a choice between the governor's recommendation and the prisoner's petition and with no 'independent' source of information, who can blame the relatively low-ranking civil servant in one of the casework branches at Headquarters for effectively rubber-stamping all but the most manifestly problematic recommendations.

If power provides one part of the explanation, discourse itself provides another. In bureaucratic discourse, those to whom decision-makers are held accountable are expected to check that bureaucratic rules, guidelines and procedures have been applied. The difficulty here is that the rules, guidelines and procedures (embodied in the Prison (Scotland) Rules, Standing Orders and Circular Instructions) are not written in such a way as to provide an effective basis for day-to-day decision-making in establishments or for checking those decisions. It is for this reason that governors' discourse can be characterised as one of 'grounded professionalism' based on their accumulated knowledge, their practical experience and their personal judgment. However, this discourse is not one with which the civil servants in the casework branches are familiar or one with which they can readily engage. Their discourse is a bureaucratic discourse based on rules, regulations and procedures and thus they lack the means (as well as the power) to challenge the governors' recommendations in all but a minority of cases where their recommendations would clearly contravene the rules.

We can illustrate this general analysis by referring, on the one hand, to each of the three areas we looked at in detail and, on the other, to our discourse matrix (see Figure 2.5 on p.46 above). As regards restoration of remission, there was virtually no guidance as to the considerations governors should apply in determining requests. As a result, there were considerable disparities between governors in the extent to which they were prepared to grant ROR. It is rather hard to analyse governors' ROR discourse since they were not very explicit about it. However, it clearly belongs in Row 2 of the matrix and, depending on their commitment to rehabilitation, normalisation or control, it can be located in one or more of Cells 4, 5 and 6. The civil servants' discourse equally clearly belongs to Row 1 of the matrix, although it was a very limited form of discourse since the only rule appeared to be a 'rule of thumb' that ROR should not be considered more than three months before the prisoner's expected release date. Thus, although professional and bureaucratic forms of discourse were both present, the former was much more fully developed than the latter. This, and the fact that governors who acted as the carriers of professional discourse had much higher status than the civil servants who acted as the carriers of bureaucratic discourse, ensured that, with very few exceptions, governors' recommendations for ROR were supported.

In relation to matters of security, the lack of articulation was even more clear-cut. Security matters were regarded as entirely within the professional competence of the governor. Governors were extremely reluctant to discuss security matters, arguing that this could in itself constitute a threat to security. However, the dominant concerns were clearly about control and governors' security discourse, such as it was, can be located in Cell 6 of the matrix. Since the Prison Rules, Standing Orders and Circular Instruments placed few constraints, other than purely procedural ones, on the exercise of this judgment, civil servants' discourse was silent on these matters. Thus, they lacked the means as well as the power to challenge the dominance of the governors' professional–control discourse and were left with no alternative to supporting governors' recommendations on issues relating to security.

Finally, in relation to transfers, the primary concerns for

governors when our study was carried out were with rehabilitation (manifested in terms of a commitment to classification and to 'upgrading' to more liberal regimes in response to good behaviour) and control (manifested in terms of a commitment to security categorisation and to 'downgrading' to more restrictive regimes for disruptive prisoners). More recently, normalisation has, to some extent, displaced rehabilitation but that need not concern us here. However, in relation to transfers, governors did not have a free hand since a variety of rules, guidelines and procedures had been developed specifying, *inter alia,* the kinds of prisoners who could be held in each establishment, the point in their sentence at which prisoners could move to semi-open and open conditions, and the application procedures which applied in this case. While governors' transfer discourse represented a confluence of bureaucratic and professional concerns, on the one hand, and rehabilitation and control concerns, on the other (represented by Cells 1, 3, 4 and 6 in the matrix), civil servants' transfer discourse was more straightforward and could be characterised as bureaucratic–rehabilitation discourse (represented by Cell 1 in the matrix). This meant that, where governors' recommendations transgressed the bureaucratic rules, guidelines and procedures referred to above, the civil servants at Headquarters were, in spite of their much lower status, sometimes prepared to over-rule the governor. However, it is important to stress that these occasions were relatively infrequent. In the final chapter (Chapter 10), we indicate briefly how these deficiencies could be remedied.

Chapter 7

The Prisons Inspectorate

Monitoring regimes and improving standards?

In this chapter, we continue our discussion of accountability with an analysis of the operation of the Prisons Inspectorate. We give an account of its origins, its brief and its structure and describe its main activities. We analyse the content of inspection reports, thematic reviews, incident reports and the Chief Inspector's Annual Report and evaluate how well the Inspectorate performs its different functions. The performance of the Inspectorate is analysed in terms of discourse and power and makes repeated references to the discourse matrix outlined in Chapter 2 above.

THE ORIGINS OF THE INSPECTORATE

The office of Her Majesty's Chief Inspector of Prisons for Scotland was set up (like that for England and Wales) following acceptance by the Government of a recommendation in the *May Report*, the *Report of the Committee of Inquiry into the United Kingdom Prison Service* (Home Office 1979). However, the proposal in the Report to set up an inspectorate referred only to England and Wales and not to Scotland. This was, at least partly, because the arguments for inspection arose in the context of a discussion of the 'unique problems' which confronted the organisation of the Prison Service in England and Wales. This discussion was introduced by noting that the organisation of prisons in Scotland had only recently been reviewed and that 'no evidence suggesting a present need for further changes' had been received (ibid.:para. 5.2). According to the May Committee, Scotland, unlike England and Wales, did 'not present significant organisational problems' (ibid.:para. 5.2).

The May Committee's recommendations on inspection were developed in response to a paper submitted by the Home Office which supported the principle of inspection but rejected the idea of an independent inspectorate (ibid.:paras. 5.54–5.60; Morgan 1985:108). The Committee accepted the validity of the Home Office's argument that an inspectorate which reported to the Minister responsible for the (English) Prison Service, even if it was located outside the Prison Department, could not be independent of government, but rejected the Home Office's conclusions. The Committee was in 'no doubt that public sentiment required that as many aspects of government, which included the prison service, as possible should be opened up to as wide an audience as possible' (ibid.:para. 5.61) and recommended 'that there should be constituted within the Home Office an independent department to be called the "Prisons Inspectorate"' (ibid.:para. 5.62).

> The Committee agreed that a Home Office Inspectorate outside the Prison Department could not be fully independent of the service, but it held that it would have credibility if the new department included personnel not recruited from prisons; its reports were published; it could make unannounced visits; and it could report on general aspects of the work of the Prison Department.
>
> (Morgan 1985:108)

The Home Secretary accepted the Committee's proposals on inspection in April 1980 and the Inspectorate for England and Wales began work in January 1981. Although the proposals did not apply to Scotland, the Secretary of State for Scotland announced the establishment of an analagous Inspectorate for Scotland in August 1980 (SHHD 1981:1) Both Inspectorates were put on a statutory basis in the Criminal Justice Act of 1982. The wording of the amendments to the respective Prisons Acts was the same except that the legislation for Scotland also gave the Chief Inspector powers to inspect legalised police cells which did not exist in England and Wales. The same wording was incorporated into the Prisons (Scotland) Act of 1989.

THE INSPECTORATE AND ITS BRIEF

The Scottish Inspectorate began its work on 1 January 1981. The terms of reference of the Inspectorate are set out in detail in its first Annual Report (HMCIP(S) 1982a) and in an Appendix to the *Report for 1980 on Prisons in Scotland* (SHHD 1981). The Chief

Inspector (CI) is a member of the Scottish Home and Health Department (SHHD) and therefore reports to the Secretary of State for Scotland, but he/she is not a member of Prisons Division. The duties of the CI are to

> inspect and report to the Secretary of State on penal establishments and legalised police cells in Scotland, and in particular on
>
> 1 Conditions in those establishments;
> 2 The treatment of prisoners and other inmates, and the facilities available to them; and
> 3 Such other matters as the Secretary of State may direct.
>
> (HMCIP(S) 1982a:para. 1.02)

Further, the terms of reference state that the

> Chief Inspector's main concern will be with the regular inspection of individual establishments. He will concentrate on such matters as the morale of staff and prisoners; the quality of the regime; the conditions of the buildings; questions of humanity and propriety; and the general efficiency of the establishment.
>
> (Ibid.:para. 1.02)

These activities have been much emphasised by the Chief Inspector over the years. Indeed, they have been almost sloganised into an emphasis on 'humanity, propriety and efficiency' (HMCIP(S) 1989e:para. 2.9).[1]

Three potentially important limitations on the CI may be noted at this stage. First, the CI's mandate is not co-extensive with the Scottish Prison Service. Thus, prison establishments but not the Headquarters of the Prison Service are liable for inspection. It follows that the petition process described in the previous chapter cannot be inspected as a whole. Second, while the CI can (and does) meet inmates during the course of inspections, individual grievances cannot be dealt with. They have to go through the channels outlined in Chapter 6 above. Third, the CI is responsible to the Secretary of State. This inevitably leads to some fettering of the independence of the office, particularly in the case of investigations of controversial issues such as prison disturbances (Scraton et al. 1991) but also in connection with routine inspections.

STRUCTURE OF THE INSPECTORATE

As we have pointed out in the previous chapter, the Inspectorate comprises a (part-time) Chief Inspector, who is appointed from outside the Scottish Prison Service, a Grade 1 and a Grade 3 prison governor (who are respectively Deputy Chief Inspector and Inspector), and a middle-ranking civil servant. Up to the end of 1989, there had been three Chief Inspectors: Philip Barry (1981–5), Tom Buyers (1985–9) and Alan Bishop (1989–). Philip Barry had worked in industry and had been Chairperson of the Scottish Parole Board; Tom Buyers came to the post from a background in the oil industry; and Alan Bishop had previously been an Under-Secretary within the Scottish Office itself.[2]

The post of Deputy Chief Inspector had, up to the end of 1989, had five incumbents. The first spent only four months in post, but the span of office for the others was around two and a half years. All have retired and none has returned to establishments or moved to Headquarters. Likewise, the post of Inspector has had five incumbents, with a replacement Inspector being appointed for the five-month span of the Inspectorate's investigation into the disturbances at Peterhead (see below). There is no pattern to the duration of their terms as Inspector, which must partly be due to operational considerations since all Inspectors (except the first who retired) have returned to governor-in-charge posts in the Prison Service.

The Inspectorate is therefore headed by a non-professional who is expected to bring a measure of independence to its activities. However, as the Chief Inspector is both an 'amateur' and part time, he has been very dependent upon the expertise of his professional governor colleagues. The Deputy Chief Inspector is a senior figure, but one who is at the end of his career. In some respects this might increase his capacity and/or desire to express and take an 'independent' line, however it might also mean that the incumbent of the office is looking forward to retirement. Certainly, it cannot be said that, until now, the post of Deputy Chief Inspector has been one that governors looking towards career development would aspire to. Further, the post of Inspector has been filled after operational considerations have been decided and, like that of Deputy Chief Inspector, has not been viewed as one of the 'plum' jobs in the Prison Service.

THE WORK OF THE INSPECTORATE

The work of the Inspectorate falls into four areas (see also Morgan 1985): in addition to routine inspections and the production of reports, the Inspectorate carries out thematic reviews; investigates incidents; and produces an Annual Report. In this section we describe each of these areas in turn.

Inspections and inspection reports

Each of the penal establishments in Scotland is inspected on a three-to-four-year cycle. The results of these inspections are written up and then submitted to the Secretary of State who gives a response to any recommendations made by the Chief Inspector before the report is published.[3] The Inspectorate aims to produce a report within three months of the inspection. However, because the Secretary of State asks for the Department's comments before the report is published, 'it is sometimes a year before they come out' (Deputy Chief Inspector).[4] This gap has been commented upon in successive Annual Reports, although the report for 1989 (HMCIP(S) 1990a) indicated that the 'gap has been, and continues to be, progressively reduced' (para. 2.12).

The Inspectorate aimed to carry out around six inspections a year as well as visiting every establishment which was not the subject of a full inspection. The time taken over each inspection varied depending on the size of the establishment, with around a fortnight being spent on the larger and more complex prisons like Barlinnie, Edinburgh and Perth and a week in smaller and more straightforward establishments like Dungavel. The Inspector (I) visited the prison beforehand to formulate a programme with the Governor. Although the Inspectorate are entitled to visit a prison without giving prior notice, they rarely did so.

During the course of the inspection, the team would examine and evaluate matters within their remit. Their concerns are reflected in the structure of their inspection reports. These reports have increased in length over the years. Taking the example of Perth Prison to illustrate this, the report of the inspection carried out in 1982 (HMCIP(S) 1982b) ran to twenty-eight pages, that on the inspection carried out in 1985 (HMCIP(S) 1985a) to twenty-six pages (reflecting in part the omission of the overall brief of the Inspectorate and of the history of Perth Prison), but that on the inspection carried out in 1989 (HMCIP(S) 1989c) ran to sixty-six pages.

The chapter headings in the reports varied from report to report but the areas covered were fairly standard. The reports began with a 'general assessment' of the prison, derived in part from the material contained in the rest of the report. This was followed by descriptions of the prison population and the available accommodation and sometimes by a general account of its history and place within the prison system. The statistics relating to population and accommodation can be of help to the outside observer as they are the only published source providing such information broken down by sentence length. It enables a picture of the differential use of the various halls in the prison to be built up and any localised overcrowding to be detected. Most reports then commented on: staff and management; discipline; control and security; regimes; work and employment; administration and the activities of the medical, social work and chaplaincy services; and the work of the various committees including the Visiting Committee, the Local Review Committee and the various domestic committees such as those responsible for Health and Safety and for Energy. The reports concluded with a summary of the recommendations made in the main body of the report and any further points worthy of note. The Secretary of State replied to the recommendations made by the Inspectorate in a statement which appeared at the beginning of the report.

Reports on inspections covered various aspects of the prison. They could range, in a matter of pages, from a consideration of the control measures applied to prisoners held in 'separate cells' to the methods used to keep food warm on journeys across the prison. Such variation can be exemplified by a brief review of the recommendations made in successive reports. Taking Perth as an example, in 1982 it was recommended that the use of the 'existing separate cells be discontinued' (HMCIP(S) 1982b:para. 10.1). This recommendation was repeated in the report for 1985, together with a call for their replacement 'with a suitable unit' (HMCIP(S) 1985a:para. 10.1). In the report for 1989, four recommendations were made: first, the 'range and quality' of the work available for prisoners needed to be improved; second, vocational training required development; third, facilities for physical education needed upgrading; and, finally, 'the extended medical facility' ought to be completed timeously (HMCIP(S) 1989c:paras. 12.1–12.4). The recommendations were usually specific to the prison under inspection, although the Inspectorate sometimes waged a campaign on one issue across different prisons, physical education being a case in point. Evidence for this can also be found in the Annual Reports considered below.

In addition to the increasing length of the prison inspection reports referred to above, there also seems to have been a change in tone and an increase in the number of recommendations made.[5] Early reports seem to have assumed a greater community of interest between the Inspectorate, governors and Headquarters than the later ones. For example, in the report on Perth Prison published in 1982, the Inspectorate maintained that 'communications between management and staff could be improved but this problem is appreciated by the Governor and will receive his attention' (HMCIP(S) 1982b:para. 2.4) and that 'The Inspectors are satisfied that the major problems of the establishment have been identified by local management and Prisons Division and that reasonable action is being taken to correct them' (ibid.:para. 2.5). By the inspection report of 1985, such agreement was rather less evident, i.e.

> In his briefing of the Inspectorate, the Governor informed us of his objective to operate, within the necessary security, a relaxed and democratic regime and to do so with as few restrictions as possible. We certainly found a general lack of tension which, considering the complex task required of Perth, is all the more commendable. We did not, however, find a universal acceptance of this objective by staff, some of whom considered that discipline, control and perhaps even security were put at risk, an opinion which we thought was not without some justification. This we discussed at some length with the Governor and we have to say that in the end our respective views were not entirely reconciled. We have therefore put our views, and those of the Governor, to the Director with particular reference to those matters affecting security.
>
> (HMCIP(S) 1985a: para. 2.1)

Later reports have had more to say about the atmosphere and culture of prisons. Thus, in the 1989 report on Perth, the Inspectorate wrote that

> Overall we were left with some feeling of unease about the prison yet the various functions, statutory and otherwise, were being

> attended to in a not improper fashion. However, an underlying malaise which we felt was insidiously affecting the establishment manifested itself clearly in two main areas. Firstly, there was the sometimes indulgent attitude of many staff towards basic matters of good order and discipline. . . Secondly, there was the apathetic attitude of many of the inmates.
>
> (HMCIP(S) 1989c:para. 2.3)

Such concerns were also reflected in the number and substance of the recommendations made in inspection reports. For example, in the report on the inspection of Barlinnie carried out in 1986, five recommendations were made (HMCIP(S) 1987c:paras. 10.1–10.5), but in the report of the inspection carried out in 1990, there were eight recommendations and a further fourteen points of note (HMCIP(S) 1990b:paras. 12.1–12.8 and 13.1–13.14). It is illuminating to compare the language used in these recommendations which are quoted in full. The recommendations made in 1987 were:

1 That every effort be made to speedily resolve the findings of the staff inspection reports.
2 That Prisons Group review their procedures for filling staff vacancies with a view to expediting the process.
3 That urgent steps be taken to have an operational Staff Training Officer in post to hasten the introduction of an appropriate training programme.
4 That arrangements be made to facilitate a staff office in each hall.
5 That greater emphasis be placed on monitoring following action on reports from the Catering Adviser and the Departmental Health and Safety Adviser on kitchen facilities and practices.

The language adopted in 1986 was rather tentative, and the approach not very hard-hitting. By 1990, the recommendations were couched in a rather different language:

1 The Prison (Scotland) Rules 1952 should be revised and brought up to date.
2 In order to meet the statutory requirement of daily exercise, the exercise pen for inmates held in the segregation unit should be completed without further delay.
3 Revised arrangements should be implemented immediately to ensure that the statutory entitlement to daily exercise for remand inmates is fully honoured.
4 If the present level of demand on the laundry cannot be

reduced then it should be refitted with more modern equipment capable in capacity of providing a reliable, efficient and quality service.

5 A proper, fully equipped gymnasium, with appropriate staff resources to mount a meaningful PE programme, should be provided.

6 It is essential that the Reception area receive close and urgent attention to remedy its many physical defects.

7 Large observation panels should be inserted into the doors of a few cubicles to help Reception staff readily and constantly monitor the wellbeing of inmates located there. Additionally, as a matter of routine, Reception staff should be informed of outgoing inmates with special health problems.

8 The present dining and sterilisation processes are not acceptable and should be brought up to standard without delay.

The mode of expression used in 1990 was rather more forceful and urgent than had been the case previously and the references to the Prison Rules and other statutory requirements in striking contrast to their absence from earlier reports. This is examined in more detail below but is clearly indicative of the increasing sharpness of reports on inspections. However, it should be emphasised that the reports were still relatively unsophisticated.

Thematic reviews

The second of the Inspectorate's areas of work is the production of thematic reviews. Topics covered include: children in prison (HMCIP(S) 1985b); social work in prisons (HMCIP(S) 1987d); staff training (HMCIP(S) 1988a); prison chaplaincy service (HMCIP(S) 1989a); and ethnic minorities (HMCIP(S) 1989b). During the course of an interview, the Deputy Chief Inspector (DCI) described how the topics were selected. He explained that, as chief adviser to the CI, he drew up a list for consideration. The DCI would discuss the list with Headquarters to identify 'problem areas', for example it might be the case that someone else was already studying some of the areas under consideration. One area where the Inspectorate has been critical in the past was that of Visiting Committees, but they did not carry out a thematic review on this subject as research on Visiting Committees had recently been carried out for the Scottish Office (McManus 1986). According to the DCI, the Inspectorate sought to avoid any duplication of work in progress or under consideration. Once the list had been drawn up, the Inspectorate team would look at it and put their proposals to the Secretary of State. DCI maintained that the Inspectorate had never been prevented from studying any particular topic, though, as the CI pointed out, this was because 'we have always done our homework first...before we put forward proposals we have talked to people'.

From this account and from the topics selected for thematic reviews, it is not clear that the Inspectorate pursues its own agenda which is independent from that of Prison Headquarters. These doubts are confirmed by examining the form and content of the reports.

The report on staff training (HMCIP(S) 1988a) was clearly written, for the most part, with an operational frame of reference. Apart from a brief consideration of training in occupations such as the police and the fire service, it gave little attention to training in other organisations and did not draw extensively on the professional expertise of staff involved in training. Furthermore, the report was overtaken by events. These points are expressed by the Chief Inspector himself in the letter to the Secretary of State which prefaced the review:

> While we were carrying out this study there was a continually rising interest in staff training within Prisons Group and throughout the Service, culminating in your statement of January 1988 with the strong commitment towards a strengthened training programme. Under the circumstances, we have felt it appropriate to work closely with Prisons Group throughout our study and have offered comments as appropriate during our investigations.
>
> (HMCIP(S) 1988a)

Although there was little detailed reference to prevailing practice in the review of staff training, the review of the chaplaincy service (HMCIP(S) 1989a) adopted a different approach. Here, the lack of fit between the activities of chaplains and the current Prison (Scotland) Rules and Standing Orders structured the review, leading to a recommendation that

> the full range of tasks of the prison chaplain as contained in statute and local orders should be reviewed and updated swiftly. The appropriate sections of the Prison (Scotland) Rules 1952 and Prisons (Scotland) Standing Orders should be amended accordingly.
>
> (Ibid.:para. 7.2)

The review also referred to 'declarations by the Council of Europe' (para. 3.31) and to the Council of Europe's Standard Minimum Rules for the Treatment of Prisoners (para. 3.49). These international references are striking because they appear so rarely in the Inspectorate's reports. However, it is significant to note that they appear in the thematic report on the chaplaincy service, a topic that is hardly of central importance for the Scottish Prison Service.

The most hard-hitting review was that carried out by Phyllida Parsloe on *Social Work Units in Scottish Prisons* (HMCIP(S) 1987d). We have already considered this in detail in Chapter 5 and here we wish only to point to the manner in which it was constructed. Unlike other thematic reports, it drew on professional expertise. Such expertise was not simply drawn upon by the Inspectorate but actually dominated the review. However, since the relationship with Headquarters was weaker on this topic, the subsequent response was both more explicit and more controversial.

We can conclude that, in the area of thematic reviews, the Inspectorate has shared a set of concerns with the managers of the Scottish Prison Service, the review of social work being the only exception to this subordinate working relationship. Through a process of negotiation, the Inspectorate has tended to censor itself and has been loath to pursue an independent line in its thematic reviews, which, in any case, have not been at the forefront of its activities.

Incident reports

The Inspectorate has carried out one major investigation into prison disturbances in Scotland: those which took place in Edinburgh between 27 October and 1 November 1986 and in Peterhead between 9 November and 13 November 1986. The then Secretary of State for Scotland, Malcolm Rifkind, appointed the Chief Inspector to conduct an inquiry on 14 November 1986. The Chief Inspector's terms of reference were:

1 To investigate allegations made by Peterhead inmates in the course of incidents which took place at HM Prison Edinburgh... and at HM Prison Peterhead...;
2 To interview, individually or in groups, Peterhead inmates who wish to put forward views;
3 To interview, individually or in groups, staff who have dealt with Peterhead inmates, who wish to put forward views;

4 To ensure that any inmate who claims to have been protesting about conditions or treatment at Peterhead Prison during either of the incidents mentioned above is given the opportunity to make his views known at interview or in writing even if he is temporarily held in an establishment other than Peterhead Prison;

5 To review the adequacy and effectiveness of procedures for responding to individual, specific complaints from inmates or groups of inmates about their treatment at Peterhead Prison; and

6 To review the use of existing channels of complaint available to inmates in relation to the matters indicated above.

(HMCIP(S) 1987b)

The Chief Inspector carried out the inquiry in three stages (ibid.: paras. 1.1–1.14). In the first, 240 interviews were conducted with prisoners and staff at Peterhead, as well as with senior governors and other members of the criminal justice system; in the second, the Inspectorate sifted the material accumulated during the first phase and visited England to examine the dispersal system; and in the third, the Inspectorate met the Director and Deputy Directors of the Prison Service as well as the Governor and Deputy Governor of Peterhead.

The report, which runs to ninety-nine pages, examines the 'history and role' of Peterhead's accommodation, regimes, support services, complaints procedures, catering, visits and letters, parole, staff, classification, and the problems of 'difficult and dangerous' prisoners. The general review which concludes the report made a number of points and developed a particular line of argument (HMCIP(S) 1987b:paras. 13.1–13.12). It maintained that there was no staff brutality at Peterhead and that the actions taken by prisoners could not be 'condoned or justified'. However, it suggested that the regime at Peterhead could be developed as it was felt to be 'dull', and standards at the prison were below those which might be expected. It recognised that there was scope for more psychological intervention and argued that more small units should be developed for the 'disruptive minority'. The Inspectorate accepted the case for building a new maximum-security prison at Peterhead, and, in general, maintained that there should be more dialogue between governors in the field and Headquarters. The report made eleven recommendations as well as twenty-eight points of note.

In the context of the current discussion, six of the Chief Inspector's recommendations are of particular importance. First, he called for the 'role of the Standing Committee on Difficult Prisoners (SCDP) [to] be revised and extended' to produce a greater measure of oversight of the handling of 'difficult' prisoners.[6] Second, more activity on the part of the Visiting Committee was recommended. Third, he called for 'careful and frequent monitoring of all complaints procedures'. Fourth, he recommended an assessment of the limitations on parole for certain categories of prisoner made by the Secretary of State in 1984. Fifth, he recommended that 'long-term inmates, except high security risks and those who were a danger to others, should, where possible, be allocated to a long-term establishment nearer to their home areas'. Finally, a call was made for 'four new, small, alternative, secure units [to] be built' (HMCIP(S) 1987b:paras. 14.1–14.11). This report exemplifies some core aspects of the work of the Inspectorate and we therefore consider it in more detail below. However, before doing so, we examine the content of the Chief Inspector's Annual Reports.

Annual Reports

Since the report for 1986 (HMCIP(S) 1987a), the reports have been written using a consistent set of headings: first, there is a review of the work of the Inspectorate in the year in question; second, some general comments are offered; third, there is a consideration of staff and management issues; fourth, an examination of regimes; fifth, an evaluation of services (or, in later reports, support services); sixth, a discussion of any more general issues which the Inspectorate feels the need to raise; and, finally, there are the Inspectorate's recommendations. Most important for our purposes are the general issues and the recommendations made. We examine these in tandem as they are interconnected in the reports.

In the early years of its operation, the Inspectorate was very concerned with the conditions under which remand prisoners were held. These were singled out for separate discussion in the reports for 1981 and 1984 (HMCIP(S) 1982a and 1985c). Both of these reports contain recommendations for the improvement of the conditions and regimes for remand prisoners. Indeed, the report for 1981 made four interconnected recommendations in this area as well as seven others. Amongst these were recommendations for the appointment of Visiting Committees to Low Moss, Longriggend and for the Legalised Police Cells. These recommendations were repeated in the report for 1983 (HMCIP(S) 1984), which also recommended a review of the method of appointing Visiting Committees.

In his report for 1984 (HMCIP(S) 1985c), the Chief Inspector recommended for the first time that the Prison (Scotland) Rules 1952 should be updated. In his report for 1985 (HMCIP(S) 1986), he expressed his concern at the lack of progress on any such revision and he repeated his recommendation in his next report (HMCIP(S) 1987a). This has clearly been a long and drawn out process as, in the Annual Report of the Prison Service in Scotland for 1989–90, it was reported that 'work was taken forward on the revision of the Prison (Scotland) Rules 1952' (SHHD 1991). However, no indication was given as to the principles underlying the revision or when this might be completed. We discuss below the difficulties that the absence of up-to-date rules pose for the Inspectorate.

In his report for 1986 (HMCIP(S) 1987a), the Chief Inspector drew attention to some issues affecting the long-term prisoner and recommended a system of 'sentence planning' for this group (for a fuller discussion of 'sentence planning', see Chapter 9 below). This theme was reiterated in his report for 1987 (HMCIP(S) 1988b) when a package of measures for long-term prisoners was proposed. In his report for 1986, the CI also recommended additional resources for staff training and, in his report for 1987, he urged that the 'momentum' in this area should be sustained. Prisoners' complaints procedures received a brief mention in the report for 1986.

The report for 1987 (HMCIP(S) 1988b) recommended an increase in the provision of physical education and doing away with dormitory accommodation, as well as some of the other issues mentioned above. The concern with physical education has run through Inspectorate reports since then. In his report for 1988 (HMCIP(S) 1989e), the retiring Chief Inspector took the opportunity to review the troubled period of 1986–8 and made six formal recommendations (the most in any one report since the first for 1981).[7] Two of these concerned the physical fabric of the penal estate, and another called for an audit of the operation of Fresh Start. The Chief Inspector also recommended an improvement in medical facilities, especially for prisoners who were HIV positive. He also called for the implementation of the proposals for small units for 'difficult' prisoners which he had made in his report on the incident at Peterhead (see above). Finally, he called for an enhanced system of classification. The report for 1989 (HMCIP(S) 1990a) recommended a policy statement on 'race relations' in Scottish prisons and again called for action on physical education.

It can be seen that a number of issues and themes have been taken up by the Inspectorate over the period of its operation. However, it is rather difficult to determine where the Chief Inspector has taken the lead and where he has been guided along certain lines by policy shifts within the Prison Service. Many of the Chief Inspector's more important recommendations, e.g. those relating to small units, classification and sentence planning, referred to initiatives that were being promoted or developed within Headquarters, while many of the others, e.g. those relating to physical education, dormitory accommodation and medical facilities, referred to deficiencies in regimes or other practices which were deemed to be inadequate. Sometimes they were acted on, sometimes not. The case of the Prison Rules was particularly problematic in this regard. Years after their updating was first recommended by the Chief Inspector, it was still not complete. We offer an explanation for this in our evaluation of the Inspectorate below.

EVALUATION OF THE INSPECTORATE

Rhodes (1981: xi) has distinguished two different ends of inspection in central and local government and other public bodies, i.e.

1 Inspection to ensure compliance with statutory requirements ('enforcement inspection');
2 Inspection to secure, maintain or improve standards of performance ('efficiency inspection').

It is appropriate to examine the work of HMCIP(S) in relation to these two ends of inspection. The potential for the Inspectorate to carry out 'enforcement inspection' is limited by the obsolescence of the Prison (Scotland) Rules 1952 and Standing Orders. We have pointed out that the Inspectorate has called for their revision many times, but with little success so far. But, despite its call for the rules to be revised, the Inspectorate has only rarely drawn attention to instances where it concluded that the rules had been breached. Even then, as the following example makes clear, its approach has been very cautious:

> our problem lay not in the authority to place certain inmates on a restricted regime but rather in whether the restrictions being carried out under the regime were actually authorised. We do understand the operational arguments which lead to a need for such reactions but continue to feel that existing Rules do not specifically give such authority.
>
> (HMCIP(S) 1986:para. 4.7)

It is important to note the diffidence in the Inspectorate's language and the Inspectorate's sympathetic understanding of operational arguments. We need to ask whether an Inspectorate which is supposedly independent of the Prison Service should show so much understanding for operational considerations which contravene the Prison Rules.

Further, the Inspectorate places little emphasis on the relevance of European or international standards. It makes very few explicit references to the *European Convention on Human Rights* (Council of Europe 1989) or the *United Nations Standard Minimum Rules for the Treatment of Prisoners* (United Nations 1984), although these could be used to inform its activities on a systematic basis in the absence of up-to-date domestic rules.

In terms of 'efficiency inspection', the Inspectorate's record is equally limited. The main problem here is that the Inspectorate does not seem to have developed a clearly articulated set of standards for itself (or to have adopted standards developed elsewhere) against which to measure standards of performance in any one prison. Although, as we have already pointed out, Inspectorate reports on prisons have increased in length, made more recommendations in a somewhat more forceful manner, and commented on the ethos and atmosphere of the prison, these reports have not been produced in accordance with a clear (and agreed) vision of what counts for good practice. To the extent that Inspectorate reports have been shaped by an implicit conception of good practice, this has changed in accordance with changes in personnel rather than in any other way.

The Inspectorate's judgments tend to be intuitive, commonsensical and rooted in experience, in particular in the experience of the governors who have been seconded to the Inspectorate. As these governors are not typically selected on the basis of their professional standing and as governors do not base their professionalism on any independent body of knowledge but rather on knowledge derived from their own experience, it is unlikely that any coherent analytically-based standards will emerge from this source. Although we find ourselves in agreement with the Inspectorate itself here in maintaining that 'it is the job of the Inspectorate to ensure, as far as lies within its power, that minimum acceptable standards are maintained' (HMCIP(S) 1990a:para. 2.9), it is clear that the Inspectorate has not succeeded and, as it is presently constituted, is unlikely to succeed in developing and articulating such a set of standards. In the next section, we explore the reasons for this state of affairs.

DISCOURSE, POWER AND THE INSPECTORATE

In the previous chapter, we explained the weakness of the petition system as a form of accountability in terms of power and discourse and we adopt the same strategy with the Inspectorate. The Inspectorate is in a weak power position with regard to the establishment and accomplishment of independent inspection. It is numerically small, and has a high turnover of staff who do not necessarily have any great commitment to it. In addition, it does not normally have recourse to an independent body of knowledge as a basis on which to make its judgments (the *Parsloe Report* (HMCIP(S) 1987d) shows how much difference this can make). Likewise, it does not draw upon research findings or refer to practices in other prison systems. As a result, its conception of good practice can be characterised as particularistic and parochial rather than general and authoritative. Consequently, 'efficiency inspection', i.e. inspection with the aim of securing, maintaining or improving standards of performance has suffered.

The power of the Inspectorate is also dependent on the status and independence of the Chief Inspector. This is particularly important given the current structural location of the Prison Inspectorate within the Scottish Home and Health Department. A comparison with the English Prisons Inspectorate lends support to this view. The English Prisons Inspectorate currently has a much higher profile than the Scottish Inspectorate. This is largely because Judge Tumin, the Chief Inspector in England, has a power base in the judiciary and his views carry considerable weight in the context of British political life, advantages that recent Chief Inspectors in Scotland, who have been drawn from industry and the civil service, have lacked. Furthermore, independence of mind and judgment are almost occupational traits for judges and the appointment of a judge as Chief Inspector is probably the best way of ensuring the independence of the Inspectorate and giving it a measure of power and authority. It would also enhance its performance of 'enforcement inspection', i.e. ensuring compliance with statutory requirements. This has been particularly weak in Scotland, and reports of the Scottish Inspectorate have made very few references to Prison Rules or Standing Orders let alone to international standards and conventions. In our view, this is in large measure due to the absence of any legal input into its activities. In this connection, it is important to consider further the role of the Chief Inspector. Judge Tumim has successfully introduced legal categories and concepts into the discourse of the English Inspectorate. By comparison, successive Chief Inspectors appear to have had much less influence on the Scottish Inspectorate's discourse. The early Chief Inspectors, who were drawn from industry, lacked an independent power base while the current Chief Inspector has his power base in the civil service. This may have led to a greater emphasis on bureaucratic concerns but all of the Chief Inspectors in Scotland have been much less powerful in relation to the governors on their staff than the current Chief Inspector in England, Judge Tumim. At this point, we turn to a more general analysis of Inspectorate discourse.

A review of 1986–8 by the Chief Inspector (HMCIP(S) 1989e: paras. 7.1–7.9) condenses the main aspects of the Inspectorate's discourse. It begins with an emphasis on the centrality of 'staff' in prisons, arguing that

> recruitment, training, organisation, morale of staff must receive continuing attention and support. Policies on promotion, assessment, terms of reference, provision of adequate communications were all seen as vital and in need of contant review, with every effort being made to link Departmental staff with those in the establishments.
>
> (Ibid.:para. 7.2)

It is clear that the Inspectorate has placed professionalism and professional development at the core of its concerns. In this respect the Inspectorate discourse occupies the professional row of our discourse matrix.

In addition to its general concern with staff training and professional development, two further strands in the Inspectorate's discourse can be identified. On the one hand, there has been a call for 'structured policies on matters such as assessment, allocation, sentence planning and progression for the long-term prisoner' (ibid.:para. 7.3). The Inspectorate has made this point in a forceful manner, as can be seen in the continuation of the above quotation,

> we have repeatedly called for improvements in current practice, which is often woefully inadequate. We raised this matter formally in our Peterhead Inquiry Report and although the matter is given some favourable consideration in *Custody and Care*, little action is yet evident. In our inspection of Edinburgh Prison, which provides the home base for the National Classification Board, this view was confirmed. Although the commitment of Board members, and their methodology, are commendable, the outcome of their work is totally frustrated by problems elsewhere in the Prison Service.
>
> (Ibid.:para. 7.3)

This concern expresses a view which can be located in Cell 1 of our matrix (see Figure 2.5 on p.46), a combination of the bureaucratic focus on a coherent system with the classificatory processes central to rehabilitation. We could give several examples of this, but will confine ourselves to one more quotation which makes the point very clearly:

> We also continue to be concerned regarding the inadequate systems for classifying long-term prisoners (LTPs) after sentence, and the lack of a clear plan for them, linked to progression towards more open conditions. Often the location of LTPs appears to be arbitrary, the result of temporary problems with accommodation or well-intentioned 'trade offs' between governors. We see a need for an ordered system, with initial assessment and classification at a suitable centre within but separate from a main prison.
>
> (HMCIP(S) 1987a:para. 3.3)

In a related fashion, the Inspectorate has called for 'active regimes', to enable staff to go about their jobs in a more professional manner, i.e.

> In almost every area – medical, psychology, education, physical education, training, social work, chaplaincy – there is a requirement for additional resources and better co-ordination of

> efforts. This is not to denigrate the very good work being carried out by dedicated staff in these spheres of activity, more a call to give them greater support and better facilities.
>
> (HMCIP(S) 1989e:para. 7.4)

This shows a connection with professional rehabilitation discourse as represented by Cell 4 of our matrix. In this respect when these sorts of concern are expressed, the Inspectorate discourse occupies the space demarcated by Cells 1 and 4. As the Chief Inspector says,

> 'Rehabilitation' as such may be outmoded, but we believe that every prisoner should be offered the means of improving self-esteem and indeed encouraged to make use of the facilities, always provided there is an element of personal commitment.
>
> (Ibid.:para. 7.4)

This reflects one important strand in the discourse of the Inspectorate, centred on the remnants of rehabilitation discourse. The second strand focuses on control, and is expressed in different ways in different contexts. To illustrate this point we offer three quotations. First, the following from the letter to the Secretary of State which prefaces the Annual Report for 1988:

> Acts of indiscipline and wanton destruction by inmates continued from 1987, but were less severe in 1988 and did not significantly disrupt our planned programme. As the year progressed there was a welcome return towards greater stability, albeit as a result of imposing strict and very limited regimes for lengthy periods on those prisons which had suffered the worst effects.
>
> (HMCIP(S) 1989e:1)

Second, from an earlier Annual Report:

> There is, of course, a small minority of the inmate population who, for their own reasons, seek to cause disruption and who present particular management problems and there are those who are inadequate or who are suffering from what is termed personality disorder.
>
> (HMCIP(S) 1986:para. 4.2)

Third, from the Report of the Peterhead Inquiry:

> We were acutely conscious of the sensitivity of the situation and the difficulties we would face with the timing of the Inquiry, instigated, as it was, hard on the heels of a major and very serious

> incident. Under these circumstances there was an inevitable degree of polarisation between staff and inmate opinion in some respects but, hearteningly, there was also a fair measure of consensus and corroboration between the two.
>
> (HMCIP(S) 1987b:para. 1.3)

and

> It must be said that we find it difficult to comprehend the logic in destroying the best facilities while, ostensibly, protesting about poor facilities.
>
> (Ibid.:para. 3.2)

We see here revealing modes of expression and shifts of emphasis. The Inspectorate desired consensus and agreement between staff and prisoners. There is nothing wrong with that but it is important to ask where and on what basis such consensus is to be found. Whose ground is 'reasonable' can be seen in the contrast between the representation of prisoners' views about the disturbances in Peterhead and those of prison staff. Hence, 'It would be true to say that most inmates we spoke with appeared very open and frank and were not in any way reticent in expressing their views for which we are grateful' (ibid.:2) is written about prisoners while 'We are grateful to the staff with whom we met for their often very reasoned opinions and the candid and forthright manner in which they expressed themselves' (ibid.:3) is written about staff.

Prisoners only appeared to be open and frank whereas staff actually were candid and forthright and had reasoned opinions. One account is presented as if it were more authentic than the other. Furthermore, the fact that the 'illogical' actions taken by prisoners in Peterhead were only performed by a small minority is used to support the case for holding them in highly controlled conditions. The logic is the same as that in the policy document *Assessment and Control* (SPS 1988b) which we examine at some length in Chapter 9 below (see also, Scraton et al. 1991). In abnormal situations, control discourse, represented by Cells 3 and 6 in our matrix, comes through clearly. However, the Inspectorate was clearly aware of the limitations of an undue emphasis on control, pointing out that control for the large majority simply cannot be sustained. Consider, for example, the following discussion in the aftermath of the disturbances which took place in Shotts Prison in September 1988:

> In the context of control, it was clearly evident that this had been fully regained by staff long before our arrival and general morale clearly reflected this. Use of the grille gates on the flats of each hall, to sub-divide the inmate population into manageable groups, was at the heart of the control system employed, and was still fully in evidence during our inspection. That such a design lends itself to swift control methods in times of trouble is not in doubt. Nor is it in doubt that staff benefit enormously from this facility in certain situations. However, and inevitably, there are also disadvantages. An over-dependence on the system leads to lack of communication between staff and inmates and, indeed, to a polarisation of attitudes on both sides of the grilles. Also, because the situation is an artificial one, the degree of true control cannot accurately be gauged. Moreover, there is a temptation to regard the fragmentation of the inmate population as 'normal', and with it a reluctance to revert to more traditional methods of running an establishment.
>
> (HMCIP(S) 1989d:para. 12.4)

Our point is that, for the Inspectorate, 'extreme' methods of control can only be justified for a minority while, for others, a more interpersonal, consensual method is required (cf. Bottoms 1980). This relies upon and is connected to improvements in classification and progression which they have been at such pains to promote (see, for example, HMCIP(S) 1987a:para. 3.3 cited above).

To emphasise the dominance of the modes of discourse referred to above, which occupy, on the one hand, Cells 1 and 4 and, on the other, Cells 3 and 6 in our matrix, we now turn to the more submerged aspects of Inspectorate discourse and to those cells which are absent from it.

The Inspectorate has given voice to the mode of bureaucratic normalising discourse which occupies Cell 2 in our matrix. For example, it has maintained that, 'the principle of aiming for "normalisation" of life within prison is generally accepted and encouragement towards a more responsible attitude to the use of money could be achieved if more practical wages were offered coupled with incentive schemes' (HMCIP(S) 1988b:para. 5.5) and 'While, in general, we favour relaxations to regimes enabling inmates to live a more "normal" life, we have advised on the need for clear instructions and information to all staff when such changes are to be introduced' (HMCIP(S) 1986:para. 4.1). These quotations reveal a mode of discourse which has tended to be subservient to the forms of control and rehabilitation discourse previously identified. However, the movement away from rehabilitation towards normalisation has eroded the Inspectorate's power base. In terms of discourse, the Inspectorate has continued to give voice to a rehabilitationist mode of discourse which 'has had its day' and this has reduced the effectiveness with which it has been able to challenge the dominant mode of discourse, i.e. the discourse of normalisation.

The weakness of legality as a mode of discourse, which we have already noted has weakened the Inspectorate further. Again, the comparison with England and Wales is illustrative. Under the influence of Judge Tumin, juridical discourse has been prominent in the reports of the English Inspectorate, giving them a status and an influence which the reports of the Scottish Inspectorate have lacked. Simple calls for the revision of the Prison (Scotland) Rules 1952 have been unsuccessful, but they would probably have carried more weight if greater attention had been given to deviations from the rules (and from other sets of agreed standards and guidelines) and, more generally, if there was a greater concern with the legal rights of prisoners.

In several respects, the Inspectorate is currently in a weak position. Its staffing and structural location undermine its potential for adopting an independent line. Moreover, it has not mobilised those forms of discourse which would enable it to comment more effectively on current penal practice. In the final chapter (Chapter 10) we offer an outline of how this position could be improved.

Chapter 8

The European Convention on Human Rights

Protecting prisoners' rights?

In Chapter 6, we outlined the different mechanisms for holding the prison system to account which exist in Scotland, distinguished three different models of accountability and assessed the effectiveness of petitions to the Secretary of State which exemplify a bureaucratic form of accountability. In Chapter 7, we analysed the role of the Prisons Inspectorate which embodies a professional form of accountability and, in this chapter, we conclude our review of accountability in the Scottish prison system through an analysis of applications from individual prisoners to the European Commission on Human Rights. As we have already pointed out in Chapter 6, only two applications for judicial review have to date been heard in the Scottish courts and less than ten cases involving Scottish prisoners have been investigated by the Parliamentary Commissioner for Administration. Since there has been a considerably larger number of applications from prisoners held in Scotland to the European Commission on Human Rights, and since these exemplify a juridical form of accountability, an analysis of these applications will enable us to assess the effectiveness of this type of accountability.

We begin this chapter by outlining the nature of the European Convention on Human Rights and the role of the two institutions (the European Commission on Human Rights and the European Court of Human Rights) which were set up to enforce its provisions. We then describe its role in relation to prisons and review some of the leading cases in this field. This is followed by a summary of twelve recent Scottish applications and an account of the ways in which they were handled. Finally, we offer an interpretation of these procedures in terms of discourse and power and assess the extent to which the Convention provides an effective mechanism of accountability. Once again, this makes repeated references to the discourse matrix first introduced in Chapter 2.

THE NATURE OF THE CONVENTION AND THE ROLE OF THE COMMISSION AND THE COURT

The European Convention on Human Rights was signed by the United Kingdom in 1950 and came into effect following ratification by ten states in 1953. The contracting states are required to secure the rights and freedoms set out principally in Articles 2–12 (and, where the state has further contracted to any of the protocols, to the rights and freedoms they establish) for all persons within their jurisdiction. The following fundamental rights and freedoms are guaranteed by the Convention: the right to life (Article 2), freedom from torture and inhuman or degrading treatment (Article 3), freedom from slavery and forced or compulsory labour (Article 4), the right to liberty and security of person (Article 5), the right to a fair and public trial within a reasonable time (Article 6), freedom from the retrospective effect of penal legislation (Article 7), the right to respect for private and family life, home and correspondence (Article 8), freedom of thought, conscience and religion (Article 9), freedom of expression (Article 10), freedom of assembly (Article 11) and the right to marry and found a family (Article 12). Articles 13–18 contain general provisions which apply to the rights and freedoms covered by Articles 2–12; for example, Article 13 requires that everyone to whom the rights and freedoms apply shall have an effective remedy before the domestic (national) courts even where the action complained of is the execution of public policy by civil servants, and Article 17 makes it clear that the rights guaranteed by Articles 9 and 10 cannot be used to defend activities which are undemocratic or aimed at the destruction of other rights guaranteed by the Convention. Article 19 establishes the structure and competence of the Commission and the Court whose role is to ensure the observance of the commitments undertaken by the contracting parties.

Thirteen of the twenty-one members of the Council of Europe have incorporated the Convention in their internal law,[1] which means that its provisions can be invoked and directly enforced in their domestic courts but the United Kingdom has not done so. The other eight members, including the United Kingdom, have recognised the right of individual petition and individuals (or groups of individuals) who allege that they have been victims of a breach of the Convention to petition the Commission.[2] However, they may only do so after all domestic remedies have been exhausted and within six months of any final domestic decision.

Administrative procedures

Once an application has been submitted, the Commission has first to decide upon the admissibility of the complaint. The Government of the state complained against may be asked to submit observations on the application (or parts of the application) by a particular date, which can often be moved back at the Government's request. Once submitted, these written observations are sent to the applicant who is then invited to comment on them. The knowledge that this occurs can, of course, affect the nature of the evidence put forward by the Government, as it may not wish to reveal particular administrative decisions and procedures to the applicant. This is particularly pertinent in the context of prisons, since the basis for decision-making is often kept secret (for critiques of Government secrecy in the UK, see Cohen and Taylor 1979 and Fitzgerald and Sim 1979). However, to strike a more optimistic note, it may be that the mere existence of the Convention has aided some of the recent liberalisation in this area.

At this point the Commission takes a decision on the admissibility of the application. A large proportion of applications are declared inadmissible. If the application is found to be admissible, the Commission will attempt to help the parties involved reach a settlement to the dispute. Such a settlement will, of course, have to come within the terms of the Convention, and the issues involved may be investigated by the Commission. The investigations and attempts to promote a 'friendly' settlement will often be prolonged and involve further submissions from the Government and the applicant. If a friendly settlement is secured the Commission will report on it.

If there is no friendly settlement, the Commission will send a report on its judgment (or judgments if there is dissention) to the Council of Ministers, which usually follows the opinion of the Commission. The Government involved or the Commission may then bring the case before the European Court of Human Rights. This happens within three months of the submission to the Council of Ministers. The Court, in turn, will adjudicate on the issues, using both written and oral evidence, and will make a decision on breach of the Convention. This may take place years after the initial application was submitted. Indeed, this may be the case even if a friendly settlement is reached.

Table 8.1 shows that only a very small proportion of individual applications are held to be admissible. In recent years, approximately 3,000 provisional files a year have been opened in response to applications or inquiries and about 600 of these applications have been officially registered.[3] However, only a small proportion of these were eventually declared admissible. This is understandable in a system of free application but it is significant that the proportion declared admissible has increased quite substantially over the period. In the eighteen years from 1955–72, it was 2.13 per cent but in the subsequent five-year periods, it increased to 3.04 per cent in 1973–7, 5.57 per cent in 1978–82 and 8.35 per cent in 1983–7.

Of the 523 cases which were declared admissible, sixty-nine cases (involving seventy-seven applicants) led to friendly settlements, seventy-four (involving 161 applicants) were decided by the Council of Ministers, 144 cases (involving 198 applicants) were brought before the Court while forty-two cases were terminated in some other way (Council of Europe 1989). Thus, the number of cases that have reached the Court has been very small – less than 150 cases over a period of more than thirty years.

National comparisons – the UK position

Applications from the United Kingdom have always constituted a substantial proportion of the total. For example, in 1983, 785 (25 per cent) of the 3,150 provisional files opened and 152 (30 per cent) of the 499 registered applications were from the UK. Table 8.2 provides a breakdown of registered applications by the country of origin.

A cursory inspection of Table 8.2 might suggest that the United Kingdom's record on human rights is significantly poorer than the other sixteen signatories to the Convention who have recognised the right of individual petition. This may indeed be the case, although it is not as clear as these figures seem to suggest. As the Home Office has pointed out, if population is taken into account the UK's record is no worse than that of many other states. However, as Table 8.3 shows, the UK still has a worse record than other states which are roughly comparable in size.

Table 8.1 Numbers of individual applications to the Commission declared admissible and non-admissible, 1955–87

	1955–72	*1973–7*	*1978–82*	*1983*	*1984*	*1985*	*1986*	*1987*	*Total*
Provisional files	na	9,560	12,598	3,150	3,007	2,831	2,869	3,675	37,690
Applications registered	5,960	2,153	2,097	499	586	596	706	860	13,457
Decisions taken	5,069	2,172	2,207	436	582	582	511	590	12,149
Applications declared inadmissible and struck off	4,745	1,919	1,785	363	450	449	375	498	10,584
Ditto after communication with respondent Government	216	287	299	44	78	63	94	61	1,142
Applications declared admissible	108	66	123	29	54*	70	42	31	523
Decision to reject taken in course of examining merits	1	7	–	–	–	–	–	–	8

Note: * Including twenty-one prisoners' correspondence cases.
Source: Council of Europe (1988:84)

Table 8.2 Registered applications by country of origin, 1981–7

	1981	*1982*	*1983*	*1984*	*1985*	*1986*	*1987*	*Total*
Austria	32	30	29	36	42	61	76	306
Belgium	22	27	18	41	33	44	64	249
Denmark	3	7	9	5	13	11	9	57
France	7	93	45	59	70	86	115	475
Germany	109	98	93	115	106	106	108	735
Iceland	–	–	–	–	1	1	1	3
Ireland	9	23	9	8	5	4	5	63
Italy	20	15	17	21	54	62	110	299
Liechtenstein	–	–	–	2	1	–	–	3
Luxembourg	–	1	7	1	1	2	1	13
Netherlands	21	24	29	45	35	48	53	255
Norway	3	2	5	4	3	3	2	22
Portugal	3	8	2	5	10	7	15	50
Spain	4	12	10	15	19	17	16	93
Sweden	8	18	46	51	64	68	77	332
Switzerland	31	42	27	49	34	50	60	293
UK	132	190	152	128	113	138	140	993
Total	404	590	498	585	604	709*	865**	4,255

Notes: * Includes one registered application from Greece.
** Includes eleven registered applications from Greece and two from Malta.

Sources: Council of Europe (1984:325); Council of Europe (1986:144); Council of Europe (1988:107)

Table 8.3 Frequency of cases, standardised by size of population

	Average no. of cases per year 1981–7	*Population mid-1981 (millions)*	*Cases per 100,000 population*	*Size of population per case*
Austria	43.7	7.5	0.0058	171,625
Belgium	35.4	9.9	0.0036	279,661
Denmark	8.0	5.1	0.0016	637,500
France	67.9	54.0	0.0013	795,287
FRG	105.0	61.0	0.0017	580,952
Iceland	0.5	0.2	0.0025	400,000
Ireland	9.0	3.4	0.0026	377,778
Italy	46.0	56.2	0.0008	1,221,739
Luxembourg	1.9	0.4	0.0048	210,526
Netherlands	36.7	14.2	0.0026	386,921
Norway	3.1	4.1	0.0008	1,322,581
Portugal	7.1	9.8	0.0007	1,380,282
Spain	13.3	38.0	0.0004	2,857,143
Sweden	47.4	8.3	0.0057	175,105
Switzerland	41.7	6.5	0.0064	155,875
UK	141.7	56.0	0.0025	395,201

These figures should also be viewed with caution and do not necessarily mean that the UK has a poor record on human rights. It may be, for example, that UK citizens are more prone, for a variety of reasons, to forward applications to the Commission than citizens of other states. This might itself be due to the fact that the European Convention has not been incorporated into UK law since domestic remedies that are available to citizens of other Convention countries are not available to United Kingdom residents. However, all in all, the United Kingdom's record does not look good.

PRISONS AND THE CONVENTION

The Convention contains a number of Articles relevant to imprisonment, and prisoners (and other groups held in detention) have always been one of the major groups using the system. The statistics in Table 8.4 confirm this.

However, as can be seen in this table, the proportion of registered applications from detained or interned applicants has decreased significantly since 1975. However, among the small number of cases to reach the Court, a substantial proportion have concerned imprisonment. As Fawcett (1985) notes, 'By the end of

Table 8.4 Registered applications from detained or interned applicants, 1955–87

Year	*Total number of applications*	*Applicants detained or interned*	*%*
1955	138	24	17
1960	291	67	23
1965	310	164	53
1970	379	133	35
1975	466	227	49
1980	390	87	22
1981	404	84	21
1982	590	91	15
1983	499	60	12
1984	586	75	13
1985	596	96	16
1986	706	96	14
1987	860	103	12

Source: Council of Europe (1988:109)

1983, seventy-two cases had been sent to the Court, of which about fifteen involved imprisonment or its conditions. Four of these latter emanated from the United Kingdom.'

The provisions of the Convention as they concern prisoners

The Convention itself does not refer specifically to imprisonment, although Article 10(3) of the Civil and Political Rights Covenant, which the United Kingdom has ratified, does specify that

> the penitentiary system shall comprise treatment of prisoners, the essential aim of which shall be their treatment and eventual rehabilitation.

Nevertheless, many of the Articles of the Convention are relevant to imprisonment and, at least in theory, should impose constraints on prison administrators and a corresponding measure of protection for individual prisoners. Houchin (n.d.) has carried out a very useful review of ECHR case law in the areas of prison work, training and education; systems of conditional release, i.e. parole; transfers, allocation and classification; prison conditions; the investigation of grievances; and medical care which demonstrates that several of the Articles have been invoked by applicants who have sought to prove that the terms and conditions of their imprisonment were in breach of the Convention. However, although some of these applications have been successful, most of them have not and the impact of the Convention on imprisonment in countries that have signed the Convention is rather slight. The following examples, taken from Houchin's review, illustrate the difficulties that prisoners have faced in their attempts to invoke the Convention as a means of challenging the terms and conditions of their imprisonment.

1 The Commission has rejected claims that interruption of a pre-arranged training programme by transfer or exclusion from training opportunities by being held out of classification in a local prison or by classification to Category A were in breach of the Convention.
2 It was early established by the Commission that the Convention conveyed no rights of choice as to where prisoners would serve their sentence.
3 In a case brought by twenty-one German prisoners which sought to challenge the legality of prison labour, the Court dismissed all the claims that were put forward, i.e. that prisoners were underpaid, that their social security payments were discontinued and that they were contributing to private profits. It found that none of these facts was in breach of the Convention.
4 At various times, it has been held that being forced to sleep without a mattress, fed on a restricted diet, kept in solitary confinement for lengthy periods or required to take exercise alone in an enclosed 'pit' were not inhuman or degrading and did not contravene Article 3 of the Convention.
5 Likewise, it has been held that the conditions under which 'strict escapee', Category A and Rule 43 (the English equivalent of Rule 36) prisoners have been held for periods of up to nine years are not in breach of the Convention.
6 The Commission has ruled that decisions relating to classification are administrative decisions and that, as such, the standards of natural justice do not apply and it has no powers to review them.

Despite this litany of failure, there have been a number of successful cases. Five of these have been brought against the United Kingdom Government and are summarised below.

Ireland v. UK

The applicants in this case had all been taken into custody for the purpose of interrogation and subjected to the 'five techniques' used by the armed forces, i.e. wall-standing, hooding, deprivation of sleep, subjection to noise, and deprivation of food and drink. The Commission found that the combined use of these techniques constituted torture and inhuman treatment in terms of Article 3, arguing that disorientation and sensory deprivation constituted 'a modern form of torture'. The Court did not go quite that far, but nevertheless concluded that, taken together, the 'five techniques' constituted inhuman treatment. As a result of the Court's judgment, the UK Government not only paid compensation to detainees who had been subjected to these techniques of interrogation but also ended their use.

Golder v. UK

The applicant in this case, Mr Sidney Golder, challenged the right of the prison authorities to prevent him from seeking legal advice. The complaint arose because he had been mistakenly identified as having been involved in an assault on a prison officer and was concerned that this incident would adversely affect his parole prospects. He petitioned the Home Secretary for a transfer to another prison and requested permission to consult a solicitor with the intention of bringing a civil action for defamation against the prison officer. Both requests were refused and Mr Golder complained to the Commission against the Home Secretary's refusal to grant him permission to consult a solicitor and against the Governor's decision to intercept his letters. The Commission dismissed the second claim on the grounds that Mr Golder had not exhausted the existing domestic remedies before making it but found that his rights of access to the courts under Article 6(1) and to respect for correspondence under Article 8 had been breached. The Government adopted a minimalist response, allowing prisoners to communicate with their solicitors if they intended to commence civil proceedings. However, where the proceedings were against the prison authorities, prisoners would have to make the nature of their complaint known to the authorities and receive a reply before initiating proceedings (this was known as the 'prior ventilation rule') and their letters could still be read by the authorities.

Silver and others v. UK

The obviously unsatisfactory nature of the prior ventilation rule did not last long since, by the time the *Golder* case was decided, another important case was in its initial stages. Seven applications, covering sixty-two instances of letters stopped by the prison authorities, had been lodged with the Commission at various dates between 1972 and 1975. One of these applicants was Mr Silver and it is by this name that the conjoined case is known.[4] In 1980, the Commission concluded that the stopping of these letters was not only in breach of Articles 6(1) and 8 but that the absence of an effective remedy for those violations was also in breach of Article 13. In 1983, the Government responded by liberalising its policy on correspondence and changing the prior ventilation rule to a 'simultaneous ventilation rule'.[5] Standing Orders were amended and, in an unusual step, made available to prisoners.[6] In the light of its acceptance of the Commission's findings, the Government then invited the Court not to make a ruling. The Court refused to take this line on the grounds that the changes in policy could not restore a right which had been violated beforehand and which was the subject of a claim under the Convention. As far as the question of adequate remedies was concerned, the Court held that, where the practice complained of was incompatible with the Convention, the remedies were inadequate and Article 13 was violated but, where they were compatible, the range of available remedies could be regarded as appropriate.

Weeks v. UK

Mr Weeks had originally been given a discretionary life sentence for armed robbery, not only for punitive but also explicitly for rehabilitative and incapacitative reasons. He had been released on parole but was recalled fifteen months later as a result of further minor offences and evidence of instability which suggested that he remained a 'persistent risk'. He complained under Article 5(4) that, at the time of his re-conviction, he was unable to have the lawfulness of his recall determined by a court or, subsequently, to have his detention reviewed at regular intervals. The Commission held and the Court ruled that there had been a breach of Article 5(4) on the grounds that the Parole Board's procedures were not sufficiently judicial. It followed that cases such as this required to be kept under regular and frequent review in just the same way as prisoners serving mandatory life sentences and prisoners who had not already been released on parole.

Campbell and Fell v. UK

Following disturbances at Albany Prison in 1976 both applicants had substantial periods of remission removed by the prison's Board of Visitors. Charged with mutiny and gross personal violence to a prison officer, Mr Campbell lost 570 days of remission, while Mr Fell lost 590 days. In addition, both men were subject to periods of cellular confinement.

Both applicants alleged that they had been refused permission to seek legal advice in connection with claims for compensation for the injuries they had incurred in the incident. In addition, Mr Fell claimed that he had been refused permission to consult his solicitors out of hearing of the prison officers. The Commission, and subsequently the Court, held that these restrictions were in breach of Articles 6(1) and 8. Mr Fell further alleged that the prison authorities had refused him permission to correspond with individuals on the grounds that they were neither relatives nor existing friends but this was also held to be in breach of Article 8.

The case was also important as a test of the fitness of Boards of Visitors to conduct disciplinary hearings. Mr Campbell alleged that he had been convicted of disciplinary charges which amounted in substance to criminal charges and should have been heard in a court of law;[7] that the Board was neither independent nor impartial; that the hearing was not held in public and the decision was not publicly announced; that he had not been allowed legal assistance or representation; and that he had not had a fair hearing. The Court dismissed most of these claims, but held that the Board's failure to make its decisions public was in breach of Article 6(1) and that Mr Campbell's inability to obtain legal assistance or representation constituted a violation of Article 6(3).

THE IMPACT OF THE ECHR ON THE SCOTTISH PRISON SERVICE

The five cases summarised above confirm that cases taken to the Commission and the Court under the Convention have had some limited impact on the administration of the Scottish Prison Service.

This impact has been felt in a small number of areas, in particular prisoners' correspondence and access to legal advice and representation, but, considered against a background of the many areas of prison administration which have been untouched by the Convention, our preliminary conclusion must be that the ECHR constitutes a rather feeble form of accountability. In order to explore further how the Scottish Prison Service sought to defend itself against applications brought under the Convention and whether, and if so to what extent, it altered its existing procedures in response to these applications, we examined the files (kept at Headquarters) relating to twelve cases which were either currently under consideration by the Commission or the Court, or had recently been considered. We also had access to relevant policy files and files describing the actions taken in previous cases and refer to those where appropriate.

As we have argued in a general way throughout this book, we are not only interested in the specific outcomes of administrative decisions, but also in the processes through which decisions are reached and the discourses that are mobilised in the course of such processes. With this in mind, we present a brief outline of the administrative procedures that are followed by the UK Government in Scottish cases. This is followed by an account of the twelve cases and then by an analysis of the ways in which they were handled in terms of the discourses employed by those concerned and the power relations between them.

Administrative procedures followed in Scottish cases

The general procedure followed is set out in Figure 8.1. The way in which applications to the Commission are dealt with has become relatively formalised over a period of years as the stages that have to be gone through have become more familiar to the participants in the process. The procedure begins with the initial application by the prisoner which is submitted on a standard form. Applications are often backed up by extensive documentation, indeed in one case a prisoner submitted his diary as evidence.[8] However, this was not on file and was probably not sent to the Government by the Commission.

As soon as an application has been received a provisional file is opened. However, there is often a delay before it is examined and a decision taken about whether or not to register it officially. Once

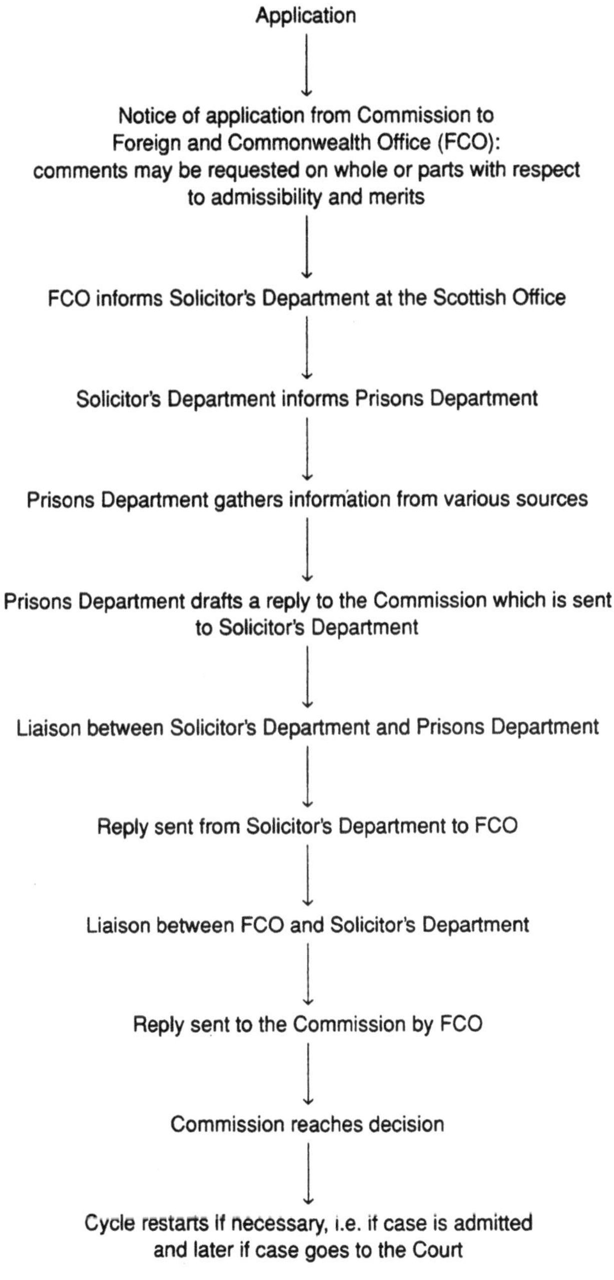

Figure 8.1 Administrative procedure followed in Scottish cases to ECHR

the application has been registered, the Commission will ask the Government to submit observations or to comment on particular aspects of the case. It seems clear that the Commission makes some kind of preliminary decision about the admissibility of an application in determining the nature of the comments asked for.

Requests for information or comment are sent by the Commission to the Foreign and Commonwealth Office (FCO) in London and any subsequent correspondence between the Government and Strasbourg goes through the FCO. Once the FCO has received a communciation from the Commission relating to a Scottish case, details are sent to the Solicitor's Department at the Scottish Office. Most of the applications were dealt with by one legal officer who would contact the Prison Service for information and instructions on how to proceed, although he would, of course, also advise on the line to be taken in replying to an application. However, his inquiries were often of a purely factual nature.

The legal officer (L) in the Solicitor's Department communicated with the Principal (P) in Headquarters of the Prison Service who was responsible for dealing with ECHR cases. P gathered the information requested although specific tasks would be delegated to members of his branch. This involved contacting those working in establishments, as well as scrutinising records held at Headquarters. The degree of difficulty involved in gathering this information obviously varied from case to case. If the case involved a complaint about medical treatment, the Chief Medical Officer would be contacted and medical records consulted. The information requested might be very specific. For example, if a prisoner complained that the nature of the visits he received was such as to infringe his rights to family life, it would be necessary to find out what the detailed procedures for visits at a particular prison were several years before. Given the scope for different interpretations of Prison Rules, Standing Orders and Circular Instructions on 'the ground', it was important, from the Government's point of view, to ensure that precise details were gathered from those who had day-to-day responsibility for the implementation of official procedures.

Once the relevant and necessary information had been obtained, a reply to the Commission would be drafted by P. This draft would then be sent to L who would revise it in consultation with P. The revised draft, with the information requested, would then be passed to the FCO in London. The legal officer dealing with the case there would then liaise with L, before it was sent to the Commission by the FCO. The Commission would then decide on the admissibility of the case or possibly adjourn it pending a decision on other cases which raised similar issues. A similar procedure to the above would be followed if the Commission asked for additional information or if further comment was requested on the merits of the case.

The parties to an application might also be invited to an oral hearing which would normally take place at the later stages of the process. The procedures adopted were formal and legalistic. The parties would be legally represented with counsel speaking from prepared texts and answering few oral questions.

Once a decision had been taken, or anticipated given the probable outcome of other cases before the Commission or the Court, there might be a follow-up set of operations within the Prison Service, involving the redrafting of Standing Orders or the drafting of new procedures. This would probably involve discussion and negotiation between legal officers in the FCO, the Solicitor's Department in the Scottish Office and civil servants at Headquarters of the Scottish Prison Service.

We now summarise the twelve cases which were either under consideration or had recently been considered by the Commission or the Court.

Shields v. UK

This application was introduced on 3 December 1975 and registered on 29 March 1976. Admissibility was examined on 10 July 1978 and the UK Government was informed that it concerned censorship of correspondence by the prison authorities and Mr Shields' resulting inability to initiate civil litigation. The Commission noted that it raised similar issues to a number of other correspondence cases, including the *Silver* case, which were before it and those parts dealing with correspondence were adjourned pending the outcome of the other cases. The other complaints raised by the applicant were declared inadmissible.

In its reply, the Government argued that the letter in question was 'suppressed for reasons other than the fact that the applicant may have been seeking legal advice' on the grounds that it contained 'statements about private individuals (including members of the judiciary) which are patently scandalous or libellous or otherwise deliberately calculated to do them harm' and noted that the applicant had not been stopped from seeking legal advice on other occasions. Furthermore, it argued that the stopping of the letter was justifiable under Article 8 since it was in accordance with the law (the Prison Rules) and 'necessary for the protection of the rights and freedoms of others'.

After the final decision of the Court in *Silver and Others v. UK*, the Government conceded that, although stopping the letter had been in accordance with Standing Orders at the time, it was a breach of Article 8 and announced that Standing Orders had been altered.

Fischer v. UK

This application was introduced on 21 June 1979 and registered on 16 August 1979. The parts of the application dealing with the applicant's transfer to Inverness Prison and the stopping of thirteen items of correspondence (which raised issues of language discrimination and unfair treatment since other prisoners' letters were not censored) were declared inadmissible by the Commission on 5 October 1981. The Government was invited to submit written observations on the admissibility and merits of the remainder of the application, which dealt with two letters from the applicant, then in the Segregation Unit in Inverness Prison. One letter, to Ms Rose Innes, had been stopped by the prison authorities because Ms Innes was campaigning for the closure of the Segregation Unit; the other, to Ms Linda Istead, c/o Ms Rose Innes, was stopped because the prison authorities considered that it was meant for Ms Innes and that Mr Fischer was attempting to circumvent the restrictions on writing to her.

The Government's observations were submitted on 23 February 1982. The Commission adjourned consideration of admissibility pending the outcome of *Silver and Others v. UK* (see above) and (again) declared the remainder of the application inadmissible. After the final judgment in the *Silver* case on 24 October 1983, the Government was invited to waive objections to admissibility. The Government agreed and submitted observations on merits on 19 June 1984.

The Commission deliberated on the merits of the case on 4 March 1985 and adopted its report on 13 March 1985. The Commission noted the Government's concession that interference with the applicant's correspondence constituted a violation of

Article 8 of the Convention and that the Standing Orders which prohibited correspondence aimed at stimulating public petition and the circumvention of censorship regulations had been withdrawn but, because the reforms had not been in place at the relevant time, unanimously found against the Government. In spite of this, the Government was opposed to the payment of compensation on the grounds that no one had suffered from the interception of the correspondence. Although no information on the outcome of this case was available, it can safely be assumed that Mr Fischer did not receive compensation.

Burke v. UK

This application, which was introduced on 2 July 1978 and registered on 5 April 1979, complained about the conditions in Peterhead and, in particular, the difficulties associated with visits at that establishment. A preliminary examination of admissibility was carried out on 30 April 1980 when further information was requested from the Government on the number and duration of visits allowed to prisoners in Peterhead, the procedures for granting supplementary visits and whether or not the applicant had requested one. After consultation, the Government replied by setting out the regulations concerning visits, explaining that the governor had discretion to grant supplementary visists but that he only did so 'infrequently' and noting that there was no record of the applicant requesting supplementary visits. The application was declared inadmissible on 10 October 1980.

McCallum v. UK

In this application, which was introduced on 31 August 1981 and registered on 16 September 1981, a variety of complaints were made. In essence the applicant complained about 'the inhuman and degrading treatment and punishment' he had received in the Inverness Segregation Unit, that his family life and correspondence had been interfered with and that there were no remedies for these conditions and issues. The applicant was supported by the Scottish Council for Civil Liberties (SCCL).

The application was registered on 4 October 1983 and the Government was invited to submit observations on the admissibility and merits of the parts of the application dealing with conditions in the Inverness Unit (under Article 3) and the availability of an effective remedy (under Article 13); those parts of the application dealing with his family life and correspondence being adjourned pending judgment in the *Silver* case. In response to this request, the Government argued that conditions in the Segregation Unit did not constitute a punishment regime and that confinement in the Unit did not reach a level of severity that would result in a breach of Article 3. The Government also argued that in aggregate the procedures that were available for reviewing prisoners detained in the Unit and the right to make representations did not breach Article 13.

The application was examined by the Commission on 9 July 1984 when it was decided that the parts relating to the conditions of detention in the Inverness Unit were inadmissible. The Government was then invited to submit further comments on the admissibility and merits of the applicant's complaints about correspondence and the availability of a remedy for his complaint in this respect. The Commission also asked for supplementary observations in respect of the applicant's complaint concerning the non-availability of a remedy for his complaints about the regime in the Inverness Unit. In response the Government admitted that several letters should not have been stopped, pointed out that procedures had since been altered with the introduction of the new Standing Order M, and listed the available remedies. In a second (undated) judgment, the Commission declared those parts of the application dealing with correspondence and remedies admissible but adjourned those parts which referred to the available remedies pending a judgment in the *Boyle and Rice* case (see below). Following the decision of the Court in *Boyle and Rice* on 27 April 1988, Mr McCallum's case eventually came to Court on 21 May 1990. His counsel conceded that 'effective judicial remedies through the national courts' were available and that there had been no breach of Article 13. In its judgment of 30 August 1990, the Court confirmed that the restrictions on Mr McCallum's correspondence constituted a violation of Article 8 but declined to award compensation.

McQueenie v. UK

This application was introduced on 1 March 1982 and registered on 17 June 1982. It originally concerned three issues. First, the applicant's failure to obtain adequate medical treatment at the prison hospital as a result of being supplied with the wrong size of surgical leg supports. Second, being stopped from writing to certain welfare organisations in connection with an attempt to persuade the Secretary of State to use his discretionary powers to submit the appellant's case to the Court of Criminal Appeal. Third, having various other letters stopped by the prison authorities.

As far as the first issue was concerned, the Commission held on 1 March 1983 that this did not amount to severe ill-treatment under Article 3 which prohibits inhumane or degrading treatment. As far as the stopping of correspondence was concerned, the case was first adjourned pending the outcome of *Silver and Others v. UK*. Once the *Silver* case was decided, the Solicitor to the Scottish Office recommended that 'in the light of the judgment. . .we should concede both the admissibility and the merits of this case'. At the first hearing on 4 March 1985, the application was declared admissible with no evidence being presented to the contrary. At a second hearing on 2 July 1985, the Commission found in favour of the appellant on the merits, arguing that interference with the applicant's correspondence was a violation of Article 8 of the Convention. As in the *Fischer* case, the Government was opposed to the payment of compensation although the prison authorities were clearly of the view that he had a stronger case than Fischer. However, a letter from Headquarters to the Solicitor's Department made it clear that the Prison Service was not prepared to concede on this issue: 'McQueenie has much better cause for complaint than Fischer and for this reason I have prepared a much fuller statement of why he should not get compensation.' No information on the final outcome of this case was available. However, as in the *Fischer* case, it can safely be assumed that Mr McQueenie did not receive compensation.

Wardlaw v. UK

This application was introduced on 6 November 1982 and registered on 11 January 1983. The applicant complained about conditions in the Inverness Segregation Unit under Article 3 of the Convention and the lack of effective remedies under Article 13. The case is very similar to the *McCallum* case (see above) and they were often considered together by the Government. For example, the arguments produced about the Segregation Unit were exactly the same. Thus, in both cases, the Government argued that transfer to the Unit was not a punishment and that conditions in the Unit did not reach the level of severity necessary for them to breach Article 3. The Government also maintained that the remedies that were generally available throughout the Scottish prison system together with the possibility of representation to the Inverness Unit Review Board and the Standing Committee on Difficult Prisoners were not in breach of Article 13. On 9 July 1984, Mr Wardlaw's application was declared inadmissible under Article 3. On 10 July 1985, it was declared admissible under Article 13, although judgment on this was adjourned pending a decision in the *Boyle and Rice* case (see below). Following the decision of the Court on 27 April 1988, both parties were invited to submit further observations on the merits of the case. However, in spite of repeated attempts to contact Mr Wardlaw, no reply was received and the application was therefore struck off.

Steele v. UK

This application, which was introduced on 24 January 1984 and registered on 24 February 1984, concerned the applicant's detention in the Inverness Segregation Unit, the procedures for keeping him in the Unit and the availability of a remedy concerning these issues. Like *McCallum*, the applicant was supported by the Scottish Council for Civil Liberties (SCCL) which claimed that he was subjected to 'inhuman and degrading' treatment in the Unit contrary to Article 3; that he was subjected to this treatment without 'notice, charge, representation, presentation of evidence, opportunity to be heard or access to an adjudication' in violation of Articles 5 and 6; and that there was no domestic remedy available to him under Article 13.

The Government was not asked for comments at this stage pending the decisions in the *McCallum* and *Wardlaw* cases (see above) but the Commission did ask for specific information on how long the applicant had been held in the Segregation Unit, what the administrative reason for his detention there was and whether the detention had had any effects on his health. With respect to this latter point, the Commission asked to see the applicant's medical records. The Solicitors' Office formulated replies to these questions but the application was struck off on 9 December 1985 after the applicant's legal representatives failed to reply to the Commission's letters.

Nelson v. UK

This application was introduced on 24 April 1984 and registered on 9 August 1984. The applicant argued that, due to his age at the time of his arrest and trial (he was 15), he was denied the possibility of remission. He was sentenced to nine years for attempted murder in 1977 under Section 206(2) of the Criminal Procedure (Scotland) Act 1975. This provides that

> Where a child is convicted and the court is of the opinion that none of the other methods of dealing with the child is suitable, the court may sentence him to be detained for such period as may be specified in the sentence; and where such a sentence has been passed, the child shall during that period be liable to be detained in such place and on such conditions as the Secretary of State shall direct.

The applicant alleged discrimination under Article 5, taken in conjunction with Article 14 of the Convention. His argument was that he had been deprived of liberty to a greater extent than he would have been if he had been sentenced in England.[9] He also alleged discrimination on age grounds since, if he had been 16 when he was sentenced, he would have been entitled to remission.

From the available evidence, it would appear that the Government expected to lose this case. Its response to the first allegation was to point out that the United Kingdom had three separate systems of law which applied to different parts of the country and functioned as separately as the different legal systems of different states. The Government went on to point out that the logic of the applicant's case would be to require the harmonisation of the separate systems of criminal law but that 'this would be a ridiculous requirement which cannot have been intended by those who drafted the Convention'. Its response to the second allegation was to question whether age was a ground for discrimination to which Article 14 applied since it was not explicitly mentioned and discrimination on age grounds was frequently justified. However, many of those involved had doubts about the strength of the Government's case. As the Solicitor to the Scottish Office wrote to a Legal Adviser in the FCO

> The weakness of our explanation is that, while it seems perfectly reasonable to have different treatments for people who actually are children, it is less easy to justify for people like the applicant

> whose sentence drags on into adulthood and who are actually detained in adult institutions. The Commission may well ask at some stage why we do not commute these sentences into equivalent young offender or adult sentences and thereafter allow remission to run. I have ignored the point.

The ploy was successful but, in his reply to the Government's observations, Mr Ashman (who was representing the applicant) pointed out an inconsistency between the Government's claim that the applicant's case was first reviewed by the Parole Board after he had served three years of his sentence and their earlier claim that his case had been kept under review throughout his sentence. The Government was forced to concede that the earlier claim was erroneous. An official at Headquarters wrote 'As a layman, it seems to me that legally and logically he [Nelson] has a point' and added, in an internal memo, 'some people within the Prison Service are doubtful about the strength of the Government's case'.

In its reply, the Government pointed out that Section 206 cases were legally eligible for release on licence and they went on to explain that an administrative practice had grown up for such cases to be reviewed a few months before the prisoner had served one-third of his sentence or one year, whichever was the later. After further correspondence between the parties, the Commission, rather surprisingly, declared the application inadmissible in November 1986.

Hodgson v. UK

This application, which was introduced on 15 October 1984 and registered on 12 February 1985, concerned the stopping of the applicant from writing to the Justiciary Office in the High Court, at the request of the Court. The request was received by the Governor of the prison in question (Peterhead) on 23 August 1984 who informed the applicant of it and instructed the censors to stop such correspondence. The applicant had received replies to requests for information from the Court. The applicant stated that he wished for further information from the Justiciary Office and access to the High Court in order to institute proceedings against his defence solicitor. A complaint he made to the Lord Chancellor about the Clerk of Justiciary was passed to the Scottish Courts Administration in December 1984, but he had not received a reply at the time when he lodged his application.

On examining the application, the Commission asked the Government to reply to questions about the basis in law for the request from the Justiciary Office to the Governor of Peterhead, whether the stopping of the mail was a justified interference with the applicant's rights in respect of correspondence under Article 8, and whether this constituted a denial of the applicant's right of access to the courts under Article 6. The Foreign and Commonwealth Office decided that there was no effective defence against the stopping of the correspondence. It was decided to withdraw the restriction on correspondence with the Court and to amend Standing Order MA4(2) to make it clear that the governor of a prison cannot use his/her discretion to stop letters to courts or public authorities. Circular 77/1985, which amended Standing Order MA4(2), was issued on 16 October 1985. The applicant was asked by the Commission if he wanted to withdraw his application, but he declined arguing that Standing Orders have no force in law. The Government disputed this. Observations on admissibility and merits were submitted by the Government on 15 May 1986 but there was no further information on the file. However, ECHR records reveal that the application was held to be inadmissible.[10]

Ross v. UK

This application was introduced on 19 November 1984 and registered on 18 February 1985. The applicant complained under Articles 5 and 6 that he was not lawfully detained because the incorrect serving of a warrant made his subsequent trial void, that he was not allowed the statutory minimum period before his trial, and that he was not provided with the necessary legal textbooks when preparing for an appeal against conviction which he intended to conduct himself. The Commission examined the application for admissibility on 6 May 1985 and invited the Government to submit written observations on the admissibility and merits of part of the application dealing with access to legal textbooks.

The Government advanced two main arguments against the applicant's complaint. First, that adequate facilities were provided and, second, that the applicant had failed to exhaust the domestic remedies available to him. The Commission decided that the application was inadmissible on 11 December 1986, stating that it could not deal with possible errors committed by domestic courts, that the applicant did have a sufficient period of time before his trial and that it had not been shown that the materials supplied were inadequate or that this prevented him from receiving a fair hearing of his appeal.

Boyle and Boyle v. UK

This application, which was brought by James and Sarah Boyle (husband and wife), raised various issues related to the first applicant's transfer from the Barlinnie Special Unit to Edinburgh Prison and the loss of the privileges he had formerly enjoyed. On 5 May 1983, the Commission declared most of the complaints inadmissible. However, the Government was asked to submit observations on those parts of the complaint concerning the applicant's correspondence and the availability of effective remedies. These were considered by the Commission and were found admissible on 6 March 1985.

Rice and Rice v. UK

This application, which was brought by Brian and John Rice (father and son) was mainly concerned with the refusal of the prison authorities to allow the son to visit his father who, it was alleged, was seriously ill and unable to travel, the restriction of prison visits to twelve hours per year, and delaying or refusing to post letters written by the son while he was in prison. As in the *Boyle* case (see above), the Commission declared most of the complaints inadmissible but asked the Government to submit observations on those parts of the case referring to the applicant's correspondence and the absence of effective remedies. These were considered by the Commission, together with the Government's observations on the *Boyle* case, and were found admissible on 6 March 1985. Thereafter the two cases were conjoined and the Government was invited to an oral hearing on the merits of both cases on 10 July 1985.

Boyle and Rice v. UK

The Government was aware that certain members of the Commission held the view that the present avenues for prisoners' complaints, i.e. to the Secretary of State, the Visiting Committee or the

Parliamentary Commissioner for Administration, did not provide the 'effective remedy' required by the Convention and clearly expected problems. Its counsel (Bruce Weir QC) argued that remedies were available for each complaint while counsel for the applicants (Anthony Lester QC) contended that these channels were ineffective, since the matters complained of were all authorised by or under statute.

The Commission reached its 'provisional opinion' after the oral hearing. It found that there were breaches of Article 13 in respect of the availability of an effective remedy and of Article 8 in respect of the stopping of correspondence. The Government was then asked if it wished to reach a friendly settlement. Officials were opposed to this since it would have required a strengthening of the available remedies and preferred the high-risk strategy of challenging the Commission's opinion in court. This line was supported by ministers although it was contrary to the general policy which had been promulgated by the Prime Minister that settlements should be sought wherever possible. The Commission reported on 7 May 1986 and decided to refer the two cases to the Court. Arguments similar to those used at the oral hearing on 6 March 1985 were put to the Court which concluded on 27 April 1988 that the available remedies were sufficient to satisfy the requirements of Article 13. The Government's high-risk strategy had paid off.

Outcomes of the Scottish applications

The issues raised by the cases outlined above and their outcomes are summarised in Table 8.5. The twelve cases raised a wide variety of issues including the censorship of correspondence, regulations concerning visits, procedures for transferring prisoners between establishments, conditions in the Inverness Segregation Unit, the availability of medical treatment, the lawfulness of detention, remission for young offenders and the existence of effective remedies. As one would expect in the light of the statistics summarised in Table 8.1 above, most of the applications were declared inadmissible by the Commission. Moreover, of those that were declared admissible, most were (eventually) held to be unsuccessful on their merits, the only exceptions being cases involving interference with correspondence. The whole process was extraordinarily time-consuming, especially for cases which

Table 8.5 Issues and outcomes in ECHR applications from prisoners in Scotland

Name of applicant	*Substance of complaint*	*Alleged infringement of convention*	*Outcome*
Shields	Interference with correspondence	Article 8	Conceded by SPS (following *Silver*)
	Inability to start legal action	Article 6	Inadmissible
Fischer	Interference with correspondence	Article 8	Part inadmissible, part conceded by SPS (following *Silver*)
	Transfer to Inverness Unit	Article 3	Inadmissible
Burke	Conditions in Peterhead	Article 3	Inadmissible
	Visits at Peterhead	Article 8	Inadmissible
McCallum	Conditions in Inverness Unit	Article 3	Inadmissible
	Interference with correspondence	Article 8	Conceded by SPS (following *Silver*)
	Interference with family life	Article 8	Inadmissible
	Lack of effective remedy	Article 13	Conceded by applicant (following *Boyle and Rice*)
McQueenie	Failure to obtain medical treatment	Article 3	Inadmissible
	Interference with correspondence	Article 8	Conceded by SPS (following *Silver*)
Wardlaw	Conditions in Inverness Unit	Article 3	Inadmissible
	Lack of effective remedy	Article 13	Conceded by applicant (following *Boyle and Rice*)
Steele	Detention in Inverness Unit	Article 3	Struck off
	Imposition of Inverness regime	Articles 5/6	Struck off
	Lack of effective remedy	Article 13	Struck off
Nelson	Remission of juvenile offender discrimination by country/age	Articles 5/14	Inadmissible
Hodgson	Interference with correspondence	Article 8	Conceded by SPS (following *Silver*)
	Denial of access to courts	Article 6	Inadmissible
Ross	Illegal detention	Articles 5/6	Inadmissible
Boyle and Boyle	Loss of privileges following transfer	Articles 5/6	Inadmissible
	Interference with correspondence	Article 8	Conceded by SPS (following *Silver*)
Rice and Rice	Denial of visit	Article 8	Inadmissible
	Visiting arrangements	Article 8	Inadmissible
	Interference with correspondence	Article 8	Conceded by SPS (following *Silver*)
Boyle and Rice*	Lack of effective remedy	Article 13	Rejected by Court

Note: * Complaint heard by European Court of Human Rights.

went to Court, and applications invariably took years to resolve. However, although the process would certainly be quicker if the Convention was incorporated into domestic law, since this would mean that remedies could be sought in the domestic courts, it is by no means certain that the outcomes would be any different and the two parties would be more equally placed if the prisoner was granted legal aid and both were represented (by advocates) in court. This is largely because the 'wide mesh' of the European Convention on Human Rights is unable to catch the 'fine grain' of domestic prison procedures and because the rights embodied in the Convention are too inchoate to be of much use to prisoners in Scotland.

Three of the applications examined above focused on the very spartan conditions in the Inverness Segregation Unit, frequently referred to as 'the cages'. These applications were backed by the Scottish Council for Civil Liberties (SCCL).[11] The Government's response to these complaints was to argue that transfer to the Unit was not made for the purposes of punishment and that conditions in the Unit were not 'inhuman or degrading' and were therefore not in breach of Article 3 of the Convention. The Government made reference to previous decisions of the Court and, in each case, the Commission declared the application inadmissible. It is therefore extremely unlikely that the Commission, in future, will hold that conditions in any Scottish prison are 'inhuman and degrading' or that prisoners will be able to use Article 3 to improve the conditions in which they are held. Things would have to get very much worse for this to occur.

Five of the applications challenged the availability of an effective domestic remedy for prisoners who wished to complain about some aspect of their imprisonment. The Government was aware of its vulnerability in this respect. Thus, in April 1985, the Director of the Prison Service wrote

> The problem is that most of the complaints taken by prisoners to the Commission cannot competently be heard by domestic courts and their basic right of petitioning the Secretary of State only brings these complaints before the authority who, formally, made the decision in the first place.

These shortcomings could have been met by incorporating the Convention into domestic law or by establishing an independent complaints procedure such as that referred to at the end of Chapter

6 above. However, both these solutions were contrary to Government policy. The Government then adopted two lines of argument. The first was to amend its own procedures, particularly in relation to correspondence, to bring them into line with the requirements of the Convention and then to argue that the question of remedies no longer applied; the second was to argue that, although individual complaints procedures might not provide effective remedies, in aggregate they met the requirements of Article 13. At the end of the day, the Court reversed the provisional opinion of the Commission and accepted these arguments. It is most improbable that the Court will, in future, reverse its decision and therefore very unlikely that prisoners will be able to use Article 13 to strengthen the existing complaints procedures.

The largest number of applications (seven in all) referred to the stopping of correspondence with solicitors, the courts, pressure groups, the media and a number of other recipients. Following the *Silver* case (see above), the Government routinely conceded that its practices had been in breach of Articles 6 and 8. Standing Orders were amended, albeit somewhat grudgingly, in a process which officials described as one of 'damage limitation', the aim being to do the minimum necessary to bring Standing Orders into line with the Convention.[12] The result was a considerable liberalisation but not the total abandonment of procedures relating to censorship. Although this is not without significance, it is worth noting that the existing policy on censorship could hardly have survived the introduction of pay phones which has given most prisoners unrestricted access to the outside world.

Although the leading cases (reviewed above) do appear to have made governors and officials aware that they are, at least in theory, accountable to a higher authority and the trickle of applications from Scotland has helped to ensure that practices are in accordance with official procedures,[13] the detailed analysis of these applications and the way in which they were handled only confirms our earlier assessment of the ECHR, namely that it constitutes a rather feeble form of accountability. In the next section, we attempt to explain why this is so.

DISCOURSE, POWER AND THE ECHR

The impact of the ECHR on Scottish prisons can be explained in terms of discourse and power. ECHR discourse is legal discourse and, as such, it belongs to the third row of our discourse matrix (see Figure 2.5 on p.46). Because of its general concern with human rights, it is not really possible to locate it unambiguously in any particular cell. However, it does contain a normalising thrust and it is therefore appropriate for it to be centred on Cell 8. The major carriers of this discourse are, of course, lawyers but, since there are no lawyers within the Scottish Prison Service, they are to be found elsewhere.

Applications from prisoners in Scotland to the Commission involve complaints against the Government and allegations that there has been a breach of the Convention. The prisoner may or may not be legally represented but the Government is invariably represented by the Solicitor's Department in the Scottish Office and its legal advisers in the Foreign and Commonwealth Office.[14] This introduces a considerable degree of assymetry into the proceedings. Even if the prisoner is legally represented his lawyer is likely to be a 'one shotter' with little or no prior experience of ECHR litigation; by comparison, the Government's legal representatives are almost certain to be 'repeat players' with a great deal of experience of handling ECHR applications (Galanter 1975). Thus, for example, the same Scottish Office solicitor handled nearly all the twelve Scottish applications reviewed in this chapter while the legal advisers in the FCO were responsible for representing the Government in about 150 new cases per year (see Table 8.2 above). Given that cases often took many years to resolve, this implies that they must have been handling several hundred cases at any one time, including a substantial number from prisoners.

The relationship between the Solicitor's Department and the Scottish Prison Service can best be understood in terms of that between a solicitor and his or her client – indeed the Solicitor's Department often referred to the Scottish Prison Service as its client. In theory, officials at Headquarters gave instructions to the Solicitor's Department; in practice, the latter often gave expert advice and determined the line of argument that was subsequently adopted. However, this did not appear to generate much conflict. In this domain at least, the solicitors were acknowledged to be the experts and their expertise was recognised and accepted without demur.

The Principal who handled ECHR cases would, on occasion, consult senior colleagues about strategy and, where major strategic decisions were involved, ministerial approval would be sought. An example of this was the decision not to accept the offer of a friendly settlement in the *Boyle and Rice* case (see above) but to refer the case to the Court instead. On strategic issues of this nature, the Government's view clearly prevailed.

The Principal with responsibility for ECHR casework would also consult governors in establishments, both to elicit information relevant to the case and to get their comments on draft replies which had been prepared for the Solicitors' Department. In the course of filling in the background to the case, governors often gave their own assessment of the prisoner and the motives underlying his application to the ECHR. This was based on their wide experience and intimate knowledge of the particular prisoner who was often described as a 'troublemaker' or a 'subversive' for whom recourse to the ECHR was a further manifestation of his tiresome behaviour. However, just as the solicitors would often 'screen out' the bureaucratic responses of officials when these were insufficiently legalistic, so officials would likewise 'screen out' the 'professional' assessments of governors when these were insufficiently bureaucratic. In terms of ECHR applications, it is clear that there was a hierarchy in which legal discourse took precedence over bureaucratic discourse which in turn took precedence over professional discourse and solicitors (in the Scottish Office and the FCO) had greater power and influence than Headquarters officials who were in turn more powerful than prison governors.

In these circumstances, a prisoner who took on the Prison Service was in a similar position to that of David when he took on Goliath. Even if the prisoner was legally represented, his chances of success were very slim indeed. This was due both to the difficulty of successfully challenging the formidable legal expertise which the Government is able to call on and to the fact that the Convention is a rather blunt instrument whose requirements are relatively easy to meet. Moreover, there is no reason to think that this situation is likely to change. The characteristics of legal discourse in ECHR cases, together with the power differential between the individual prisoner and the Government machine, explain why it is that the ECHR has made so little impact on the Scottish Prison Service and why this situation is likely to continue.

Albeit perhaps to a lesser degree, similar arguments can be applied to the two other mechanisms of legal accountability referred to in Chapter 6 above. There have only been two applications for judicial review to date in Scotland and both of these were unsuccessful. This is, in part, due to the fact that new and streamlined procedures for obtaining a judicial review of administrative action were not introduced in Scotland until 1985, some eight years after analagous procedural reforms were introduced in England and Wales (Page 1991). Although this might suggest that there could be more applications in future when the procedure becomes better known, other considerations make this prospect unlikely. The inequality between the parties (which is certainly not as marked as in ECHR cases but is nevertheless still substantial) and the 'green light' jurisprudence of judicial review (Harlow and Rawlings 1984) which, in effect, holds that 'everything is allowed save that which is expressly forbidden'[15] together explain why the judiciary has been so reluctant to question administrative decision-making and why this situation is likely to persist.

There have been rather more applications from prisoners in Scotland to the Parliamentary Commissioner for Administration (PCA). The fact that the procedure is not an adversarial one and that the PCA carries out its own investigations in an inquisitional manner should work to a prisoner's advantage in that he is not placed in a disadvantageous position *vis-à-vis* the Government. However, the lack of direct access to the PCA and the fact that he can intervene only after receiving a complaint from an MP,[16] together with the narrowness of the test which the PCA applies ('maladministration giving rise to injustice'), and the very restrictive interpretation which has been given to it, have greatly reduced the PCA's potential impact (Justice 1977).

Chapter 9

Recent developments in penal policy

Towards enterprising managerialism

In our discussion of institutional and discursive change in the first two chapters of this book, we examined developments in penal policy up to the mid-1980s. As we developed some of our main themes in subsequent chapters, we referred to the emerging pressures on the Scottish prison system, in particular to overcrowding and the hostage-taking incidents which took place in many prisons. Since the mid-1980s, at least partly in response to these pressures, the Scottish Prison Service has produced a series of policy documents in an attempt to recast the management of the adult, male, long-term prison system. In this chapter we examine these documents in terms of the discourse matrix set out in Chapter 2 above. We consider them in the order in which they were produced in order to highlight the changing course of the debates and struggles which took place during this period. Although we make few explicit references back to our analysis of administrative decisions and mechanisms of accountability in Chapters 3–8, our account of policy in this chapter is both informed by and, we hope, consistent with our earlier accounts of administrative practices.

The period in question (1985–92) is short but can be divided into three phases. We begin by analysing *Custody and Care* (Scottish Prison Service 1988a) and *Assessment and Control* (Scottish Prison Service 1988b) which together represent the first phase. We then turn to *Opportunity and Responsibility* (Scottish Prison Service 1990a), the key document of the second phase. Finally, we conclude by examining *A Shared Enterprise* (Scottish Prison Service 1990b) and *Organising for Excellence* (Scottish Prison Service 1990c), both of which are products of the third phase.

FIRST STEPS TOWARDS A NEW POLICY

In 1979, the *May Report*, the *Report of the Committee of Inquiry into the United Kingdom Prison Services*, concluded that 'the rhetoric of treatment and training has had its day and should be replaced' (Home Office 1979: para. 4.27). However, the Committee refused to espouse the concept of 'humane containment', which was favoured by most of the academic critics of rehabilitation (e.g. Morris 1974; King and Morgan 1980), on the grounds that this concept was far too negative to serve as the aim of imprisonment, and instead advocated its own concept of 'positive custody'. The Report had potentially far-reaching implications for the Scottish Prison Service and the Scottish Office set up a number of Working Parties to formulate detailed policies in the light of its recommendations. However, there appeared to be little sense of urgency and, after several years, few of the Working Parties had reached the stage of producing a final report. Some of the interim and and draft reports were leaked to the press (see, for example, the *Report of the Departmental Working Group on Prison Education* (SHHD 1987a) referred to in Chapter 5 above) but there were no new policy initiatives. Although this was a matter of considerable concern to a small band of prison reformers, the political parties and the general public seemed largely indifferent (Kinsey 1988).

This situation lasted until 1985 when the first of two separate developments created a crisis for Scottish prisons and encouraged the Government to adopt a greater sense of urgency. As the figures detailed in Table 1.4 (on p.19) show, there was a sharp upsurge in the inmate population in 1985. Between 1973 and 1984, the average daily inmate population in Scottish penal establishments exceeded 5,000 in only two years (1978 and 1983) but, by 1985, receptions into custody were the highest on record (18,985 on remand and 24,532 under sentence) and the average daily population had risen to 5,273. Per head of population, the number of receptions into prison was the highest in Europe and the prison population was second only to that of Northern Ireland (Council of Europe 1987; Nicholson 1987). In 1986, the average daily population was the highest ever recorded (5,588) although the number of receptions into custody fell slightly below the 1985 levels. In 1987, there was a further drop (of 2.5 per cent) to 5,446 in the average daily population, with particularly sharp reductions in the number of remands, fine-defaulters and young offenders.

However, the number of prisoners serving determinate sentences of three years or more and the number serving life sentences increased by 7 per cent to 1,247 and by 35 per cent to 615 respectively, the highest numbers ever recorded (SHHD 1988a).

The second set of developments made the crisis far worse and effectively forced the Scottish Office to reformulate its prisons policy. In 1986 and 1987 there was the unprecedented series of hostage-taking incidents in which major damage was done to the fabric of several establishments (Scraton et al. 1988 and 1991). Although roof-top protests and hostage-taking incidents are not new phenomena in British prisons (Fitzgerald 1977), the number and scale of these incidents attracted a considerable degree of public and media interest to which the Scottish Office clearly had to respond.

Several factors eased the pressure of increased numbers on establishments. Between 1986 and 1987, an extra 675 places were provided with the completion of the refurbishment of Greenock Prison and the opening of Phase II of Shotts Prison. In addition, in 1987, the use of four establishments was changed to transfer under-utilised places in the male Young Offenders' Institution (YOI) system to the hard-pressed adult, male, long-term prison (LTP) establishments. Under the plans known as Grand Design (see also, Chapter 3 above), 320 places were transferred to the adult LTP system when Glenochil and Noranside YOIs became adult prisons and Greenock and Dumfries Prisons became YOIs. However, the nature of the problems confronting the Prison Service was such that a solution required more than a reallocation of establishments to the different sectors, as is shown by the continuation of disturbances in prisons after these changes were completed. The policy response to this crisis began with the iteration of the 'task' for the Scottish Prison Service by the Secretary of State in October 1985 (Scottish Prison Service 1988a: para. 2.4). Its main elements were as follows:

1 to keep in custody untried or unsentenced prisoners, and to ensure that they are available to be presented to court for trial or sentence;
2 to keep in custody, with such degree of security as is appropriate, having regard to the nature of the individual prisoner and his offence, sentenced prisoners for the duration of their sentence or for such shorter time as the Secretary of State may determine in cases where he has discretion;
3 to provide for prisoners as full a life as is consistent with the

facts of custody, in particular making available the physical necessities of life; care for physical and mental health; advice and help with personal problems; work, education, skill training, physical exercise and recreation; and opportunity to practice their religion;

4 to promote and preserve the self-respect of prisoners;
5 to enable prisoners to retain links with family and community; and
6 to encourage them to respond and contribute positively to society on discharge.

This task was reiterated by the Secretary of State in a speech given to representatives of the Scottish Prison Service in January 1988 (Rifkind 1989) and is repeated and elaborated upon in *Custody and Care* (*C & C*) (published in March 1988), which set out a framework of aims and objectives for the future management of prisons in Scotland, and in *Assessment and Control* (*A & C*) (published in October 1988), which detailed the approach of the Scottish Prison Service towards the particular problems of 'violent and disruptive inmates'.

In addition to these two discussion papers, two other policy documents of note were published in the same period. In October 1988 the Government published a consultation paper on *Fines and Fine Enforcement* (SHHD 1988b) which canvassed a number of proposals, including the experimental introduction of day fines, which were intended, *inter alia*, to reduce the number of fine defaulters who serve terms of imprisonment and, in March 1989, the *Report of the Review Committee on Parole and Related Issues in Scotland* (*the Kincraig Report*) (SHHD 1989a). Its principal recommendations – that parole should be restricted to prisoners serving sentences of more than five years who would become eligible when they had served half their sentence, and that prisoners serving shorter sentences would receive conditional remission at this point – should lead to a reduction in the amount of time spent in custody and thus in the prison population. These two policy documents feed into the general policy domain that is represented for prisons by *C & C* and *A & C*.

An outline and critique of the Phase 1 proposals

C & C was divided into four main parts dealing with: first, the task and responsibilities of the Scottish Prison Service (SPS); second, policy and priorities for inmates; third, planning for individual establishments; and fourth, training and development of staff. We briefly examine each of these in turn.

C & C reaffirmed the 'task' of the SPS summarised above, but also made it clear that:

> The appropriate balance of elements of the task is a matter of judgment based on experience, specialised advice, perception of the risk or positive potential of inmates and availability of facilities or resources.
>
> (Para. 2.12)

Although priority was given first to security and then to control, the balance between the various tasks and thus the aims and objectives of the SPS was left open. As we argue below, this was deeply problematic. *C & C* outlined the legal framework of imprisonment in Scotland and set out proposals to produce a consolidation of the Prisons (Scotland) Act 1952 and subsequent amendments; and to amend and update the Prison (Scotland) Rules, which likewise dated from 1952, and the Standing Orders derived from them. It also examined the alterations in prison capacity outlined above and introduced plans to keep the number of places for different types of prisoner under review.

In examining policy and priorities for inmates, *C & C* considered the nature of initial classification of long-term prisoners to establishments and discussed the role of the National Classification Board (see Chapter 3 above). It proposed that 'regime prospectuses' be drawn up for every prison and made available to prisoners. It advocated the introduction of 'sentence planning' for all long-term inmates, arguing that 'the aim is to get the individual to come to terms with his sentence and to complete it as peaceably and constructively as possible' (para. 9.4) and that '"sentence planning" in the sense of continuous assessment and dialogue with the inmate should begin immediately the sentence is known' (para. 9.8). As we demonstrate below, these proposals had important implications for *A & C.*

To facilitate such 'sentence planning' *C & C* proposed that each establishment should produce a 'regime plan'. In general, it was suggested that unnecessary disparities between establishments should be removed so as to ensure 'parity of regimes' between prisons holding similar types of prisoner (Chapter 12). The pressure for this came from the fact that Grand Design and the hostage-taking incidents led to an unprecedented number of transfers between establishments which, in turn, drew attention to differences in facilities and privileges and provoked a substantial amount of adverse comment and disgruntlement. *C & C* concluded by arguing for more and better staff training (Chapter 13) and setting out the roles of governors and staff (Chapter 14).

The second document, *A & C*, consisted of three main parts: first, an analysis and criticism of explanations for the recent spate of incidents in Scottish prisons which then developed the idea of the need for 'control risk profiles' of individuals; second, an explication of plans for the future pattern of specialised units for 'difficult' prisoners in the Scottish Prison Service; and third, a very brief update on *C & C*.

A & C began with a consideration of the reasons that had been given by inmates for the recent spate of disturbances in Scottish prisons. The reasons examined were: ill-treatment by staff; overcrowding and conditions of accommodation; changes in parole policy; quality of regimes and availability of privileges; the remoteness of Peterhead and the difficulties this creates for visits. Except for the remoteness of Peterhead, all these reasons were refuted. However, the reasoning in the report is highly suspect. First, the 'logic' involved is fatally flawed. The analysis sought to infer from the possible (or known) consequences of an act that it was not rational for the actor to engage in it. This presupposes a particular kind of rationality, which was then used to evaluate explanations for observed forms of social action. The two quotations below illustrate this well.

> The changes in parole policy introduced in 1984 have been cited as a third reason behind the recent incidents. It is alleged that the introduction of the new policy led to a 'loss of hope' on the part of many long-term inmates. Irrespective of the fact that all cases continue to be seen by the Parole Board with the same frequency as previously, so that the Board has the opportunity to make a case for exceptional circumstances, it is puzzling that inmates allegedly protesting about their release prospects should take part in action which is likely to have the effect of extending the period they spend in custody (either through loss of remission or award of additional sentences). It is also noticeable that the incidents continued even after the Secretary of State's announcement, in December 1987, of a thorough review of parole policy in Scotland under the chairmanship of Lord Kincraig.
>
> (Para. 2.5.3)

> Quality of regimes and availability of privileges have on occasion been advanced as reasons for particular incidents. But again, the practical effect of a major incident is likely to be simply that regimes and privileges are further restricted, even if temporarily, while staff restore the necessary control.
>
> (Para. 2.5.4)

In both cases the conclusions were the same: protesting against the more restrictive parole policy introduced in 1984, the quality of regimes or the availability of privileges was irrational, therefore changes in parole policy, the quality of regimes and the availability of privileges could not constitute explanations for the incidents.

Second, *A & C* transformed 'reasons' (a non-judgmental characterisation) into 'justifications':

> In themselves, the various reasons which have been given by inmates as justification for the incidents do not, on investigation, give any justification at all for the actions taken.
>
> (Para. 2.6)

It would, of course, be quite proper to cite all the reasons given as possible explanations for a pattern of events without arguing that they justified the events. Explanations and justifications are not necessarily synonymous.

The rejection of these reasons allowed *A & C* to argue that the explanation for disruption lay with the individual (see also Scraton et al. 1991 and Sim 1992):

> rather than looking to changes in the way in which the Prison Service as a whole goes about its task (although clearly this is an area which must be kept under review) a more productive approach may be to concentrate attention on the individual personality and 'repertoire' of particularly disruptive and violent inmates.
>
> (Para. 2.11)

A & C attempted to provide a profile of this type of inmate, maintaining that 'violent and disruptive prisoners tend to display a combination of the following features' (para. 2.12).

The list of features comprised: a hostile attitude towards authority; an inability to come to terms with their sentence or its length; the experience of being separated from their families; peer-group pressure from the criminal community; an inability to live to order;

the intensifying effect of the prison environment; drugs; and personality disorder. This catalogue is quite incoherent in its own terms in that it covers personality attributes, experiences, attitudes and behaviour. Thus, it was unlikely to form a satisfactory basis for the set of diagnostic tests proposed in *A & C*.

By adopting this strategy, the 'problem' for the SPS became that of identifying those prisoners who potentially exhibited these features in order to remove them from the mainstream of prison life. In order to do this, continuous assessment of prisoners was required. The link back to the proposals made in *C & C* is clear. The use which was envisaged for continuous assessment in *A & C* undercut the potentially worthwhile aspects of this strategy outlined in *C & C*. In addition, it was clear that the SPS was planning a substantial expansion of 'alternative units' to accommodate these 'violent and disruptive' prisoners.

According to *A & C*, at the beginning of 1988, there were facilities for seventy-eight such prisoners as follows:

Aberdeen	5	
Barlinnie	8	Special Unit
Inverness	5	Segregation Unit
Peterhead	60	10-cell unit, B Hall, separate cells, A Hall
Total	78	

In 1987, a further sixty places were to be added when Shotts' E Hall re-opened as a 'half-way house' to hold and assess 'difficult' prisoners moving to or from Peterhead. This brought the total to 138 places but five additional places were subsequently provided in Perth E Hall and a further twelve in a new unit at Shotts (see below). This would have brought the total to 155 places. However, *A & C* announced that plans were in hand for sixty more places in a large maximum security unit at Shotts and possibly another sixty in a similar unit at Peterhead, although the latter would have replaced some of the sixty already there. Assuming that the ten-cell unit (opened in 1984) was to be retained, and the rest of Peterhead decommissioned or used for other purposes (an optimistic assumption in the light of past experience and current trends), this would have resulted in an increase of seventy over the number of places available earlier in 1988 and an overall total of 225 places.

It was clear that the SPS was set on this expansionist course without being clear about the exact number of places that were required. Indeed, according to *A & C*:

> Previous surveys, in October 1983 and January 1985, have suggested that the Scottish Prison Service requires between 100 and 200 places for maximum security or enhanced control of previously or potentially violent or disruptive adult male inmates.
> (Para. 3.4)

Thus, the proposals in *A & C* would have provided even more places in special units than the upper limit of the estimate made three years previously.

Despite setting the SPS on an expansionist course, *A & C* provided little information about the nature of the regimes that were to be operated in these different units. There were some positive hints, for example, the report stated that 'A new unit for long-term inmates, drawing on the experience of the Barlinnie Special Unit, is being developed at Shotts prison' (para. 1.15) and outlined some features of the regime for this unit in para. 9.12. Nevertheless, we feel that our general point holds good. The only reference to the regimes in the large maximum security units at Shotts and Peterhead was to 'the most stringent conditions of security and control' (para. 8.4.2). We believe that this relates to the central problem with *C & C*, i.e. its failure adequately to specify the aims and objectives of the SPS or to achieve a balance between the different aspects of the 'task'. Because of this, the SPS was unable to detail the relationship between the task and the prison regimes that would give effect to it. This problem applied with particular force to regimes in the units for 'difficult and disruptive' prisoners.

A further problem related to the size and location of these units. Having rejected without much argument the Chief Inspector's recommendation for four new units of fifteen places each (HMCIP(S) 1987b), *A & C* opted instead for one or more sixty-place units but ignored the problems of managing units of this size. Moreover, although *A & C* stated that the physical planning of the units 'must obviously be based upon detailed planning and design of regime, routine and operation' (para. 8.8.3), it gave the impression that the physical planning of the units was already in hand but provided no evidence of any detailed thinking about the regimes in these units. It would seem that the SPS had, despite a ritual genuflection towards the primacy of regimes, not really learned the lessons of Glenochil (as outlined in the *Chiswick Report*) (SHHD 1985), namely that the design of an establishment imposes a powerful influence on prison regimes and routines.

Power and discourse in Phase 1

With the publication of *C & C*, it looked as if the SPS was moving in the direction of normalisation and legality. Examples of normalisation discourse were the commitment, as part of the task of the SPS, 'to provide for prisoners as full a life as is consistent with the facts of custody' and 'to enable prisoners to retain links with family and community'. Control discourse was still discernible but rehabilitation was more or less absent. Elements of legality discourse can be seen in giving long-term prisoners a degree of choice in where they spent the majority of their sentence and in the attempt to ensure some kind of parity of regimes so that, as far as possible, prisoners serving similar sentences and at similar stages of sentence would be treated more or less equally. However, to the extent that change was to be imposed on the system by Headquarters, it is not altogether surprising that bureaucratic discourse was clearly still in the ascendency.

The discourses of normalisation and, to a lesser extent, legality which can be found in *C & C* were undermined by the discourse which permeates *A & C*. Take the following for example:

> The priority is prevention and this means that judgements have to be taken which anticipate possible or intended trouble. The test of preventive measures cannot be 'proof beyond a reasonable doubt' because the only such proof would be the actual occurrence of the events which it is hoped to prevent. Necessary intervention in advance of anticipated trouble, therefore, will always be open to objections that it is unfair or unreasonable.
>
> (Para. 4.9.2)

The abandonment proposed here of criteria of proof infringes the very basis of claims to normalisation or legality. Two strands of criticism can be advanced: the proposal can be criticised in terms of justice, even if what was proposed had been possible; and in terms of practicality since there were no grounds for believing that what was proposed could actually be made to work. The initial thinking was, as we have pointed out earlier, woolly and the mechanisms for carrying out the exercise were unlikely to lead to the development or specification of reliable or valid diagnostic tests in practice.

Many of the proposals in *A & C* entailed an increased reliance on strategies of control and reflected the growing influence of control discourse. Given the absence of legality, this was particularly worrying. The thrust of *A & C* undermined that of *C & C* and, taken together, the two documents heralded greater centralisation and a greater emphasis on control within the prison system.

Overcrowding and the volatility of Scottish prisons gave the centre the opportunity to take control of the SPS. *C & C* and *A & C* were both written by civil servants and both reflect a bureaucratic response to the problems facing the SPS. These two documents attempted to alter the direction of the Scottish Prison Service from the centre in a 'top–down' fashion (Sabatier 1986). *C & C*, which appeared just after Grand Design, reflects a composite bureaucratic–normalisation discourse and can be represented by Cell 2 of our discourse matrix (see Figure 2.5 on p.46) while *A & C*, which was written against a background of continuing unrest, represents a composite bureaucratic–control discourse and can be represented by Cell 3 of the matrix. There was little input from governors to either document and little mention of modes of professional intervention in them. In addition, the arguments on small units advanced by HMCIP(S), which were presumably supported by his professional staff, were disregarded in *A & C*. Further, by not thinking through the precise nature of the regimes to be operated in these units, no countervailing force could be articulated in opposition to the refuge of an uncritically accepted form of control discourse. However, while a good deal of the response to *C & C* was positive, *A & C* was received very negatively. This led to some re-thinking and it was in this context that *Opportunity and Responsibility* appeared.

FINDING A NEW LANGUAGE

The Government invited comments on *C & C* and *A & C*, the latter to be submitted within six weeks of its publication, and promised to take account of the comments received in developing its strategy which was to be announced 'early in 1989'. These plans were eventually revealed, some fifteen months later than promised, in March 1990 in *Opportunity and Responsibility* (*O & R*) (SPS 1990a). *O & R* is a remarkable document, not only for the candour with which the SPS acknowledged the inadequacy of *A & C* and took into account the criticisms that this provoked, but also for questioning many of the taken-for-granted assumptions about and practices in Scottish prisons and for developing a positive and coherent philosophy of imprisonment.

An outline and critique of the Phase 2 proposals

O & R was divided into two parts. In the first (Chapters 2–4), the context for a review of policy was outlined, pressures for change were identified and recent developments in the prison system were described. In the second (Chapters 5–9), a framework for developing the long-term prison system was proposed. We briefly consider each part in turn.

It is significant that Part 1 began with a review of penal philosophy and the aims of imprisonment. This was a welcome step as it recognised that agreement on aims and objectives is a prerequisite for developing a coherent strategy and a set of policies that will give effect to it. It accepted that the SPS found itself in a philosophical vacuum when confidence in the 'treatment model' declined and that the 'justice model' failed to engender much enthusiasm. Consequently Chapter 2 outlined a new philosophy based on the twin assumptions that prisoners should be treated as 'responsible' persons and that the prison system should aim to offer prisoners a full range of opportunities for 'personal development' and 'the resolution of personal problems'. Chapter 3 reviewed some of the factors which contributed to the problems experienced by the SPS in the late 1980s. Noting that many of those who commented on *A & C* felt that its analysis of the violent incidents which occurred in the period 1986–8 concentrated excessively on individual pathology, *O & R* identified a number of external and internal factors, including overcrowding, Grand Design, the differential liberalisation of regimes, drugs and deterrent sentencing, changes in parole policy and the role of Peterhead Prison in the system, which contributed to the problems experienced in the mid-1980s. The approach adopted in *O & R* entailed the almost total rejection of that adopted in *A & C* and no punches were pulled in admitting the extent to which the problems of the SPS were created by its own policies and the discursive difficulties that it encountered at that time. Chapter 4 examined some of the key developments from 1988–90, drawing attention to the 10 per cent reduction in the prison population, the fall in the number of prisoners held under Rule 36,[1] the reduced dependence on Peterhead for holding prisoners presenting what *O & R* referred to as 'management problems', and improvements in staff training.

Part 2 was more programmatic. Reacting to the views expressed by many of those who responded to *A & C* that it placed too much emphasis on the identification, segregation and containment of potentially disruptive prisoners, Chapter 5 made it clear that the main solution for prisoners with difficulties lay in better quality mainstream establishments rather than in purpose-built control units. It reiterated the view, outlined above, that

> we should regard the offender as a person who is responsible, despite the fact that he or she may have acted irresponsibly many times over in the past, and that we should try to relate to the prisoner in ways which would encourage him or her to accept responsibility for their actions by providing him or her with opportunities for responsible choice, personal development and self-improvement.
>
> (Para. 5.5)

Central to this approach were proposals for sentence planning, which would allow the prisoner to participate at each stage in planning his or her sentence, and the need to structure opportunities in a sensible and appropriate manner. Although this entailed the retention of a system of progression, *O & R* suggested that it would be helpful to distinguish three aspects of regimes, namely the minimum elements a prisoner should receive by right ('the threshold quality of life'), 'appropriate opportunities' and 'privileges', with what were previously regarded as privileges being progressively incorporated into the basic threshold quality of life in prison.

Chapter 6 then spelled out *O & R's* conception of normalisation, which entailed the provision of 'regimes which allow prisoners the opportunity to live as normal lives as possible and as may be consistent with the requirements of security and order' (para. 6.3) and pointed to the need to review practices in three areas, namely 'access to families', 'quality of life' and 'preparation for release'. Here *O & R* was at its most liberal, advocating increased home leave for most prisoners, promising to set up a Working Party to examine the possibility of providing 'family visits' for those prisoners who would not be eligible for home leave, and setting as policy objectives the provision to every prisoner of a room of his own and the abolition of 'slopping out'.

Chapter 7 made it clear that security categorisation should refer only to security concerns and not to the prisoner's response to staff or to the stage reached in his or her sentence. In a particularly significant analysis of the need to achieve a balance between security, order and regime, *O & R* pointed out that 'an oversecure establishment will have pressure exerted on its control and regime elements' (p.43) and suggested that more long-term prisoners should be placed in lower security categories from the beginning of their sentence. The effect of this would be to alter the balance between the numbers of prisoners in security categories A to D. Moreover, by allocating prisoners to an appropriate hall rather than an appropriate establishment, the number of available options would be greatly increased.

The role of small regimes within the mainstream was considered in Chapter 8 and that of small units in Chapter 9. Chapter 8 proposed the eventual subdivision of existing accommodation into discrete small regimes and categorically rejected the extremely contentious proposals put forward in *A & C* to build a sixty-place maximum security complex at Shotts Prison. In place of *A & C*'s expansionist aim of providing sufficient maximum security accommodation to accommodate all potentially violent and disruptive prisoners, *O & R* proposed as a 'rule of thumb' that roughly 1 per cent of inmates, i.e. about fifty at any one time, should be accommodated in small units, whose

> value. . .lies as much in the ability to pioneer innovative approaches, the lessons of which can be applied to the mainstream generally, as in the capacity to provide for a limited number of prisoners who are having difficulty settling into their sentence.
> (Para. 9.16)

With the commitment to establish another small unit for up to twelve difficult prisoners in Edinburgh, the proposals in *O & R* represented a reduction of about fifty maximum security places over the number proposed in *A & C*. One consequence of this was the retention of Peterhead 'in the medium term', i.e. for the foreseeable future.

In spite of its many positive features, there were a number of problems with *O & R*. Although *O & R* represented, on the one hand, a confluence of bureaucratic and professional discourses, its failure to accommodate legal discourse was a matter of some considerable concern. This constitutes the basis of our first set of criticisms. Our second set of criticisms follows from the conception of normalisation which was utilised in *O & R*. The SPS's prior commitment to normalisation seems to us to be at odds with the thrust of some of the key proposals in *O & R*.

Although *C & C* outlined proposals for consolidating the Prisons (Scotland) Act 1952 and subsequent amending legislation, and for revising and updating the Prison (Scotland) Rules and the Standing Orders derived from them, *O & R* made no reference to this. More significantly, it made few references to prisoners' rights or the means by which they can be enforced. In accordance with prevailing Government rhetoric, *O & R* emphasised prisoners' responsibilities, their need to make choices and to face the consequences of their decisions (see further Keat 1991:10–11). This runs the risk that, in the absence of any reference to prisoners' rights, prisoners may find themselves in a very vulnerable position if and when they act 'irresponsibly' and take decisions that land them in trouble. In such circumstances, prisoners may still be moved, against their will, to a small unit or, *in extremis*, placed on Rule 36,[2] or deprived of visits or of opportunities and other privileges without having any really effective means of redress. Ministers and the public were, in effect, invited to place their trust in the SPS to get things right by making the appropriate response to the prisoners' behaviour. Although *O & R* did promise a review of existing procedures for dealing with requests and grievances (see Chapter 6 above), its discussion of accountability was very disappointing. The view conveyed, that once all the developments proposed in *O & R* were introduced prisoners would have no need to complain, was utopian in the extreme.

The definition of normalisation which was adopted in *O & R* (cited above) and its relationship to the provision of opportunities, also raises a number of problems. If the yardstick for living as normal a life as is consistent with the requirements of security and order is the kind of life the offender could lead outside prison, where few opportunities for personal development and self-improvement, education, training or employment may be available and where, in any case, little pressure may be exerted on the offender to take advantage of them, then this may not be consistent with the provision of opportunities and the encouragement which prisoners will need if they are to take advantage of them. In fact, the concept of normalisation may even be an impediment to the development of such opportunities.

Although the view of the May Committee that 'the notion of "treatment" or a "coerced cure" is a contradiction in terms and that a much more achievable goal is "facilitative change"' (para. 2.10), one positive feature of rehabilitation was its ability to command resources and the pressure it could bring to bear on prisoners. Whether *O & R* will be equally successful must remain to be seen. However, the absence of any reference to the need for effective external monitoring leaves the SPS at the mercy of the Government of the day which may or may not supply the resources required to bring about improvements in prisoners' quality of life and in the opportunities necessary for personal development and self-improvement.

O & R gave very little detail about the kinds of opportunities that should be available for long-term prisoners and, in particular, for those with serious personal and personality problems or about the roles that education, social work, psychology and psychiatry might be expected to play. Nevertheless, in spite of the reservations outlined above, its commitment to the provision of opportunities for 'personal development' and 'the resolution of personal problems' enabled it to bring rehabilitation back in, albeit in a 'new old' form (DiIulio 1991) which resonates with the idea of the form propagated in the nineteenth century (see Chapter 7 above). As Coyle (1991:263) has written:

> The concept of rehabilitation, properly understood as change coming from within a person is sound. What was fundamentally flawed was the notion that this could be imposed by external agencies. . . In theory it should have been possible to confirm the correct understanding of the word rehabilitation and to exclude from it the erroneous accretions. In practice, this additional baggage has become so much a part of the essential understanding of the word that it has proved impossible to separate the rhetoric from the reality.

Because of this, it became necessary 'to find a new form of words with which to restate the belief that the prisoner can make positive use of his time in prison' (ibid.) and that the state, which deprives the prisoner of his liberty, has a duty to provide the means to make this possible. The concept of 'opportunities' would appear to provide that new form of words.

Power and discourse in Phase 2

O & R represented a substantial advance on *C & C* and *A & C*. It attempted to articulate a clear philosophy of imprisonment and the role of the prisoner. The philosophy was more than a combination of normalisation (as developed in *C & C*) and control (as exemplified by *A & C*) in that it also contained a third ingredient, opportunity, which, as we have just explained, represented a revised and updated form of rehabilitation. As far as the role of the prisoner was concerned, responsibility was the key concept. *O & R* envisaged a prison system which, while retaining a strong centre, devolved responsibility to those working in the field and to prisoners themselves. The document, which was the product of close collaboration between civil servants and Headquarters governors, proposed an alliance between bureaucratic concerns with the smooth running of the system as a whole and professional concerns for some degree of autonomy from the centre. The approach of *O & R* was much less heavy-handed than that articulated in the earlier documents. However, this new alliance of professional and bureaucratic concerns effectively squeezed out legal concerns, rights being swamped by responsibilities. Thus, the discursive structure of *O & R* is rather complex. It represents, on the one hand, a combination of bureaucratic and professional discourses and, on the other, a confluence of rehabilitation (in its new form), normalisation and control discourses and inhabits the space defined by Rows 1 and 2 of the discourse matrix.

O & R can be seen as advocating an alliance of professionals and bureaucrats, under the combined aims of rehabilitation, normalisation and control. It was a very optimistic document in that it believed that new relationships could be forged. However, it was only able to do this because it played down conflict and ignored issues of power. For example, its characterisation of the relationship between prison officers and prisoners as one of mutual interdependence and of the role of the prison officer as a facilitator, i.e. as a kind of 'social worker in the halls', were both unsatisfactory, since they harmonised the interests of prison officers and prisoners. The authors of *O & R* failed to recognise that the relationships between prisoners and all those in authority over them are imbued with power. This is why prisoners need protection and why the neglect of prisoners' rights was of such significance.

O & R reflected and indeed articulated many of the core concerns of Government policy. However, it is in subsequent developments that such concerns become even clearer as the SPS moved towards the construction of itself as an enterprise Prison Service.

TOWARDS AN ENTERPRISING SCOTTISH PRISON SERVICE

The latest policy thinking on the SPS is exemplified in two representative documents: *A Shared Enterprise* (*ASE*) and *Organising for Excellence* (*OFE*). The former is an 'outline corporate strategy' produced from within the SPS Planning Unit in March 1990. The latter is a 'Review of the organisation of the Scottish Prison Service' carried out in consultation with the SPS by Coopers and Lybrand Deloitte and published in December 1990. We begin our outline of the latest phase of SPS thinking with an account of the key contents of *ASE*.

An outline and critique of the Phase 3 proposals

ASE sets out a 'corporate strategy' for the SPS. It begins with a 'mission statement', which asserts that the 'mission' of the SPS is

> to keep in custody those committed by the courts; to maintain good order in each prison; to care for prisoners with humanity; and to provide all possible opportunities to help prisoners to lead law-abiding and useful lives after release.
>
> (Para. 2)

This mission statement is derived from the task of the SPS set out by the Secretary of State in 1985 (see above) and reiterated in successive policy statements. *ASE* examines the legal framework of the SPS, which it terms the 'mandate', and recognises the difficulties posed by current legislation for the objectives promoted in the task and the mission statement, pointing out that

> The Prison Rules reflect an underlying philosophy of the role and purpose of the Prison Service (the 'treatment and training' of inmates) which is not that to which most people would subscribe in 1990.
>
> (Para. 4.4.3)

However, such difficulties are not thought to be of great importance by the authors of the document, who conclude that 'in practice, the legislation does not inhibit the work of the Service' (para. 4.4). The language used here is illustrative of a rather dismissive attitude to legal discourse.

ASE then develops a 'SWOT' (strengths, weaknesses, opportunities and threats) analysis of the SPS. Of particular relevance are some of the weaknesses identified, in particular the claim that 'there is a dysfunction between the field and Headquarters resulting in a "them and us" mentality which is highly detrimental to the success of the organisation' (para. 5.3.1), and that there has been a lack of 'strategic management' (para. 5.3.2) which 'has been reflected in outmoded management approaches, characterised by an inappropriate emphasis on administrative styles of management at Headquarters, and inappropriate individualistic/charismatic management styles in establishments' (para. 5.3.3).

The consideration of opportunities and threats examines the forces in the external environment which could influence the objectives of the SPS. In relation to opportunities, the document welcomes the new emphasis on managerialism (see further Pollitt 1990) since 'ministerial initiatives for improved management effectiveness in the civil service are very much in sympathy with some of the changes which may be identified as necessary' (para. 6.4). Although there is little evidence of increased judicial intervention (see Chapter 8 above), legal challenges are still represented as a threat. According to *ASE*,

> The increased trend amongst inmates to resort to judicial review, willingness of the courts to undertake review of administrative actions, and pressure for inmates' rights will impose additional pressures and costs on the Service.
>
> (Para. 6.10)

ASE defines four strategic priorities for the SPS. These are: first, 'to define, assert and give effect to the values and principles by which the SPS will operate'; second, 'to improve the quality of service to prisoners, so as to provide them with as full, active and constructive a life as possible'; third, 'to foster good staff relations, and to help staff develop their skills and abilities in support of the aims and mission of the SPS'; and, finally, 'to develop the appropriate organisational structure and management style to deliver the service as efficiently, effectively and economically as possible' (para. 7.2). These priorities are then discussed more fully. *ASE* frequently restates and develops themes in *O & R*, for example in its treatment of prisoners' responsibilities. Although *ASE* has very little to say about prisoners' rights, or about the characteristics of a 'rights based' approach to prisoners, it repeatedly asserts that rights entail responsibilities, claiming that 'whereas the treatment philosophy tended to see the prisoner as the "irresponsible client", the "rights-based" approach sees the prisoner as an individual with responsibilities' (para. 8.12). It does 'recognise the importance of. . .allowing prisoners the opportunity of having their sentences or conditions of imprisonment reviewed by due process of law' (para. 8.10) and 'value[s] highly the need for proper grievance procedures. . .and for accountability. . .through the processes of government and the courts' (para. 9.9). However, it is not clear whether these 'commitments' are any more than ritual genuflections since, as we have shown in previous chapters, the existing procedures are extremely ineffective and *ASE* does not contain any proposals for improving or enhancing them. As far as prisoners are concerned, the authors of the report 'place high value on encouraging the prisoner to accept responsibility for his action while in prison' and see the role of the SPS as 'facilitating the personal development of the prisoner throughout his sentence' (para. 8.13). Normalisation for the prisoner 'through greater access to his family and by retaining his self-respect' (para. 8.14) and professionalism for staff 'which will allow them to carry out their roles competently, effectively and with a caring compassion' (para. 8.17) are both advocated. However, just as there is no discussion of mechanisms for giving some effect to prisoners' rights, so there is likewise no discussion of procedures for ensuring the achievement of professional standards.

The management of the SPS apparently wishes 'to pursue and engender a sense of teamwork and shared enterprise which will provide us all with a sense of ownership of the policies and practices of the service' (para. 8.18), and this position is asserted increasingly strongly as the document proceeds.

The desire to create a framework of teamwork led the SPS to commission a review of its management structure. The resulting document (*OFE*) proposes a revised structure to replace the seven Headquarters divisions, each under the control of a Deputy Director who is responsibile to the Director, by one which consists of four Directorates, each under the control of a Director reporting to a Chief Executive. The four Directorates would have responsibility for Strategy and Planning, Human Resources, Prisons, and Finance and Information Systems, and the Director of Prisons would act as Deputy Chief Executive. The report also proposes a new Prisons Board made up of the Chief Executive, the four Directors and two non-executive members appointed by the Secretary of State.

The detailed proposals, most of which were implemented in

1992, need not detain us here, but it is important to consider the 'objectives and principles' of the organisational review as these exemplify current thinking. They are to: first, 'delineate between strategic planning and operational management'; second, 'devolve greater authority and managerial accountability to establishment level'; third, 'establish financial control and management information systems which support devolution of authority to establishments, whilst ensuring prison management can be held accountable to the Director and top management'; fourth, 'create the basis for building a unified service in which headquarters and prison staff share a common culture, value system and career opportunities'; fifth, 'maintain Ministerial accountability for overall direction and control of SPS'; sixth, 'establish and maintain a coherent line management structure with a clear chain of command between the Director and Governors-in-charge'; seventh, 'support the development of a Service which sets and achieves key strategic objectives rather than reacts to events'; and finally, 'deliver higher standards of service and improved value for money' (Executive Summary: para. iv). It is clear that these objectives reflect many of the Government's current concerns (Pollitt 1990).

Although *ASE* and *OFE* both reflect the importance of accountability within the SPS, the forms of accountability they refer to are always internal and hierarchical and both are suspicious of legal discourse. As with *O & R*, the emphasis is on the SPS putting its own house in order: a philosophy in the end of 'trust us'. We believe that external controls need to be far higher up the agenda. One illustrative example is *OFE*'s very brief discussion of 'Casework, Grievances and Complaints' (paras. 4167–70) where it is stated that, in the interest of giving local management more influence over the management of prisoners' sentences, establishments could take greater control over, *inter alia*, petitions. Although it may indeed be desirable for more decisions to be taken, within agreed guidelines, and for more grievances to be dealt with in the prison in the first instance, this will not be sufficient to ensure accountability.

As with *ASE*, *OFE* appears to regard legal challenges as a hindrance to good management rather than a central part of it. Rights in this document always entail responsibilities, but they should apply with particular force to prisoners who are regarded as 'irresponsible' because limits need to be placed on what can be done to them and because responsibility is, in many cases, a loaded term. At the moment it is still the SPS that defines what responsibility is. Control rests with management. We develop these points further by analysing *ASE* and *OFE* in terms of power and discourse.

Power and discourse in Phase 3

ASE and *OFE* have little to say about what prisons are for and are primarily concerned with how prisons should be run. Thus, they are to be seen as examples of means discourse rather than ends discourse (see Chapter 2 above). The aims of imprisonment are taken as given, settled by the earlier policy documents, in particular by *O & R*. They also avoid any direct reference to the question of power. However, in spite of that, they outline a particular strategy for the mobilisation of power. Whereas *O & R* proposed an alliance between the bureaucratic concerns of civil servants and the professional concerns of prison governors, *ASE* and *OFE* take this one stage further. What is proposed is a fusion of power-holders. In effect, they advocate abolishing the distinction between civil servants and prison governors as both become managers of the 'shared enterprise'. As the Director of the Scottish Prison Service explained in an interview (Nelson 1990:7) 'I must confess that I am very unimpressed by models. I'm more interested in managing the system better. The key element is training of senior people in management skills. . .being good general managers.' Furthermore, the logic extends even beyond these groups: the two documents assert that prison officers and prisoners also share in the operation of the system. However, the problem is that real and fundamental differences exist between these groups. Further, despite all talk of devolution of power, the system remains hierarchical. It is, after all, the centre which will decide on the nature and extent of the decentralisation of power. Given the difficulties involved in such a strategy, it is clear that a strong and very powerful rhetoric will be needed to give it any chance of success. This is provided by the discourse of enterprise. Such a discourse places a particular emphasis on the unification of the service, and indeed on the creation of a 'common culture' (Pollitt 1990:23) which all share. Enterprise provides the rhetoric under which the proposed reorganisation of the Prison Service is to take place.

Locating the current policy documents in our discourse matrix, it is clear that legalism (represented by row 3), despite its occasional presence, is only evident in very muted form. Thus, for example, *ASE* and *OFE* contain no references to the case for adopting minimum prison standards or to the arguments for appointing an independent Prisons Ombudsman or to the need for strengthening the Prisons Inspectorate and the only references to accountability in these documents are to hierarchical internal mechanisms which are not particularly effective. In terms of means discourses, the current terrain is no longer defined by a combination of Rows 1 and 2, but rather by a new row which represents a complete fusion between them. The strategy outlined in the two documents aims to reduce the differences between the bearers of bureaucratic and professional discourses, since such differences have in the past led to conflict. *OFE* is quite explicit:

> The administrative civil servants have tended to adopt a paper-based management approach, where direction has been exercised through written prescription and by control of the inputs to the service, but often with little information on how policies were being applied or on the outputs being delivered. Lacking effective accountability, direction and training, Governors have often adopted a 'charismatic' and individualistic approach to managing their establishments. These differences of style and approach have sometimes made it difficult for the two groups to co-operate.
>
> (Para. 3006)

Thus, *OFE* concludes that '[t]here is a need to develop a more integrated service perspective, which will produce benefits by improving co-operation between Headquarters and prisons and encourage career movement between Headquarters and establishments' (ibid.). Thus, a unified workforce is to be the bearer of a common culture.

POWER, DISCOURSE AND RECENT DEVELOPMENTS IN PENAL POLICY

In this chapter we have traced the movements in Scottish penal policy as it responded to the crisis of the mid-1980s. It is important that the shifts in emphasis and the resulting changes in policy are recognised for what they are. We have argued that they can be understood in terms of power and discourse. The strategies outlined in *C & C* and *A & C* were clearly centralising ones which reflected the power bases of their authors (civil servants at Headquarters). Since then, a new strategy has been developed which attempts to foster a common sense of ownership of the SPS. The policies outlined in *O & R* implied an alliance between administrative civil servants and professional governors, while the latest thinking in *ASE* and *OFE* takes this one stage further by proposing a new form of managerial fusion. Whether or not the power relations between the two existing groups of power-holders, i.e. between civil servants and prison governors, will allow this symbiosis to take place is another matter. However, it will certainly be assisted by the decision, announced by the Secretary of State for Scotland in February 1992, that the Scottish Prison Service would be given agency status as from 1 April 1993 since all staff will then become employees of the agency.[3]

The discursive site of this fusion between the two existing groups of power-holders is a specific form of managerial discourse which is heavily influenced by the enterprise culture and can be described as enterprise discourse. In the current political context this is a powerful discourse, which can be detected in many different areas of social life (Keat and Abercrombie 1991). The effect of this is to replace Rows 1 and 2 (representing bureaucratic and professional forms of discourse) in our 3 x 3 discourse matrix with a single row (representing a managerial form of discourse) in a new 2 x 3 discourse matrix. Whereas *O & R* occupies the space delineated by Rows 1 and 2 of the old matrix (Figure 9.1), *ASE* and *OFE* inhabit the space defined by Row 1 of the new matrix (Figure 9.2).

	Rehabilitation	Normalisation	Control
Bureaucracy	O & R	O & R	O & R
Professionalism	O & R	O & R	O & R
Legality	–	–	–

Note: O & R = *Opportunity and Responsibility* (Scottish Prison Service 1990a)

Figure 9.1 'Old' discourse matrix

	Rehabilitation	Normalisation	Control
Managerialism	ASE/OFE	ASE/OFE	ASE/OFE
Legality	–	–	–

Notes: ASE = *A Shared Enterprise* (Scottish Prison Service 1990b);
OFE = *Organising for Excellence* (Scottish Prison Service 1990c)

Figure 9.2 'New' discourse matrix

Although *ASE* and *OFE* do not refer specifically to the roles of prison professionals, like the industrial managers, education officers and social workers analysed in Chapter 5 above, it is clear that the new managerialism espoused in these reports could equally provide a means of integrating these groups into the Scottish Prison Service. How desirable that would be is quite another matter.

The Government has been active in promoting managerial solutions to organisational problems and what is being attempted by the SPS reflects the pervasive impact of the ideology of managerialism on policy-making in Government. As Pollitt argues, under the Conservatives there has been 'a growing emphasis on decentralising management responsibilities once financial targets and other norms have been (centrally) fixed' (Pollitt 1990:55). Although such strategies are often silent about the power relations between different groups of institutional actors, this can be seen as a deliberate ploy on the part of the centre. In the case of *ASE* and *OFE*, their silence on power relations operates to disguise an attempt to mobilise power for particular ends and to concentrate power in such a way as to increase social control. This is connected to the absence of legality as a clearly articulated discourse. Despite all the current talk of citizens' rights and institutional accountability, one of the weaknesses of recent policy documents is the lack of attention given to these concerns. As Scraton et al. argue in relation to the hostage-taking incidents referred to earlier in this chapter, 'despite the liberal, progressive vocabulary of the new strategy, there remained the problem within the long historical tradition of imprisonment concerning the dichotomy between control/restraint and treatment/rehabilitation, as well as questions concerning prisoners' rights and institutional accountability' (Scraton et al. 1991:38). Although the latest policy documents contain a number of positive features, the integration between the existing power-holders which they propose and the managerial discourse which they espouse can only lead to the centralisation of power and to more wide-ranging and more effective forms of social control. Such developments call for a greater emphasis on prisoners' rights and external forms of accountability than can be found in any of the policy documents reviewed in this chapter and, for this reason, they can, at best, be given a rather guarded welcome.

Chapter 10

Conclusion

Discourse, power and justice

In this concluding chapter, we pull the different strands of our argument together and assess the contribution of our book to the sociology of imprisonment. The chapter is in four parts dealing first with our theoretical position, second with our particular empirical focus, third with the normative position we adopt, and fourth with an example of how our approach enables us to contribute to debates over policy.

THEORETICAL CONTRIBUTION

In the course of this book we have attempted to develop a new sociology of imprisonment. The theoretical and analytic claims which characterise this new approach can be summarised under three headings: the centrality of power and discourse, the need for specificity and the importance of social change.

The centrality of power and discourse

Our theoretical perspective, which focuses on the roles of dominant groups within the Scottish prison system, has much in common with what DiIulio (1991) has called the 'new, old penology'. Our focus on the disparate concerns of administrators, governors and other, somewhat less powerful, groups of prison professionals which runs through the book, reflects our dissatisfaction with holistic and overly-coherent accounts of individual prisons and the prison system as a whole. Our approach draws attention to the rich variety of regimes and practices which co-exist in different prisons, each of which is a complex and highly differentiated organisation, and throughout the entire prison system.

Our theoretical position asserts the centrality of internal power struggles between dominant groups within the prison system. That is not to say that external or contextual factors are unimportant. However, it is to argue that their significance lies in their ability to structure the power relations between internal staff groups and to shape the outcome of the power struggles between them (for a very successful illustration of this position, see Faugeron and Houchon 1987). Although it might be argued that our theoretical position overemphasises conflict and denies the reality of social order, that is not our view. Social order can and does result from accommodations and trade-offs between groups which are in a conflictual relationship with each other. Our approach neither implies a Hobbesian war of all against all nor assumes the 'normality' of social order. Rather, it regards social order as a phenomenon which can be explained in terms of the outcomes of political struggles and the accommodations reached between dominant groups.

Drawing on Mannheim's work on the sociology of knowledge (in particular Mannheim 1952), we assert that groups in particular settings produce discourses that reflect their interests. These discourses, which consist of relatively coherent sets of ideas and symbols, act as resources to be fought over and as a means of domination. Thus discursive struggles lie at the heart of the power struggles with which we are concerned.

Our focus on powerful groups and their associated discourses draws on the work of Abercrombie et al. (1980). Like them, we have been less concerned with the ways in which the discourses we have identified can be used to incorporate dominated groups like prison officers and prisoners or to legitimate the prison system with the general public, and more concerned with the ways in which they are used to secure the coherence of dominant groups, like administrators and governors, and of domination as such. However, while Abercrombie et al. make their abstract arguments in terms of broad historical changes, we have attempted to develop them in the context of a prison system in which struggles over power and discourse are readily apparent.

Applying this model to the Scottish prison system in the years between 1985 and 1990, when there was a vigorous struggle between dominant groups over ideas and for control, throws new light on what was at stake and attests to the validity of the theoretical assumptions on which the model is based.

The need for specificity

Accounts of imprisonment which draw attention to the interconnectedness of power and discourse are often prone to overgeneralisations. In the Introduction we acknowledge that the work of Foucault (1979) was an important influence on our thinking. However, we are particularly critical of two aspects of his work. First, he tends to neglect the variations in discourse which exist at any given point in time. Second, he makes general claims about the nature and functions of imprisonment derived from a single case-study, and on this basis proposes a set of 'universal maxims of the good "penitential condition"' which, by virtue of their universality, are invariant to changes in time and place.

We have tried to ensure that our own work suffers from neither of these shortcomings. We have drawn attention to the many combinations of power and discourse which co-exist at any one point in time; the generalisations we seek to make are all at the level of method rather than substance; and, by seeking to subject several of Foucault's universal maxims to empirical scrutiny, we have demonstrated that they are not only contestable but actually contested. Thus, our book makes it clear that the maxims outlined by Foucault represent a beginning for sociological inquiry rather than an end point for it.

The importance of social change

One comment that was repeatedly made to us as we carried out our fieldwork was that we were studying Scottish prisons at a bad time because so much was changing and it was far from clear what the final outcome would be. However, the theoretical position we have adopted suggests the converse, i.e. that it was a particularly good time to be studying Scottish prisons. The turbulence of the times, the arguments between representatives of dominant groups and the struggles for control actually helped us to construct our theoretical framework. At the same time, our theoretical framework enabled us to see the processes at work particularly clearly and to understand a prison system in a state of flux. Using an iterative procedure based on 'wide reflective equilibrium' (Rawls 1972:46–53) we achieved a mutual adjustment between our theoretical framework and the subjects of our empirical study. Thus, those who might wish to criticise our approach for being too static and too much concerned with classification, will have seriously misunderstood one of its central features, i.e. its origins in and contribution to the study of social change.

EMPIRICAL FOCUS

Our study is mainly concerned with the management of adult, male, long-term prisoners in Scotland. Although they constitute the largest and most problematic of the different groups of prisoners which together make up the Scottish prison population, they are not synonymous with it. We have largely ignored the situation of other groups, i.e. prisoners on remand, short-term prisoners, female prisoners and young offenders, and this needs to be borne in mind in assessing the validity of our account of the Scottish Prison Service as a whole.

In the course of this book, we have applied our analytic framework to the study of numerous discrete areas of decision-making within the Scottish prison system, e.g. classification, transfers, regimes and various forms of accountability, and to the policy-making process. However, although our concerns have been wide-ranging, our study has not attempted to be exhaustive. We have ignored some areas of decision-making, e.g. visits, punishments and disciplinary hearings, and the role of psychologists and psychiatrists, and have only touched on others, e.g. parole, transfers to open conditions and the role of special units, some of which are of considerable importance to prisoners and prison staff (Wozniak and McAllister 1992). This also needs to be borne in mind in assessing our overall conclusions.

Rather than attempting to produce an exhaustive analysis of day-to-day decision-making or of policy-making, we have sought to demonstrate the utility and versatility of our analytic framework and to contribute to an understanding of the crisis which the Scottish Prison Service faced in the period between 1985 and 1990. However, it is clear that our analytic framework could equally be applied to the situation of other groups of prisoners, to other areas of decision-making, to other periods of time and to other prison systems. Although we have not done this ourselves, we are keen to encourage further work of this nature.

NORMATIVE IMPLICATIONS

Our attempt to apply a theoretical framework grounded in the sociology of knowledge to a concern with the justice inherent in and delivered through administrative processes, has led us to focus on the discourse of justice. In this context, we think that the distinction we have drawn between a justice of ends (concerned here with arguments about what prison is for) and a justice of means (concerned with arguments about how prisons should be run) is of considerable importance. Our typologies of ends and means discourses are, perhaps, rather too tidy. Nevertheless, they do represent an honest attempt to describe the major discourses which we found in play in the Scottish prison system at the time. It is, however, important to stress that it is most unlikely that the same discourses, with identical characteristics, would be found elsewhere.

Since justice is a normative concept, our concern with justice discourse enables us to engage with normative issues. Thus, in the book, we have not only sought to describe existing policies and practices but also to formulate a clear normative position on the future of imprisonment. Unlike most of the participants in this debate, we do not champion a single set of aims or a particular set of procedures for achieving them. Each of the ends discourses we have identified, and likewise each of the means discourses is 'coherent and attractive' (Mashaw 1983:23) and has much to offer. Furthermore, the various discourses are not 'mutually exclusive' but are, rather, 'highly competitive' (ibid.). Thus although 'the internal logic of any one of them tends to drive the characteristics of the others from the field as it works itself out in concrete situations' (ibid.), the task for policy-makers should be to produce an optimum balance between these different discourses. This balance will be different in different concrete situations but the goal of the Scottish Prison Service (and likewise of other prison systems) should be to produce a synthesis of what is best in each of the discourses we have identified. This would appear to have been achieved by *Opportunity and Responsibility* (SPS 1990a) in respect of specifying the ends of imprisonment, i.e. deciding what prison is for, although it has clearly not yet been attained by *A Shared Enterprise* (SPS 1990b) or *Organising for Excellence* (SPS 1990c) in relation to specifying the means of imprisonment, i.e. deciding how prisons should be run. That a synthesis has now been found between rehabilitation (in its new voluntaristic form), normalisation and control is a considerable achievement. However, the attempt to integrate the two main groups of power-holders (administrative civil servants and prison governors) is fraught with problems and the failure to embrace legal discourse as a means of holding the power-holders to account is a matter of some considerable concern.

We conclude this chapter, and our book, by demonstrating how the approach we have developed enables us to contribute to debates over policy. Since Chapters 6, 7 and 8 are concerned with different mechanisms of accountability, we now consider here how the overall accountability of the Scottish Prison Service could be improved.

APPLICATION TO POLICY: HOW TO STRENGTHEN THE ACCOUNTABILITY OF THE SCOTTISH PRISON SYSTEM

In Chapter 6, we showed how the bureaucratic form of accountability embodied in the petition system was in practice unable to offer an effective challenge to the professionalism inherent in governors' decision-making or to provide an effective mechanism of accountability, and attempted to explain why this should be so. For it to be more effective, the Prison Rules and Standing Orders will have to be rewritten in such a way as to set out clear criteria for decision-making and allocate responsibility for particular decisions to officials at appropriate levels of seniority within the Scottish prison system. This is an essential prerequisite both to improving the internal arrangements for administrative review and to introducing an external check on internal decision-making in the form of an independent Prisons Ombudsman (see, e.g., Birkenshaw 1985) along the lines advocated by most of the prison reform groups. The appointment of an independent Prisons Ombudsman for England and Wales was recommended by the Woolf Committee (Home Office 1991a) and subsequently accepted by the Home Secretary. However, it is a matter of some concern that this proposal was rejected by a Scottish Working Group (SPS 1992) in favour of an extremely complex (and probably unworkable) set of proposals intended merely to introduce an 'independent element' with a reformed set of grievance procedures (Adler 1993).

In Chapter 7, the logic of our argument led to a set of proposals which would strengthen the Inspectorate, enhance its capacity to enforce compliance with statutory requirements and improve standards of performance (Rhodes 1981). First, changes are needed in the staffing of the Inspectorate. We believe that the office of Chief Inspector of Prisons is an important one which should be filled by an individual of some social standing who can command a power base. The need for independence suggests that the Chief Inspector would most appropriately be a judge or other senior member of the legal profession. Further, the staff of the Inspectorate should be professionals with a stake in making a mark during their time there. A period at the Inspectorate should be seen as an important stage in the career development of every governor and not as a period of rest and recuperation in a 'backwater'. Second, the Inspectorate should take the lead in developing and articulating a set of professional standards which could then be applied consistently across the prison system as a whole. Prisons could then be inspected in a more consistent and authoritative manner. Third, the Inspectorate needs to pay far more attention to the discourse of legality. As we have made clear, we think the best way of bringing this about would be through the appointment of a judge as Chief Inspector. Fourth, the remit of the Inspectorate needs to be extended to include Headquarters as well as individual establishments. Finally, the Inspectorate should seek to address a wider audience. At the moment, its work tends to be directed inwards, towards the Secretary of State and those in charge of the prison system. Although the Inspectorate's Annual Reports are published as Command Papers and hence can be purchased from HMSO, reports on inspections are only available from the Inspectorate and members of the public would need to make a considerable effort to obtain them. Of course, it is unlikely that many members of the public would wish to do so but the press could play an important role in filtering the contents of such reports and presenting them to the public. For this to be the case however, the Inspectorate will need to be more hard-hitting and publicity-seeking.

As we showed in Chapter 8, none of the mechanisms of legal accountability we considered provides a particularly effective means of holding the Scottish Prison Service to account or of safeguarding the rights of Scottish prisoners. Incorporation of the European Convention on Human Rights might help by speeding up proceedings and reducing the power differential between the parties but is unlikely to make much difference overall. If legal accountability is to be taken seriously, legal discourse will need to be strengthened and the imbalance of power between the individual prisoner and the prison authorities will need to be redressed at the same time. A legal framework which not only guarantees 'general rights' but also establishes 'special rights' for prisoners (Richardson 1984), together with an accessible set of procedures which prisoners can invoke to secure their rights and ensure that they are enforced, would need to be introduced. Although such reforms could be implemented on a European or an international basis, they would almost certainly be more effective if they were designed and introduced domestically.

If the overall accountability of the prison system is to be strengthened, it is clear that it will be necessary to make progress on several fronts at the same time. This is because the existing bureaucratic, professional and legal mechanisms of accountability are all deficient in themselves and all in need of strengthening, and because the demands of bureaucratic, professional and juridical accountability are competitive rather than mutually exclusive (Mashaw 1983). Thus it is really a question of balance. The first priority must be to revise the Prison Rules and Standing Orders in such a way as to reflect the desired trade-off between the three ends discourses, i.e. between discourses of rehabilitation, normalisation and control. However, a second, and almost equally important, priority should be to revise the Prison Rules and Standing Orders so as to produce an enhanced trade-off between the three means discourses, i.e. between discourses of bureaucracy, professionalism and legality. Each of these discourses emphasises the virtues of a different principle of organisation – administrative rules and regulations in the case of bureaucratic discourse, discretion and standards of service in the case of professional discourse, and the rights of subjects in the case of legal discourse. But, while arguments can be advanced in favour of each of these principles, arguments can also be advanced against them. Thus, while rules hold out the prospect of greater consistency and of ensuring that like cases are treated alike, they can lead to excessive rigidity unless they are continually revised and give a great deal of power to the organisation, in this case the prison system. While discretion allows for greater flexibility and facilitates creativity, it can easily permit the intrusion of moral judgments and give a great deal of power to the officials who are entrusted with it, in this case prison staff. Finally, while rights can lead to a greater sense of independence among subjects and allow for appeals to an adjudicating authority, they can also promote litigiousness and give too much power to individual rights-holders, in this case prisoners.

One of the aims of securing an appropriate trade-off between the three means discourses and an optimum balance between the respective claims of administrative rules and regulations, professional discretion and standards of service, and the rights of prisoners should be to devolve as much decision-making as possible away from the centre. Many of the requests which are currently transmitted through petitions and answered at Headquarters could equally well be dealt with in individual establishments if the Prison Rules and Standing Orders provided sufficiently clear criteria for decision-making. Only when the Prison Rules and Standing Orders have been revised in this way will it be possible to devise an appropriate set of mechanisms to ensure that those who take decisions are accountable for the decisions they take and that the decisions are in accordance with the agreed aims and policies of the organisation. If organisational discourse is to represent a balance between each of the two sets of discourses described above, and is to embrace all the cells in the discourse matrix, then a variety of mechanisms of accountability will need to be developed. They will need to include internal/hierarchical review, peer-type assessment and independent adjudication, although each will clearly need to assume a more developed form than it has at present.

Notes

INTRODUCTION

1 The research was funded by the ESRC (Grant Number E 0625 0031) under its Crime and Criminal Justice Initiative and, to a lesser degree, by the Nuffield Foundation.

2 Our reasons for not including female prisoners were that there were so few of them (the average daily population of adult, female, long-term prisoners in 1988 was less than fifty), they were all held in one establishment (Cornton Vale, the only prison for women in Scotland) which has recently been the subject of two major studies (Carlen 1983 and Dobash et al. 1986). In addition, a serious comparative study would have called for substantial modifications to the research design adopted here.

3 In 1988 the average daily population of adult, male, long-term prisoners was about 1,900, out of an overall average daily population of just over 5,000. In addition there were about 1,400 short-term prisoners, 800 prisoners on remand and 850 young offenders (all male) and a total of about 150 female prisoners (Scottish Home and Health Department 1990b).

4 We comment on the status of our data sets as they are introduced. We refer to interviewees and those we observed by letters and numbers as follows:

A1–A8	Administrators of various grades (specified when cited)
G1–G10	Governors-in-charge of prisons
G11–G15	Deputy Governors
G16–G18	Governors (regimes) or Training Governors
G19	HQ Governor
G20–G26	Grade 5 (Assistant) Governors
I1–I7	Industrial Managers (with responsibility for work in prisons)
E1–E4	Education Officers
S1–S5	Social Workers of different grades
01–05	Others (specified when cited).

All the interviews were tape-recorded and detailed notes, including verbatim quotations, taken afterwards.

5 The incidents in Scotland were the subject of an official report by Her Majesty's Chief Inspector of Prisons (Scotland) (1987). They were also the subject of an unofficial report by the Gateway Exchange (1987). For another unofficial view see Scraton et al. (1988 and 1991). The results of the inquiry chaired by Lord Justice Woolf into the disturbances at Strangeways Prison in Manchester are set out in Home Office (1991a).

6 It is important to note that these are generalisations; Jacobs (1977) is historical, Sykes (1958) and Goffman (1961) do consider wider theoretical issues, and Jacobs (1977) and Sykes (1958) do address those in power.

7 There is, of course, a well-established tradition of work which focuses on the prison system as a whole. See, for example, Bottomley (1973), Fitzgerald (1977), Fitzgerald and Sim (1979), Rutherford (1986), Stern (1987) and, most recently, Coyle (1991) and Cavadino and Dignan (1992).

1 INSTITUTIONS, ACTORS AND TRENDS IN IMPRISONMENT

1 Over a twenty-year period at the end of the eighteenth century, 134 convicted criminals were sentenced to death in Scotland and ninety-seven of these were actually executed. During the same period, in London and the County of Middlesex (which together had a population about half the size of that in Scotland), 1,910 convicted criminals were sentenced to death and 890 were executed. This pattern continued until well into the nineteenth century (Coyle 1991:23).

2 Following a review by Coopers and Lybrand Deloitte (Scottish Prison Service 1990c), a new management structure was recently introduced. This consists of a Chief Executive and four Directors, each of whom is responsible for a major area of activity. The Chief Executive and the four Directors, together with two non-executive members from outside the Scottish Prison Service, constitute a Prisons Board, whose role is to provide strategic advice to the Chief Executive.

3 In the fully elaborated topographical model, the criminal courts were included in the outer ring of legal accountability. However, in the simplified model, it seemed more appropriate to place them on a par with the Parole Board. The reasons for this are set out on p.13 above.

4 Holding a prisoner on remand is subject to the following limits of time in Scotland. In summary criminal proceedings a court may, without calling upon the accused to plead guilty or not guilty to the charge, remand the person for up to seven days (or twenty-one days in exceptional cases) to allow time for inquiry into the case. In solemn criminal proceedings, an untried prisoner must receive an indictment within eighty days of the date of committal and, if the indictment is not served within this period, must be released, although the person may still be prosecuted for the offence. If the indictment is served within eighty days, the trial must begin within 110 days of the committal date. If this time limit is not met, the prisoner must be released and no

further proceedings may be taken against the person for that offence. Where the prosecution is under summary proceedings and the accused has been remanded in custody, the trial must begin within forty days of bringing the summary complaint in court.

5 Prisoners serving sentences of more than five days become eligible for release when they have served two-thirds of their sentence. Only loss of remission imposed as a punishment for an offence against prison discipline can extend this period and then only for the length of sentence imposed by the court. Parole was introduced into Scotland, as well as England and Wales, by the Criminal Justice Act 1967 and, since then, prisoners serving determinate sentences have become eligible for release on parole after serving one-third of their sentence or twelve months, whichever expires later. The procedure for releasing offenders serving indeterminate sentences is necessarily somewhat different. A preliminary sift is carried out after about three years and the prisoner is then given some indication, taking into account any recommendation by the trial judge and the Secretary of State's policy on parole, of when the case is likely to be reviewed. Scotland has its own Parole Board, whose members include judges, psychiatrists, criminologists, social workers and lay members, which is appointed by the Secretary of State for Scotland. See Chapter 4 below.

6 However, according to the UN Crime Survey, Scotland had a lower prison population per 100,000 recorded crimes than many other European countries including Northern Ireland (which had the highest rate), Italy, Austria, (West) Germany, Greece, England and Wales and France. Only Finland, the Netherlands and Sweden recorded lower rates (Home Office 1991b).

7 In 1984, the Secretary of State for Scotland announced that prisoners convicted of certain crimes, including murder in the course of armed robbery, murder of a police or prison officer, and sexual or sadistic murders of young children, should serve a minimum of twenty years. This restrictive policy brought Scotland into line with England and Wales, where the Home Secretary had introduced a similar policy the year before.

2 DISCOURSES AND DISCURSIVE STRUGGLES

1 Mannheim has often been seen as a kind of naïve relativist who had a simple faith in the goodness of intellectuals. For a rebuttal of such claims see Longhurst (1989:75–83).

2 We are indebted to Nick Abercrombie and Scott Lash for discussions on this subject.

3 For a fuller account of prison labour in nineteenth-century Scotland, see Dobash (1983).

4 For an interesting consideration of his critical stance and a response to Left realist criminology's particular sense of its political task, see Cohen (1990:30) where Taylor (1990) is the target.

5 One can imagine other forms of control discourse which focus on other disruptive influences, e.g. the inmate subculture.

3 CLASSIFICATION: THE CORE OF THE PRISON SYSTEM

1 For a useful discussion of the problems of Durkheim and Mauss's approach, see Rodney Needham's *Introduction to Durkheim and Mauss* (1963).

2 All prisoners appearing before the National Classification Board take two tests: a 'Graded Arithmetic–Mathematics Test' and 'The Millhill Vocabulary Scale, Form 1 Junior' test. At Edinburgh, the tests are taken in the morning, prior to the meeting of the Board in the afternoon. At Barlinnie, the prisoners sit the tests immediately before the meeting of the Board in the morning.

3 The prisoner's 'warrant' is his file which is opened at the beginning of his sentence. It follows him from establishment to establishment during his prison career and contains a record of all the things which happen to him during his sentence. Factual details, such as age, home area, sentence and offence are listed on the front cover.

4 These data, and those summarised in Tables 3.6 and 3.7, were provided for us by the Induction Officer at Edinburgh Prison.

5 Until the opening of Phase II in May 1987, Shotts Phase I could only provide accommodation for sixty prisoners, most of whom worked in the laundry.

6 Very few prisoners took up the option of petitioning. In 1986, only seventeen of the 3,405 petitions submitted referred to classification. However, 458 of those submitted requested transfer to another establishment and a further seventy-nine were appealing against transfer. See Chapter 6 below.

7 Largely as a result of the unprecedented increase in the number of long-term prisoners during 1986 and 1987 (see Chapter 1 above) and the consequent overcrowding.

8 This shop was used as a workplace for sex offenders (and others who were deemed to be in need of protection) in Edinburgh Prison.

9 This means, of course, that in the past those wishing to be classified to Peterhead, as some prisoners undoubtedly did, could get there very easily by refusing to take induction tests.

10 Noranside, which had been an open institution for young offenders of all sentence ranges, became Scotland's second open prison. See Chapter 1 above.

11 Grand Design was made possible by the relative stability of the young offender population. The average daily population of male young offenders was 982 in 1984, 969 in 1985, 1,051 in 1986 and 961 in 1987. Over the same period, the average daily population of male adult LTPs increased by 50 per cent from 1,215 in 1984 to 1,431 in 1985, 1,725 in 1986 and 1,862 in 1987 (SPS 1988a:Appendix 1). The effect of Grand Design was to transfer 320 places from YOIs to the adult LTP system. See, also, Chapter 9 below.

12 At three out of the four meetings we observed after Grand Design, various members of the industrial staff deputised for the industrial manager. This contrasted to the situation prior to Grand Design when the industrial manager was always present.

13 The basic conditions for an immediate transfer to Penninghame are that the prisoner

1 has no history of sexual offences (excluding incest);
2 has not served a custodial sentence for any offence involving violence;
3 has not previously received a custodial sentence of more than nine months; and
4 has not actually spent more than a total of one year in custody in the previous five years.

There were also other considerations which could mean that an immediate transfer to Penninghame would be inappropriate. These are that the prisoner:

1 has further charges to face;
2 is an appellant;
3 has other legal, medical or domestic business to attend to that could not be carried out adequately if he were transferred to Penninghame;
4 is unsuitable for open, dormitory conditions because of his medical condition, personality, conduct or domestic circumstances; and
5 has other characteristics in his circumstances (including his own attitude to Penninghame) that point to his being kept in closed conditions.

(SHHD 1983)

4 TRANSFERS AND CAREERS: REINFORCING CLASSIFICATION

1 Transfer data were collected from the prison register of each long-term prison visited. In most cases, the data covered a two-year period prior to data collection but, in some cases, a shorter period had to be selected. This was because the role of several establishments changed during 1987. Shotts Phase II opened in May 1987 (prior to that, Phase I provided accommodation for only sixty prisoners, most of whom worked in the laundry). At the same time, and as a consequence of Grand Design, Glenochil and Noranside, which used to be YOIs, became adult prisons while Dumfries and Greenock, which used to be adult prisons, became YOIs. Although movements into and out of Shotts were collected for a two-year period, movements into and out of Glenochil and Noranside were only collected over one year. This exercise generated a data set of 3,476 prisoners. It does not constitute a random sample of long-term prisoners in Scotland as no data on the movements of long-term prisoners into and out of individual establishments were collected for Barlinnie, Dumfries or Greenock. This resulted in a substantial under-representation of prisoners from the west of Scotland in our sample. Prisoners who moved between these three prisons during the period in question will not have been picked up by our sampling procedure; prisoners who moved between one of these three prisons and another long-term prison should have been

picked up once (from the records of the other prison); while prisoners who moved between any of the other long-term prisons should have been picked up twice (from the records of both prisons). The breakdown of the transfer sample was as follows:

Prison	*Number*	%
Aberdeen	130	3.7
Dungavel	270	7.8
Edinburgh	673	19.4
Glenochil	611	17.6
Noranside	175	5.0
Penninghame	207	6.0
Perth	728	20.9
Peterhead	196	5.6
Shotts	486	14.0
Total	3,476	100.0

Due to the unavailability of appropriate data at Headquarters, careers data were collected in prisons. In each of the long-term prisons we visited we selected a sample of up to fifty prisoners and recorded a considerable amount of information from the prisoner's warrant (file) which accompanies him throughout his prison career. When the number of long-term prisoners in the establishment was less than fifty, the sample was stratified by length of sentence. In other cases, a 100 per cent count was taken. Names were selected from the prison register and the information extracted from the file which the holding establishment keeps on each prisoner. The breakdown was as follows:

Prison	*Number*	%
Aberdeen	51	11.9
Barlinnie	14	3.3
Dungavel	48	11.2
Edinburgh	51	11.9
Glenochil	65	15.2
Noranside	27	6.3
Penninghame	23	5.4
Perth	50	11.6
Peterhead	50	11.6
Shotts	50	11.6
Total	429	100.0

2 Rule 36 of the Prison (Scotland) Rules 1952 states that 'if it is desirable for the maintenance of good order and discipline, or in the interests of a prisoner, that he should not be employed in association with others' arrangements may be made 'for him to work in a cell and not in association'. However, in practice, Rule 36 is used to remove prisoners from all association. Recommendations from the governor require the authorisation of the Visiting Committee or the Secretary

of State, in practice the latter. They are dealt with in a rather perfunctory way at Headquarters (see Chapter 6 below). Authorisation is given for one month at a time. Rule 36 is the equivalent of Rule 43 in England and Wales.

3 We examined at Headquarters the files of all the lifers who had been paroled in 1975, 1981 and 1986, some seventy-nine cases in all, comprising fourteen from 1975, forty-one from 1981 and twenty-four from 1986. We have no reason to think that there is anything special about any of these years and a comparison of the three cohorts provides a valuable opportunity to describe and explain how the Scottish prison system dealt with lifers over the period in question.

4 For example, nine out of thirteen (69.2 per cent) of prisoners with an Edinburgh classification served ten years or less compared with six out of twelve (50.0 per cent) of those classified for Perth and two out of thirteen (15.4 per cent) of those classified for Peterhead or Aberdeen. By comparison, eleven out of thirteen (84.6 per cent) of prisoners with a Peterhead or Aberdeen classification served more than ten years compared with six out of twelve (50.0 per cent) of those classified for Perth and four out of thirteen (30.8 per cent) of those classified for Edinburgh. The modal sentence for those who were paroled in 1975 was eight to nine years; for those who were paroled in 1981, it was nine to ten years and for those paroled in 1986 it was ten to eleven years.

5 Where parole is supported by Headquarters, it is very unusual for it not to be recommended by the Parole Board. Between 1985 and 1989, 135 cases of prisoners serving life sentences were referred to the Parole Board for decision. In all of these cases parole was supported by Headquarters and in all but one of them, parole was recommended. In addition, 294 cases which were not supported by Headquarters (for whatever reason) were referred to the Parole Board for information (Parole Board for Scotland 1990: Table 2). Parole was not recommended in any of these cases.

6 Membership of the Parole Board includes criminologists, psychiatrists, psychologists and social workers, as well as members of the judiciary. It has a lay chairman and a number of lay members.

7 In 1988, a Select Committee of the House of Lords was set up to examine, *inter alia*, whether the life sentence should be the maximum or the mandatory penalty for murder (Windlesham 1989). In many other countries, it is the maximum penalty and is reserved for the most heinous crimes. If the life sentence became the maximum penalty, it would follow that, in other less heinous cases, the judge would impose a determinate sentence.

5 REGIMES: THE POWER OF THE GOVERNORS AND THE MARGINALISATION OF OTHER PROFESSIONALS

1 See Chapter 4, note 2 above.

2 In the aftermath of the hostage-taking incidents, sixty prisoners were held under lockdown conditions in Peterhead. This meant that there

were insufficient prisoners available to service the establishment. In these circumstances, the Governor suggested and Headquarters agreed that essential domestic jobs, e.g. kitchen orderly, cook and 'passman', should be allocated to short-term prisoners from Aberdeen.

3 Under the Special Escorted Leave (SEL) scheme, leave for all or part of a day is granted on the understanding that the prisoner places himself under the supervision of his escort and follows his/her instructions. Prison officers (and civilian instructors) act as escorts but the scheme is voluntary and they do not get paid. Prisoners must be C or D category. The scheme operated in Edinburgh as well as Dungavel.

4 G3 did believe that progression could (and should) be achieved through transfer to another prison.

5 It is not entirely clear why this should be so since many 'outside' organisations operate systems of progression, paying higher wages and giving better employment protection and more prerequisites to longer-serving staff, giving priority to those who have spent time on a waiting list etc.

6 The published statistics include separate figures for adult prisoners and young offenders. The figures in Table 5.1 refer to adult prisoners only.

7 The remainder were awaiting or under punishment, recent admissions, sick/disabled (and not required to work) or in full-time education.

8 This is, of course, much higher than the proportion of men in the national workforce who now work in manufacturing industries (approximately 25 per cent).

9 Fresh Start was implemented on 1 November 1987. It gave the majority of staff a new pay and conditions package and blurred the distinction between officer grades and governor grades by introducing a unified grading structure.

10 Under normalisation, prisoners would be paid the 'going rate' for working (see Ruxton 1989).

11 The Working Group contained one HMI (Inspector of Schools) who resigned in June 1986 and was not replaced and the Principal of Perth College of Further Education. Although it contained three prison education officers and two prison teachers, it was rather short on educational expertise. Nevertheless, its recommendations sought to enhance the professional standing of education in the prison service.

12 In 1984–5, the resources available for education under the prisons vote amounted to £699,000 for Scotland and £12,065,000 for England and Wales. Although no direct comparisons can be made, the Report of the Working Group 'felt there was a clear indication that the resources being made available to Scottish Penal Institutions compared unfavourably with those in England and Wales (SHHD 1987a:para. 7.1).

6 PETITIONS TO THE SECRETARY OF STATE: HANDLING REQUESTS AND SETTLING GRIEVANCES?

1 Visiting Committees broadly parallel Boards of Visitors in English Prisons. On the latter see Vagg (1985), Maguire (1985) and Morgan et al. (1985).

2 Under the provisions of Section 16 of the Prisons (Scotland) Act 1877, prisoners may also ask to see a sheriff or a justice of the peace when they visit a prison. However, since sheriffs and magistrates only visit prisons rarely, if at all, this route no longer constitutes an effective means for the redress of grievances. Prisoners may also exercise their constitutional right to petition the Queen and Parliament but few choose to do so.
3 In subsequent years, the number of petitions declined. The number of petitions received by the Scottish Prison Service fell to 3,697 in 1989 and to 2,888 in 1990.
4 It would appear that petitions are used much more frequently in Scotland than in England and Wales. In 1986, there were 3,351 petitions in Scotland corresponding to a rate of approximately 60 petitions per 100 prisoners. In 1987–8, the first year for which a complete set of figures is available, there were 14,420 petitions in England and Wales (7,401 at Headquarters and 7,419 at Regional Offices), corresponding to a rate of approximately 30 per 100 prisoners, i.e. less than half the Scottish rate (HM Prison Service 1989:Table 4).
5 Since it is a disciplinary offence under the Prison Rules to make 'false and malicious allegations against an officer' (Rule 42(19)) and to make 'repeated and groundless complaints' (Rule 42(16)) sealing a petition may also provide a measure of protection to a prisoner who might otherwise find himself on a disciplinary charge.
6 Corresponding to Ditchfield and Austin's Type I reply, i.e. '"fully considered", subject matter mentioned'. The other categories they use are 'expanded' which 'contains some form of explanation or personalisation, subject matter mentioned'; Type II '"fully considered", no subject matter mentioned'; and Type III '"sympathetically considered", no subject matter mentioned' (Ditchfield and Austin 1986:53).

7 THE PRISON INSPECTORATE: MONITORING REGIMES AND IMPROVING STANDARDS?

1 This stands in contrast with the activities of the Chief Inspector for England and Wales who, since the early 1980s, has placed greater emphasis on thematic reviews of general policy issues across institutions (Morgan 1985:112).
2 The appointment, on his retirement, of a very senior Scottish Office civil servant, who had previously been directly accountable to the Secretary of State for Scotland, led to further questioning of the independence of the Inspectorate.
3 During the course of an interview with the Inspectorate, this process was described in the following way by the CI. 'About a week after the inspection, the Inspectorate will say to the Governor "have we got the story right?"' After this the Inspectorate will go to Prisons Group, present their findings and then ask for comments. They will ask 'is this right on policy matters?' CI stated that 'In that process we can

communicate a lot about our findings and we are beginning to see the shape of the report which is then written up in draft.'

4 The Deputy Chief Inspector pointed out that, for example, the report of the inspection of Dumfries that was carried out in September 1986 had still not appeared by September 1987, leading to a 'loss of impact'.

5 A related point was made by the Deputy Chief Inspector during the course of an interview. He maintained that the reports had moved away from the 'bricks and mortar' approach of earlier reports, to become more concerned with regimes.

6 As the Chief Inspector's report points out,

> The SCDP has seven members comprising a lay Chairman, two representatives nominated by the Governors' Committee and two nominated by the SPOA Executive, a psychiatrist and a member of Prisons Group. There is no minimum or fixed period of office. The Committee has no executive powers and its functions include:
>
> (a) To advise the Scottish Home and Health Department on the allocation and management of prisoners referred to it by the Department because of difficulties created by their unruly, violent and/or subversive behaviour; and
>
> (b) The Committee may, if its experience suggests that alternative regimes or units are desirable for the management of violent, unruly and/or subversive prisoners, make recommendations on the subject to the Department.

7 The number of recommendations in each Annual Report is:

1981	11
1982	2
1983	3
1984	2
1985	0
1986	3
1987	4
1988	6
1989	2
1990	8

8 THE EUROPEAN CONVENTION ON HUMAN RIGHTS: PROTECTING PRISONERS' RIGHTS?

1 Austria, Belgium, Cyprus, France, Germany, Greece, Italy, Luxembourg, Netherlands, Portugal, Spain, Switzerland, Turkey.

2 This is now possible in all the Convention countries except Cyprus and Turkey.

3 In 1986 and 1987, there was a considerable increase in the number of registered applications. The number increased from 596 in 1985 to 706 in 1988 and 860 in 1987 (Council of Europe 1988).

4 One of the cases related to *Silver* was the Scottish case brought by *Shields*. This is discussed in some detail below.

5 The 'simultaneous ventilation rule' did not last long. In *R. v. Home Secretary, ex parte Anderson* (1984), the Divisional Court in England held that it constituted an impediment to the right of access to the courts.

6 In Scotland, Standing Order M was issued in July 1983. It outlined a revised set of procedures governing communications by correspondence and, in order to meet ECHR views, was published and made available to inmates. It was divided into seven points dealing with correspondence, visits to inmates, petitions and complaints, communications with MPs and MEPs, communication with consular and Commonwealth officials, ECHR and litigants. Among the major changes which it introduced were the simultaneous ventilation rule, greater freedom in the choice of correspondents, relaxation of censorship (the main object of censorship was henceforth to check that letters did not include objectionable matters), removal of the prohibition on visits by ex-prisoners, reduced surveillance during visits and access to solicitors for prisoners who wished to commence litigation.

7 In Scotland, tacit practice for the last few years has been to not allow cases to be passed to the Visiting Committee but, rather, to involve the Procurator Fiscal with a view to criminal prosecution in the courts where the case is too serious to be dealt with by the governor (Roberts 1991:32).

8 A number of these applications were supported by the Scottish Council for Civil Liberties (SCCL).

9 In Scotland, remission (of one-third of the sentence) did not apply to those who were imprisoned as children. By contrast, those who were imprisoned as children in England were entitled to remission under Section 103(2) of the Criminal Justice Act 1967.

10 No record appears in the ECHR's annual *Stocktaking Supplement* which lists all the applications that have been declared admissible. See, for example, Council of Europe (1988).

11 One of these cases was abandoned as a result of SCCL's failing to reply to requests for further information from the Commission.

12 See note 6 above.

13 In the course of preparing submissions in the *Rice* case, the Solicitor's Department in the Scottish Office noticed that prisoners in Barlinnie were not receiving the minimum visiting requirements laid down in Standing Order Mb. It was pointed out that this would constitute a breach of Article 8 (which lays down that procedures must be 'in accordance with the law') and would undermine the Government's own contention, frequently expressed, that the Secretary of State would always uphold the rights of prisoners under Standing Orders. The Prison Service was advised to 'rectify this [situation] with all possible speed' and it would appear that this was done.

14 Some prisoners were represented by pressure groups, in particular by the Scottish Council for Civil Liberties (SCCL). However, their expertise was no match for the legal expertise which the Government could call on.

15 By contrast, a red light jurisprudence of judicial review, in effect, holds that 'everything is forbidden save that which is expressly allowed'.

16 Direct complaints may be forwarded, with the complainant's consent, to the constituency MP with the request that he decide whether or not to refer the complaint back formally.

9 RECENT DEVELOPMENTS IN PENAL POLICY: TOWARDS ENTERPRISING MANAGERIALISM

1 See Chapter 4, note 2 above.
2 See Chapter 4, note 2 above.
3 When *OFE* was published in December 1990, the Scottish Prison Service was not a candidate for agency status. The arguments for and against agency status are set out in paras. 6010–11 and the report expresses the hope that this will be helpful to Ministers in reaching an eventual decision on the issue.

List of cited cases

JUDICIAL REVIEW ETC.

England and Wales

R. v. Home Secretary, ex parte Anderson (1984) 1 All ER 920
Raymond v. Honey (1982) 1 All ER 759 and (1983) 1 AC 1
R. v. Board of Visitors of Hull Prison, ex parte St Germain (1978) 2 WLR 598 (Divisional Court) (1979) 1 All ER 701 (Court of Appeal) and (1979) 3 All ER 545 (House of Lords)

Scotland

Leech v. Secretary of State for Scotland (OH) 1991 SLT 910, (IH) 1993 SLT 365
Thomson v. Secretary of State for Scotland 1989 SLT 343

EUROPEAN COMMISSION AND COURT OF HUMAN RIGHTS

England and Wales

Campbell and Fell v. UK, Application Nos. 7819/77 and 7878/78, Declared admissible 6/7/78 and 14 & 19/3/81, Report 12/5/82, Judgment No.60 (28/6/84)
Golder v. UK, Application No. 445/70, Declared admissible 30/3/71, Report 1/6/73, Judgment No.11 (21/2/75)
Ireland v. UK, Application No. 5310/71, Declared admissible 1/10/72, Report 15/1/76, Judgment No.18 (18/1/78)
Silver and Others v. UK, Application Nos. 5947–5953/72, Declared admissible 4/10/77, Report 11/10/80, Judgment No.46 (25/3/83 and 24/10/83)
Weeks v. UK 9789/82, Declared admissible 17/1/84, Report 7/12/84, Judgment Application No.93 (2/3/87)

Scotland

Boyle and Boyle v. UK, Application No. 9659/82, Declared admissible 6/3/85
Boyle and Rice v. UK, Report 7/5/86, Judgment No.120 (27/4/88)
Burke v. UK, Application No. 8586/79
Fischer v. UK, Application No. 7512/79
Hodgson v. UK, Application No. 11392/85
McCallum v. UK, Application No. 9511/81, Declared admissible 10/7/85, Report 4/5/89, Judgment No.178 (30/8/90)
McQueenie v. UK, Application No. 9917/82
Nelson v. UK, Application No. 11077/84
Rice and Rice v. UK, Application No. 9658/82, Declared admissible 6/3/85
Ross v. UK, Application No. 11396/85
Shields v. UK, Application No. 7742/76
Steele v. UK, Application No. 10778/84
Wardlaw v. UK, Application No. 10239/82, Declared admissible 10/7/85

References

Note: Earlier versions of material which appears in this book are marked with an asterisk.

Abercrombie, N., Hill, S. and Turner, B. S. (1980) *The Dominant Ideology Thesis*, London: Allen and Unwin.

Abercrombie, N., Hill, S. and Turner, B. S. (1986) *Sovereign Individuals of Capitalism*, London: Allen and Unwin.

Abercrombie, N., Hill, S. and Turner, B. S. (eds) (1990) *Dominant Ideologies*, London: Unwin Hyman.

Abercrombie, N. and Longhurst, B. (1981) 'Mannheim's Soul: a Comment on Vallas', *Sociology*, 15(3), 424–427.

Abercrombie, N. and Longhurst, B. (1983) 'Interpreting Mannheim', *Theory, Culture and Society*, 2(1), 5–15.

*Adler, M. (1991) 'Prisoners' Rights and Prison Conditions in Scotland' in F. Dünkel and D. van Zyl Smit (eds) *Imprisonment Today and Tomorrow: International Perspectives on Prisoners' Rights and Prison Conditions*, Deventer, The Netherlands: Kluwer, 493–535.

Adler, M. (1993) 'Prisoners' Rights: A Litmus Test for a Civilised Society', *Scottish Affairs*, 3, 111–117.

*Adler, M. and Longhurst, B. (1989) 'The Classification of Long-term Prisoners in Scotland' in E. Wozniak (ed.) *Current Issues in Scottish Prisons: Systems of Accountability and Regimes for Difficult Prisoners* (Scottish Prison Service Occasional Paper, No.2/1989), Edinburgh: Scottish Office, 21–45.

*Adler, M. and Longhurst, B. (1990) 'The Future of Imprisonment in Scotland: A Critique of Policy' in A. Brown and R. Parry (eds) *The Scottish Government Yearbook 1990*, Edinburgh: Unit for the Study of Government in Scotland, University of Edinburgh, 226–242.

*Adler, M. and Longhurst, B. (1991a) 'Power, Discourse and Justice: Prisons in Scotland Today' in V. Ferrari (ed.) *Laws and Rights*, Milano: Dott A. Giuffrè Editore, 461–496.

*Adler, M. and Longhurst, B. (1991b) 'The Future of Imprisonment in Scotland: A Great Leap Forward?' in A. Brown and D. McCrone (eds) *The Scottish Government Yearbook 1991*, Edinburgh: Unit for the Study of Government in Scotland, University of Edinburgh, 209–216.

*Adler, M. and Longhurst, B. (1992a) 'The Future of Imprisonment in Scotland' in J. Muncie and R. Sparks (eds) *Imprisonment: European Perspectives*, Hemel Hempstead: Harvester Wheatsheaf, 166–176.

*Adler, M. and Longhurst, B. (1992b) 'Discourse and Decision Making in Scottish Prisons' in D. Downes (ed.) *Unravelling Criminal Justice*, London: Macmillan, 73–95.

*Adler, M. and Longhurst, B. (1992c) 'Discourse, Power and Justice: Towards a New Analysis of Accountability in Scottish Prisons' in K. Bottomley, J. Fowles and R. Reiner (eds) *Criminal Justice: Theory and Practice*, London: British Society of Criminology in association with the Institute for the Study and Treatment of Delinquency, 241–272.

Advisory Council on the Penal System (1968) *The Regime for Long-Term Prisoners in Conditions of Maximum Security*, London: HMSO.

American Friends Service Committee (1971) *Struggle for Justice*, New York: Hill and Wang.

Barnes, B. (1977) *Interests and the Growth of Knowledge*, London: Routledge and Kegan Paul.

Barnes, B. (1988) *The Nature of Power*, Cambridge: Polity.

Becker, H. S. (1967) 'Whose Side are We On?', *Social Problems*, 14(3), 239–247.

Bettsworth, M. (1989) *Marking Time: A Prison Memoir*, London: Macmillan.

Birkenshaw, P. (1985) 'An Ombudsman for Prisoners' in M. Maguire, J. Vagg and R. Morgan (eds) *Accountability and Prisons: Opening Up a Closed World*, London: Tavistock, 165–174.

Bloor, D. (1982) 'Durkheim and Mauss Revisited: Classification and the Sociology of Knowledge', *Studies in History and Philosophy of Science*, 13(4), 267–297.

Bottomley, A. K. (1973) *Decisions in the Penal Process*, London: Martin Robertson.

Bottoms, A. E. (1980) 'An Introduction to "The Coming Crisis"' in A. E. Bottoms and R. H. Preston (eds) *The Coming Penal Crisis: A Criminological and Theological Exploration*, Edinburgh: Scottish Academic Press, 1–24.

Bottoms, A. E. and McLean, J. D. (1976) *Defendants in the Criminal Process*, London: Routledge and Kegan Paul.

Boyer, B. (1984) 'From Discretionary to Bureaucratic Justice', *Michigan Law Review*, 82, 971–980.

Boyle, J. (1977) *A Sense of Freedom*, London: Pan.

Boyle, J. (1985) *The Pain of Confinement: Prison Diaries*, London: Pan.

Cameron, J. (1983) *Prisons and Punishment in Scotland from the Middle Ages to the Present*, Edinburgh: Canongate Press.

Carlen, P. (1983) *Women's Imprisonment*, London: Routledge and Kegan Paul.

Cavadino, M. and Dignan, J. (1992) *The Penal System: An Introduction*, London: Sage.

Clarke, D. H. (1982) 'Justifications for Punishment', *Contemporary Crises*, 6, 25–57.

Clegg, S. (1989) *Frameworks of Power*, London: Sage.

Clemmer, D. (1958) *The Prison Community*, New York: Holt, Rinehart and Winston.

Cohen, S. (1985) *Visions of Social Control: Crime, Punishment and Classification*, Cambridge: Polity.
Cohen, S. (1990) *Intellectual Scepticism and Political Commitment: The Case of Radical Criminology*, Amsterdam: University of Amsterdam.
Cohen, S. and Taylor, L. (1972) *Psychological Survival: The Experience of Long-term Imprisonment*, Harmondsworth: Penguin.
Cohen, S. and Taylor, L. (1979) *Prison Secrets*, London: National Council for Civil Liberties/Radical Alternatives to Prison.
Conley, J. (1980) 'Prisons, Production and Profit: Reconsidering the Importance of Prison Industries', *Journal of Social History*, 14(2), 257-275.
Cooke, D. (1989a) 'The Barlinnie Special Unit' in E. Wozniak (ed.) *Current Issues in Scottish Prisons: Systems of Accountability and Regimes for Difficult Prisoners* (Scottish Prison Service Occasional Papers, No.2), Edinburgh: Scottish Office, 116–130.
Cooke, D. (1989b) 'Containing Violent Prisoners: An Analysis of the Barlinnie Special Unit', *British Journal of Criminology*, 29(2), 129–143.
Council of Europe (1984) *Stock-taking on the European Convention on Human Rights, the First Thirty-Years: 1954–1984*, Strasbourg.
Council of Europe (1986) *Stock-taking on the European Convention on Human Rights*, Supplement 1985, Strasbourg.
Council of Europe (1987) *Prison Information Bulletin*, No.9, Strasbourg.
Council of Europe (1988) *Stock-taking on the European Convention on Human Rights*, Supplement 1987, Strasbourg.
Council of Europe (1989) *The European Convention on Human Rights*, Strasbourg.
Council of Europe (1990) *Prison Information Bulletin*, No.15, Strasbourg.
Coyle, A. (1986) 'The Organisational Development of the Scottish Prison Service with Particular Reference to the Role and Influence of the Prison Officer', unpublished Ph.D. Thesis, University of Edinburgh.
Coyle, A. (1987) 'The Scottish Experience with Small Units' in A. E. Bottoms and R. Light (eds) *Problems of Long-term Imprisonment*, Aldershot: Gower, 228–248.
Coyle, A. (1991) *Inside: Rethinking Scotland's Prisons*, Edinburgh: Scottish Child.
Dant, T. (1991) *Knowledge, Ideology and Discourse: A Sociological Perspective*, London: Routledge.
Day, P. and Klein, R. (1987) *Accountabilities: Five Public Services*, London: Tavistock.
DiIulio, J. J., Jr (1987) *Governing Prisons: A Comparative Study of Correctional Management*, New York: Free Press.
DiIulio, J. J., Jr (1991) 'Understanding Prisons: The New Old Penology', *Law and Social Inquiry*, 16(1), 65–114.
Ditchfield, J. and Austin, C. (1986) *Grievance Procedures in Prisons: A Study of Prisoners' Applications and Petitions*, Home Office Research Study, No. 91 London: HMSO.
Dobash, R. P. (1983) 'Labour and Discipline in Scottish and English Prisons: Moral Correction, Punishment and Useful Toil', *Sociology*, 17(1), 1–27.

Dobash, R. P., Dobash, R. E. and Gutteridge, S. (1986) *The Imprisonment of Women*, Oxford: Basil Blackwell.
Douglas, M. (1975) *Implicit Meanings: Essays in Anthropology*, London: Routledge and Kegan Paul.
Durkheim, E. and Mauss, M. (1963) *Primitive Classification*, Chicago: University of Chicago Press.
Faugeron, C. and Houchon, G. (1987) 'Prison and the Penal System: From Penology to a Sociology of Penal Policies', *International Journal for Sociology of Law*, 15, 393–422.
Fawcett, Sir J. (1985) 'Applications of the European Convention on Human Rights' in M. Maguire, J. Vagg and R. Morgan (eds) *Accountability and Prisons: Opening Up a Closed World*, London: Tavistock, 61–78.
Fitzgerald, M. (1977) *Prisoners in Revolt*, Harmondsworth: Penguin.
Fitzgerald, M. and Sim, J. (1979) *British Prisons*, Oxford: Basil Blackwell.
Fleisher, M. S. (1989) *Warehousing Violence*, Newbury Park, London and New Delhi: Sage.
Fogel, D. (1975) *We are the Living Proof, The Justice Model for Corrections*, Cincinnati: W. H. Anderson.
Foucault, M. (1979) *Discipline and Punish: The Birth of the Prison*, Harmondsworth: Penguin.
Foucault, M. (1981) *The History of Sexuality: Volume One, An Introduction*, Harmondsworth: Penguin.
Galanter, M. (1975) 'Why the "Haves" Come Out Ahead: Speculations on the Limits of Legal Change', *Law and Society Review*, 9, 95–160.
Garland, D. (1985) *Punishment and Welfare: A History of Penal Strategies*, London: Gower.
Garland, D. (1990) *Punishment and Modern Society: A Study in Social Theory*, Oxford: Clarendon Press.
Garland, D. and Young, P. (eds) (1983) *The Power to Punish: Contemporary Penality and Social Analysis*, London: Heinemann.
Gateway Exchange (1987) *The Roof Comes Off: Report of the Independent Enquiry into the Protests at Peterhead Prison*, Edinburgh.
Gilboy, J. (1988) 'Administrative Review in a System of Conflicting Values', *Law and Social Inquiry*, 13(3), 515–579.
Goffman, E. (1961) 'On the Characteristics of Total Institutions: Staff–Inmate Relations' in D. R. Cressey (ed.) *The Prison: Studies in Institutional Organisation and Change*, New York: Holt, Rinehart and Winston, 68–106.
Goffman, E. (1968) *Asylums: Essays on the Social Situation of Mental Patients and Other Inmates*, Harmondsworth: Penguin.
Gouldner, A. W. (1968) 'The Sociologist as Partisan: Sociology and the Welfare State', *American Sociologist*, May, 103–116.
Greenberg, D. (1983) 'Reflections on the Justice Model Debate', *Contemporary Crises*, 7, 313–327.
Harlow, C. and Rawlings, M. (1984) *Law and Administration*, London: Weidenfeld and Nicolson.
Henderson, D. (1987) 'Prison Education Neglected', *Times Education Supplement (Scotland)*, 11 September.
Hesse, M. (1974) *The Structure of Scientific Inference*, London: Macmillan.
Hill, S. (1990) 'Britain: The Dominant Ideology Thesis after a Decade?' in

N. Abercrombie, S. Hill and B. S. Turner (eds) *Dominant Ideologies*, London: Unwin Hyman.
HM Chief Inspector of Prisons for Scotland (1982a) *Report for 1981*, Cmnd 8619, Edinburgh: HMSO.
HM Chief Inspector of Prisons for Scotland (1982b) *Report on HM Prison Perth*, Edinburgh: Scottish Office.
HM Chief Inspector of Prisons for Scotland (1984) *Report for 1983*, Cmnd 9401, Edinburgh: HMSO.
HM Chief Inspector of Prisons for Scotland (1985a) *Report on HM Prison Perth*, Edinburgh: Scottish Office.
HM Chief Inspector of Prisons for Scotland (1985b) *Children in Prison*, Edinburgh: Scottish Office.
HM Chief Inspector of Prisons for Scotland (1985c) *Report for 1984*, Cmnd 9636, Edinburgh: HMSO.
HM Chief Inspector of Prisons for Scotland (1986) *Report for 1985*, Cmnd 9909, Edinburgh: HMSO.
HM Chief Inspector of Prisons for Scotland (1987a) *Report for 1986*, Cm 260, Edinburgh: HMSO.
HM Chief Inspector of Prisons for Scotland (1987b) *Report of an Inquiry into Prisoner Grievances at HM Prison Peterhead*, Edinburgh: Scottish Office.
HM Chief Inspector of Prisons for Scotland (1987c) *Report on HM Prison Barlinnie*, Edinburgh: Scottish Office.
HM Chief Inspector of Prisons for Scotland (1987d) *Report on Social Work Units in Scottish Prisons (The Parsloe Report)*, Edinburgh: Scottish Office.
HM Chief Inspector of Prisons for Scotland (1988a) *Report on Staff Training in the Scottish Prison Service*, Edinburgh: Scottish Office.
HM Chief Inspector of Prisons for Scotland (1988b) *Report for 1987*, Cm 541, Edinburgh: HMSO.
HM Chief Inspector of Prisons for Scotland (1989a) *Report on Chaplaincy in the Scottish Prison Service*, Edinburgh: Scottish Office.
HM Chief Inspector of Prisons for Scotland (1989b) *Report on Conditions and Arrangements for Accommodating Persons Detained Under the Immigration Act 1971 and Members of Ethnic Minority Groups*, Edinburgh: Scottish Office.
HM Chief Inspector of Prisons for Scotland (1989c) *Report on HM Prison Perth*, Edinburgh: Scottish Office.
HM Chief Inspector of Prisons for Scotland (1989d) *Report on HM Prison Shotts*, Edinburgh: Scottish Office.
HM Chief Inspector of Prisons for Scotland (1989e) *Report for 1988*, Cm 725, Edinburgh: HMSO.
HM Chief Inspector of Prisons for Scotland (1990a) *Report for 1989*, Cm 1380, Edinburgh: HMSO.
HM Chief Inspector of Prisons for Scotland (1990b) *Report on HM Prison Barlinnie*, Edinburgh: Scottish Office.
HM Prison Service (1989) *An Improved System of Grievance Procedures for Prisoners' Complaints and Requests: Report by a Working Group*, London: Home Office.
Home Office (1966) *Report of the Inquiry into Prison Escapes and Security (The Mountbatten Report)*, Cmnd 3175, London: HMSO.

Home Office (1979) *Report of the Committee of Inquiry into the United Kingdom Prison Services (The May Report)*, Cmnd 7673, London: HMSO.

Home Office (1984) *Managing the Long-term Prison System: Report of the Control Review Committee*, London: HMSO.

Home Office (1988) *The Parole System in England and Wales: Report of the Review Committee (The Carlyle Report)*, Cm 532, London: HMSO.

Home Office (1991a) *Report on the 1990 Prison Disturbances in England and Wales (The Woolf Report)*, Cm 1456, London: HMSO.

Home Office (1991b) *A Digest of Information on the Criminal Justice System: Crime and Justice in England and Wales*, London: Home Office Research and Statistics Department.

Houchin, R. (n.d.) 'Prisons, ECHR, the Courts and the Parliamentary Commissioner: What have Twenty Years of Supervision Achieved?', unpublished paper.

Hudson, B. (1987) *Justice Through Punishment: A Critique of the 'Justice'*, Model of Corrections, Basingstoke: Macmillan.

Hutchinson, A. (1988) 'Why the Powder Keg Blew', *The Scotsman*, 8, 9, 10, 11 and 12 August.

Ignatieff, M. (1978) *A Just Measure of Pain: The Penitentiary in the Industrial Revolution*, London: Macmillan.

Irwin, J. (1970) *The Felon*, Englewood Cliffs, NJ: Prentice Hall.

Irwin, J. and Cressey, D. R. (1962) 'Thieves, Inmates and the Inmate Culture', *Social Problems*, 10, 142–155.

Jackson, G. (1971) *Soledad Brother: The Prison Letters of George Jackson*, Harmondsworth: Penguin.

Jacobs, J. B. (1977) *Stateville: A Penitentiary in Mass Society*, Chicago: University of Chicago Press.

Justice (1977) *Our Fettered Ombudsman*, London: Justice.

Justice (1983) *Justice in Prison*, London: Justice.

Keat, R. (1991) 'Introduction: Starship Britain or Universal Enterprise?' in R. Keat and N. Abercrombie (eds) *Enterprise Culture*, London: Routledge, 1–17.

Keat, R. and Abercrombie, N. (eds) (1991) *Enterprise Culture*, London: Routledge.

Kelly, T. (1987) 'Changes in the Prison Population', paper to a Conference on 'The Uses of Custodial Sentences in Scotland: Justification, Purposes and Effects', Centre for Criminology and the Social and Philosophical Study of Law, University of Edinburgh.

Kettler, D., Meja, V. and Stehr, N. (1984) *Karl Mannheim*, Chichester: Ellis Horwood and London: Tavistock.

King, R. D. and Elliot, K. W. (1977) *Albany: Birth of a Prison, End of an Era*, London: Routledge and Kegan Paul.

King, R. D. and Morgan, R. (1980) with J. P. Martin and J. E. Thomas, *The Future of the Prison System*, London: Gower.

Kinsey, R. (1988) 'The Politics and Ideology of the Prison Crisis' in D. McCrone and A. Brown (eds) *Scottish Government Yearbook 1988*, Edinburgh: Unit for the Study of Government in Scotland, 103–122.

Law, J. (ed) (1986) *Power, Action and Belief: A New Sociology of Knowledge?* (Sociological Review Monograph 32), London: Routledge and Kegan Paul.

Legge, K. (1978) 'Work in Prison: The Process of Inversion', *British Journal of Criminology*, 18(1), 6–22.
Little, M. (1990) *Young Men in Prison: Criminal Identity Explored Through the Rules of Behaviour*, Aldershot: Dartmouth.
Loader, C. (1985) *The Intellectual Development of Karl Mannheim: Culture, Politics and Planning*, Cambridge: Cambridge University Press.
Longhurst, B. (1984) 'Towards the Developed Sociology of Knowledge', unpublished Ph.D. Thesis, University of Lancaster.
Longhurst, B. (1988) 'On Interpretation: A Note', *Theory, Culture and Society*, 5(1), 127–135.
Longhurst, B. (1989) *Karl Mannheim and the Contemporary Sociology of Knowledge*, Basingstoke: Macmillan.
Lukes, S. (1974) *Power: A Radical View*, London: Macmillan.
McManus, J. (1986) *Visiting Committees in Scottish Penal Establishments*, Central Research Unit Papers, Edinburgh: Scottish Office.
McManus, J. (1988) 'Prisoners' Rights' in S. Backett, J. McNeill and A. Yellowlees (eds) *Imprisonment Today: Current Issues in the Prison Debate*, Basingstoke: Macmillan, 104–124.
McNeill, J. (1986) 'Imprisonment for Fine Defaulters: A Punishment for Poverty', *SCOLAG*, 116, 70–73.
McNeill, J. (1988) 'Classification Procedures in Scottish Prisons: "Sweeties for the Good Boys?"' in S. Backett, J. McNeill and A. Yellowlees (eds) *Imprisonment Today: Current Issues in the Prison Debate*, Basingstoke: Macmillan, 36–52.
McVicar, J. (1974) *McVicar by Himself*, London: Hutchinson.
Maguire, M. (1985) 'Prisoners' Grievances: The Role of Boards of Visitors' in M. Maguire, J. Vagg and R. Morgan (eds) *Accountability and Prisons: Opening Up a Closed World*, London: Tavistock, 141–156.
Maguire, M., Vagg, J. and Morgan, R. (eds) (1985) *Accountability and Prisons: Opening Up a Closed World*, London: Tavistock.
Mannheim, K. (1952) 'Competition as a Cultural Phenomenon' in K. Mannheim, *Essays on the Sociology of Knowledge*, London: Routledge and Kegan Paul, 191–229.
Mannheim, K. (1953) 'Conservative Thought' in K. Mannheim, *Essays on Sociology and Social Psychology*, London: Routledge and Kegan Paul, 74–164.
Mannheim, K. (1986) *Conservatism: A Contribution to the Sociology of Knowledge*, London: Routledge and Kegan Paul.
Maranville, D. (1984) 'Review of J. L. Mashaw: Bureaucratic Justice', *Minnesota Law Review*, 69, 325–347.
Martinson, R. (1974) 'What Works? – Questions and Answers about Prison Reform', *Public Interest*, 35, 22–54.
Mashaw, J. (1983) *Bureaucratic Justice*, London and New Haven: Yale University Press.
Mathiesen, T. (1965) *The Defences of the Weak: A Sociological Study of a Norwegian Correctional Institution*, London: Tavistock.
Matthews, R. (1987) 'Decarceration and Social Control: Fantasies and Realities' in J. Lowman, R. J. Menzies and T. S. Palys (eds) *Transcarceration: Essays in the Sociology of Social Control*, Aldershot: Gower, 338–357.

Matthews, R. (1989) 'Alternatives to and in Prisons: A Realist Approach' in P. Carlen and D. Cook (eds) *Paying for Crime*, Milton Keynes: Open University Press, 128–150.

Melossi, D. and Pavarini, M. (1981) *The Prison and the Factory: The Origins of the Penitentiary System*, London: Macmillan.

Morgan, R. (1985) 'Her Majesty's Inspectorate of Prisons' in M. Maguire, J. Vagg and R. Morgan (eds) *Accountability and Prisons: Opening Up a Closed World*, London: Tavistock, 106–123.

Morgan, R., Maguire, M. and Vagg, J. (1985) 'Overhauling the Prison Disciplinary System: Notes for Readers of the Prior Committee's Report' in M. Maguire, J. Vagg and R. Morgan (eds) *Accountability and Prisons: Opening Up a Closed World*, London: Tavistock, 217–226.

Morris, N. (1974) *The Future of Imprisonment*, Chicago: University of Chicago Press.

Morris, T. and Morris, P. (1963) *Pentonville: A Sociological Study of an English Prison*, London: Routledge and Kegan Paul.

Murray, K. (1987) 'And How to Alter It for the Benefit of All', *The Scotsman*, 14 January.

Needham, R. (1963) 'Introduction' in E. Durkheim and M. Mauss, *Primitive Classification*, Chicago: University of Chicago Press, vii–v–viii.

Nelson, S. (1990) 'A Corporate Approach' (interview with Peter McKinlay, Director of the Scottish Prison Service), *Community Care*, 25 January, 6–7.

Nicholson, G. (1987) 'Do We Need to Jail so Many?' *The Scotsman*, 13 October.

Nicholson, L. and Millar, A. (1989) *An Evaluation of the Fines Officer Scheme*, Central Research Unit Papers, Edinburgh: Scottish Office.

Norrie, A. W. (1982) 'Marxism and the Critique of Criminal Justice', *Contemporary Crises*, 6, 59–73.

Page, A. (1991) 'Judicial Review in the Court of Session' in M. Adler and A. Millar (eds) *Socio-Legal Research in the Scottish Courts Volume 2*, Central Research Unit Papers, Edinburgh: Scottish Office, 55–65.

Parole Board for Scotland (1990) *Report of 1989*, Cm 451, Edinburgh: HMSO.

Paternoster, R. and Bynum, T. (1982) 'The Justice Model as Ideology: A Critical Look at the Impetus for Sentencing Reform', *Contemporary Crises*, 6, 7–24.

Pollitt, C. (1990) *Managerialism and the Public Services: The Anglo-American Experience*, Oxford: Blackwell.

Rawls, J. (1972) *A Theory of Justice*, Oxford: Clarendon Press.

Renton, J. (1987) 'Time to Stop Going Over the Top', *The Scotsman*, 21 January.

Rhodes, G. (1981) *Inspectorates in British Government*, London: Allen and Unwin.

Richardson, G. (1984) 'Time to Take Prisoners' Rights Seriously', *Journal of Law and Society*, 11(1), 1–31.

Richardson, G. (1985) 'The Case for Prisoners' Rights' in M. Maguire, J. Vagg and R. Morgan (eds) *Accountability and Prisons: Opening Up a Closed World*, London: Tavistock, 19–28.

Rifkind, M. (1989) 'Penal Policy: The Way Ahead', *Howard Journal of Criminal Justice*, 28(2), 81–90.

Roberts, P. (1991) 'The Impact of European Court of Human Rights Decisions on Penal Policy in the United Kingdom', unpublished MSc dissertation, University of Edinburgh.

Rusche, G. and Kirchheimer, O. (1968) *Punishment and Social Structure*, New York: Russell and Russell.

Rutherford, A. (1986) *Prisons and the Process of Justice*, Oxford: Oxford University Press.

Ruxton, S. (1989) *Fair Pay for Prisoners*, London: Prison Reform Trust.

Sabatier, P. A. (1986) 'Top Down and Bottom Up Approaches to Implementation Research: A Critical Analysis and Suggested Synthesis', *Journal of Public Policy*, 6(1), 21–48.

Schroeter, G. (1990) 'Review of B Longhurst: Karl Mannheim and the Contemporary Sociology of Knowledge', *Contemporary Sociology*, 19, 2.

Scottish Home and Health Department (1976) 'Selection Procedure for Transfer to More Open Conditions', *Circular No.73/1976 (Criminal)*, Edinburgh: Scottish Office.

Scottish Home and Health Department (1981) *Prisons in Scotland, Report for 1980*, Cmnd 8421, Edinburgh: HMSO.

Scottish Home and Health Department (1983) 'Selection of Prisoners for Open Conditions', *Circular No.89/1983 (Criminal)*, Edinburgh: Scottish Office.

Scottish Home and Health Department (1985) *Report of the Review of Suicide Precautions at HM Detention Centre and HM Young Offenders Institution, Glenochil (The Chiswick Report)*, Edinburgh: HMSO.

Scottish Home and Health Department (1987a) *Report of the Departmental Working Group on Prison Education*, Edinburgh: Scottish Office.

Scottish Home and Health Department (1987b) 'Upgrading to Semi-Open and Open Conditions' *Circular No.21/1987 (Criminal)*, Edinburgh: Scottish Office.

Scottish Home and Health Department (1988a) 'Prison Statistics Scotland 1987', *Statistical Bulletin No.7*, Edinburgh: Government Statistical Service.

Scottish Home and Health Department (1988b) *Fines and Fine Enforcement: A Consultation Paper*, Edinburgh.

Scottish Home and Health Department (1989a) *Parole and Related Issues in Scotland: Report of the Review Committee (The Kincraig Report)*, Cm 598, Edinburgh: HMSO.

Scottish Home and Health Department (1989b) *Prisons in Scotland, Report for 1987*, Cm 551, Edinburgh: HMSO.

Scottish Home and Health Department (1990a) *Prisons in Scotland, Report for 1988–9*, Cm 998, Edinburgh: HMSO.

Scottish Home and Health Department (1990b) 'Prison Statistics Scotland 1989', *Statistical Bulletin No.5*, Edinburgh: Government Statistical Service.

Scottish Home and Health Department (1991) *Prisons in Scotland, Report for 1989–90*, Cm 1499, Edinburgh: HMSO.

Scottish Home and Health Department (n.d.) *Prison (Scotland) Standing Orders*, Edinburgh: Scottish Office.

Scottish Prison Service (1988a) *Custody and Care: Policy and Plans for the Scottish Prison Service*, Edinburgh: Scottish Office.

Scottish Prison Service (1988b) *Assessment and Control: The Management of Violent and Disruptive Prisoners*, Edinburgh: Scottish Office.

Scottish Prison Service (1990a) *Opportunity and Responsibility: Developing New Approaches to the Management of the Long-term Prison System in Scotland*, Edinburgh: Scottish Office.

Scottish Prison Service (1990b) *A Shared Enterprise: Outline Corporate Strategy for the Scottish Prison Service*, Edinburgh: Scottish Office.

Scottish Prison Service (1990c) *Organising for Excellence: Review of the Organisation of the Scottish Prison Service*, Edinburgh: Scottish Office.

Scottish Prison Service (1992) *Right and Just: A Revised System for Dealing with Prisoners' Requests, Grievances and Complaints*, Edinburgh: Scottish Office.

Scottish Prison Service and Social Work Services Group (1989) *Continuity Through Co-operation: A National Framework of Policy and Practice Guidance for Social Work in Scottish Penal Establishments*, Edinburgh: Scottish Office.

Scraton, P., Sim, J. and Skidmore, P. (1988) 'Through the Barricades: Prison Protest and Penal Policy in Scotland', *Journal of Law and Society*, 15(3), 247–262.

Scraton, P., Sim, J. and Skidmore, P. (1991) *Prisons Under Protest*, Milton Keynes: Open University Press.

Sim, J. (1992) '"When You Ain't Got Nothing, You Got Nothing to Lose": the Peterhead Rebellion, the State and the Case for Penal Abolition' in K. Bottomley, T. Fowles and R. Reiner (eds) *Criminal Justice: Theory and Practice*, London: British Society of Criminology in association with the Institute for the Study and Treatment of Delinquency, 273–300.

Smith, K. (1989) *Inside Time*, London: Harrap.

Stephen, I. (1988) 'The Barlinnie Special Unit: A Penal Experiment' in S. Backett, J. McNeill and A. Yellowlees (eds) *Imprisonment Today: Current Issues in the Prison Debate*, Basingstoke: Macmillan, 125–138.

Stern, V. (1987) *Bricks of Shame: Britain's Prisons*, Harmondsworth: Penguin Books.

Sykes, G. (1958) *The Society of Captives: A Study of a Maximum Security Prison*, Princeton: Princeton University Press.

Taylor, I. (1990) 'Sociology and the Condition of English City: Thoughts from a Returnee', *Salford Papers in Sociology*, No.9, Department of Sociology: University of Salford.

Taylor, I. (1991) 'A Social Role for the Prison: Edward Carpenter's Prison, Police and Punishment (1905)', *International Journal of the Sociology of Law*, 19, 1–26.

United Nations (1984) *Standard Minimum Rules for the Treatment of Prisoners*, New York: Department of Public Information (United Nations).

Vagg, J. (1985) 'Independent Inspection: The Role of the Board of Visitors' in M. Maguire, J. Vagg and R. Morgan (eds) *Accountability and Prisons: Opening Up a Closed World*, London: Tavistock, 124–137.

Vagg, J., Morgan, R. and Maguire, M. (1985) 'Introduction: Accountability and Prisons' in M. Maguire, J. Vagg and R. Morgan (eds) *Accountability and Prisons: Opening Up a Closed World*, London: Tavistock, 1–15.

Whatmore, P. B. (1987) 'Barlinnie Special Unit: An Insider's View' in A. E. Bottoms and R. Light (eds) *Problems of Long-Term Imprisonment*, Aldershot: Gower, 249–260.

Windlesham, Lord (1989) 'Life Sentences: The Paradox of Indeterminacy', *Criminal Law Review*, 244–252.

Woldring, H. (1986) *Karl Mannheim. The Development of His Thought: Philosophy, Sociology and Social Ethics, with a Detailed Bibliography*, ASSEW/ Maastricht: Van Gorcum.

Wozniak, E. (1989) 'Inverness Segregation Unit' in E Wozniak (ed.) *Current Issues in Scottish Prisons: Issues of Accountability and Regimes for Difficult Prisoners* (Scottish Prison Science Occasional Paper No. 2) Edinburgh: Scottish Office, 86–115.

Wozniak, E. and McAllister, D. (1991) 'Facilities, Standards and Change in the Scottish Prison Service: The Prison Survey 1990/92', paper to British Criminology Conference, University of York, July.

Wozniak, E. and McAllister, D. (1992) *The Prison Survey* (Scottish Prison Service Occasional Papers No.1/1992), Edinburgh: Scottish Office.

Young, P. (1987) 'The Concept of Social Control and its Relevance to the Prisons Debate' in A. E. Bottoms and R. Light (eds) *Problems of Long-Term Imprisonment*, Aldershot: Gower, 97–114.

Young, P. (forthcoming) *Punishment, Money and Legal Order*, Edinburgh: Edinburgh University Press.

Index

For Product Safety Concerns and Information please contact our EU representative GPSR@taylorandfrancis.com
Taylor & Francis Verlag GmbH, Kaufingerstraße 24, 80331 München, Germany

www.ingramcontent.com/pod-product-compliance
Ingram Content Group UK Ltd.
Pitfield, Milton Keynes, MK11 3LW, UK
UKHW022111190926
475702UK00013B/1375
* 9 7 8 1 1 3 8 8 7 9 9 2 8 *